Strength Guide

This guide will help you choose a cigar with a strength you enjoy, whether it be mild, medium, or full-bodied.

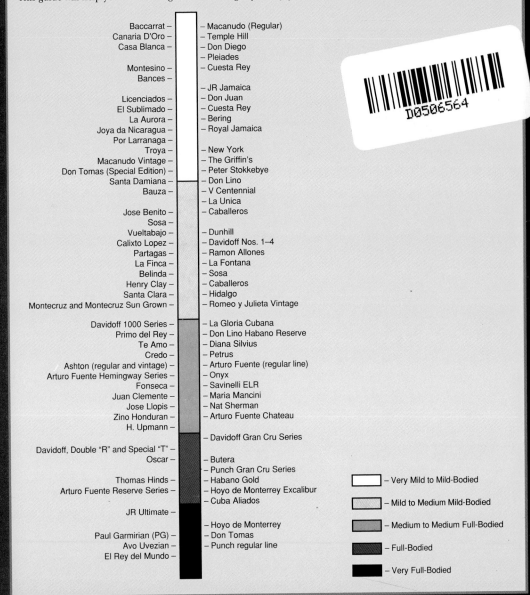

Baccarrat –	– Macanudo (Regular)
Canaria D'Oro –	– Temple Hill
Casa Blanca –	– Don Diego
	– Pleiades
Montesino –	– Cuesta Rey
Bances –	
	– JR Jamaica
Licenciados –	– Don Juan
El Sublimado –	– Cuesta Rey
La Aurora –	– Bering
Joya da Nicaragua –	– Royal Jamaica
Por Larranaga –	
Troya –	– New York
Macanudo Vintage –	– The Griffin's
Don Tomas (Special Edition) –	– Peter Stokkebye
Santa Damiana –	– Don Lino
Bauza –	– V Centennial
	– La Unica
Jose Benito –	– Caballeros
Sosa –	
Vueltabajo –	– Dunhill
Calixto Lopez –	– Davidoff Nos. 1–4
Partagas –	– Ramon Allones
La Finca –	– La Fontana
Belinda –	– Sosa
Henry Clay –	– Caballeros
Santa Clara –	– Hidalgo
Montecruz and Montecruz Sun Grown –	– Romeo y Julieta Vintage
Davidoff 1000 Series –	– La Gloria Cubana
Primo del Rey –	– Don Lino Habano Reserve
Te Amo –	– Diana Silvius
Credo –	– Petrus
Ashton (regular and vintage) –	– Arturo Fuente (regular line)
Arturo Fuente Hemingway Series –	– Onyx
Fonseca –	– Savinelli ELR
Juan Clemente –	– Maria Mancini
Jose Llopis –	– Nat Sherman
Zino Honduran –	– Arturo Fuente Chateau
H. Upmann –	
	– Davidoff Gran Cru Series
Davidoff, Double "R" and Special "T" –	
Oscar –	– Butera
	– Punch Gran Cru Series
Thomas Hinds –	– Habano Gold
Arturo Fuente Reserve Series –	– Hoyo de Monterrey Excalibur
	– Cuba Aliados
JR Ultimate –	
	– Hoyo de Monterrey
Paul Garmirian (PG) –	– Don Tomas
Avo Uvezian –	– Punch regular line
El Rey del Mundo –	

– Very Mild to Mild-Bodied

– Mild to Medium Mild-Bodied

– Medium to Medium Full-Bodied

– Full-Bodied

– Very Full-Bodied

Cigar Rating Sheet

Copy this rating sheet and use it to keep a record of all the cigars you try.

CIGAR RATING SHEET

Cigar Brand_____   Size Name_____

Length/Ring Gauge_____   Purchase Date_____

Box or Individual_____   Smoking Date_____

Cigar Band

Packaging_____

Price (Per Cigar or Box)_____

Where Purchased _____

_____

Meal/Beverage _____

Overall Appearance and Presentation of Cigar_____Points (Max. 20)   **Grade**_____

Wrapper Color_____   Consistent Color within Box?_____

Oily/Dry?_____   Veiny/Smooth?_____

Cap Construction _____   Packaging_____

Ease of Cutting _____   Construction (soft, hard?)_____

Lighting and Burning Properties_____Points (Max. 15)   **Grade**_____

Even Initial Light?_____   Even Burn? Initial?_____50%?_____75%?_____

Ash (solid and white/black and crumbly?)_____ Burn rate (fast, perfect, slow?)_____

Resting Smoke (light and even/smouldering?)_____   Require Re-Lighting?_____

Construction_____Points (Max. 30)   **Grade**_____

Initial Draw?_____50%?_____75%?_____ Wrapper Stays Intact?_____

Taste_____Points (Max. 35)   **Grade**_____

Light, Medium, Full-Bodied?_____   Bitter/Harsh/Smooth?_____

Sweet/Salty?_____   Bland/Vegetal/Spicy/Peppery?_____

Describe Any Changes in Body or Flavor_____

_____

Aroma (rich and smooth/strong and acrid?)_____ Finish_____

Comments_____

_____

_____

Total Score/Grade_____

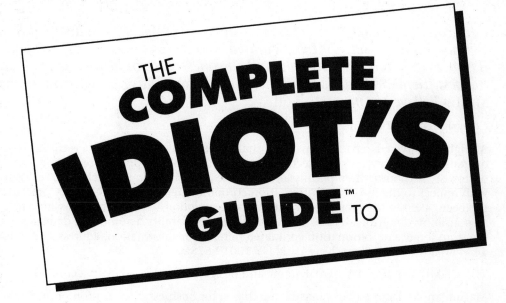

THE COMPLETE IDIOT'S GUIDE™ TO

Cigars

by Tad Gage

alpha books

A Division of Macmillan Reference
A Simon and Schuster Macmillan Company
1633 Broadway, New York, NY 10019-6785

I dedicate this book to the memory of three special people: Industry giant Herman Lane, founder of Lane Limited, who I was proud to call a friend. Barry Levin, a tobacconist, honorable businessman, industry maverick, and the best friend and business partner anyone could have. And my mom, who always believed in me.

Macmillan Publishing books may be purchased for business or sales promotional use. For information please write: Special Markets Department, Macmillan Publishing USA, 1633 Broadway, New York, NY 10019.

International Standard Book Number: 0-02-861975-7
Library of Congress Catalog Card Number: 97-073159

99 98 97   4 3 2 1

Interpretation of the printing code: The rightmost number of the first series of numbers is the year of the book's printing; the rightmost number of the second series of numbers is the number of the book's printing. For example, a printing code of 97-1 shows that the first printing occurred in 1997.

Printed in the United States of America

Publishing Brand Manager
Kathy Nebenhaus

Executive Editor
Gary M. Krebs

Senior Editor
Nancy Mikhail

Director of Editorial Services
Brian Phair

Development Editor
Jennifer Perillo

Production Editor
Phil Kitchel

Copy Editor
Cindy Morrow

Illustrator
Judd Winick

Designer
Glenn Larsen

Cover Designer
Michael Freeland

Indexer
Chris Barrick

Production Team
Tricia Flodder, Mary Hunt, Pamela Woolf

Contents at a Glance

Contents

Foreword

"Any cigar smoker is a friend because I know how he feels."

—French poet Alfred de Musset

One of my most cherished cigar memories occurred when my father and I were unceremoniously escorted out of Victoria's Secret. This exile had nothing to do with lingerie...it was merely due to what my father was holding in his hand: a cigar. The store manager believed that the fragrance of dad's Macanudo did not mix well with the floral-scented potpourri permeating the boutique. I, on the other hand, cherished the sweet aroma. To me, it was a peaceful, reassuring scent that conjured feelings of familiarity and contentment. I have never questioned why my father smokes cigars, and today I have grown to share his love of cigars, as well as feel a special camaraderie with him over our alliance.

Cigar smokers share a common bond that transcends gender, age, and social status. More than merely a "smoke," cigars are a symbol of earned relaxation—a smoky elixir of salvation that allows your mind to wander and your heart to dance. As the sweet smoke surrounds you, it somehow stimulates innovative thought as it melts away the stress of the day. Inspired by the cigar's romantic beginnings, many precarious business deals, heated discussions, and family disputes have been resolved with the magical puff of a cigar.

One of the primary missions behind the launch of *SMOKE* magazine was to create a publication for the everyday cigar smoker—a journal for men and women from all walks of life who appreciate cigars. The message was that you don't have to own an island or employ a butler to enjoy the pleasures of cigars. Likewise, on the pages that follow, *The Complete Idiot's Guide to Cigars* dispels the "millionaire mystique" of cigars and reintroduces this wonderful pastime in an understandable, fun, and contemporary format.

Focusing this guide on the beginner, Tad Gage covers every facet of cigar culture and enlightens even the educated cigar smoker. What I like most about *The Complete Idiot's Guide to Cigars* is that it can be used as a reference manual or simply read straight through. Either way, this vital guide serves as a valuable tool for the novice, as well as required reading for even the most well-seasoned cigar hound.

Alyson R. Boxman
Executive Editor of *SMOKE* Magazine

Introduction

"You're doing a *Complete Idiot's Guide to Cigars*? Cool! I'm really interested in cigars, but I don't know anything about them. All those brands are really confusing. I've got to buy a copy. Will you sign it?"

I've heard this time and again from friends and associates ever since I began working on this book. They all confess to knowing very little about cigars, but are hungry for more information. Some have smoked quite a few cigars, while others have enjoyed only one or two with friends.

Cigars can seem intimidating, especially if you're standing in a shop, toe-to-toe with dozens of cedar boxes filled with countless cigars. This can be daunting, but it's also the beginning of an adventure. With a keen eye, a discriminating palate, and enough knowledge, you can find your prize. I'd love to help guide you.

I frequently draw comparisons between wine and cigars. In many ways, they're a lot alike—from the care and skill needed to make a fine product, to the fact that the more you learn, the more fun you'll have. As with wine, you can jump right in and start enjoying cigars. With time and experience, you'll gain a greater appreciation of what you like and why you like it.

How to Use This Book

Whether you've never smoked a cigar before or you've enjoyed a lot of stogies and want to know more, you can use this book to enhance your cigar experience. I've designed this book to help guide you on your own adventure through the world of cigars: A place where you can own and consume a bit of lore and legend, relax in your own private world of warm tropical breezes, and enjoy a flavor sensation unlike anything else on earth.

In this book, you'll learn how to

➤ Speak the language of cigars

➤ Understand what makes a good cigar

➤ Identify a potentially great smoke on sight

➤ Quickly weed out "wannabe" cigars that are premium in price only

➤ Make good cigar-buying decisions at all price points

➤ Relax and enjoy cigars and other premium tobacco products

If you want a no-nonsense approach to understanding cigars, this book is for you! Here's where you'll find the information you need:

Part 1, Lighting Up, Kicking Back, provides all the basic knowledge you need to start appreciating and enjoying cigars: where to find them; how to talk about them; and how to select, cut, and light them. Heck, you don't have to know *everything* to enjoy a great cigar, so light up and start reading!

Part 2, Cigar Trek—In Search of Perfection, covers the finer points of understanding and appreciating different shapes, sizes, and styles of cigars. You'll learn a bit about how cigars are made differently throughout the world, and how to compare them. Finally, you'll learn the fact and fantasy about Cuban cigars, including all the things the guys selling $50 Cuban cigars don't want you to know.

Part 3, Portrait of the Cigar as a Young Leaf: Where Cigars Grow Up, discusses the fascinating details about how and where cigar leaf is grown, why the curing and aging process (which you never see) is so important, the gentle art of making cigars, and how to judge the finer points of good cigar leaf.

Part 4, "Turbo Smoke": Adding to Your Enjoyment, explains how manufacturers put the all-important finishing touches on cigars, what makes an attractive visual presentation, and how to judge a cigar by looks (and beyond). You'll begin to understand why cigars are such delicate creatures; how they make their way from a warm, tropical climate to your local retailer; and how you can make sure you get your money's worth.

Part 5, Eat, Drink (Smoke), and Be Merry, is where you put all your new-found knowledge to work. This section offers tips in cigar etiquette; helps you cope with objections to your cigar; provides advice on matching cigars with food, drink, and literature; and talks about ways to supplement your enjoyment of premium cigars with other fine tobacco products.

Extras

Along the way, you'll find tips and tidbits that will help you more fully enjoy cigars and dazzle your friends with little-known facts. Here's what you'll find in each box:

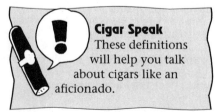

Cigar Speak
These definitions will help you talk about cigars like an aficionado.

Tobacco Leaves
These are just plain fun quotes and quotables about cigars, as well as how Lady Tobaccum has been praised in literature.

Blowing Smoke
These cautions highlight important, more involved facts you should know about cigars and tobacco, and how to cut through the smoke and mirrors to find the truth about cigars.

Hot Tip
These snippets of red-hot information help guide you through the world of cigars.

Cigar Esoterica
These little-known facts will make you smile, allow you to amaze your friends, and help you understand more about the lore and legend of cigars and tobacco.

Acknowledgments

I'd like to thank the cigar manufacturers who hung in there during the industry's tough times, and who supported me and my magazine. Thanks to cigar manufacturers Paul Garmirian and the Fuente family, retailers Diana Gits of Up Down Tobacco and Chuck Levi of Iwan Ries, Harry Kuchma (my guide through the world of spirits), and my Alpha Books editors for their assistance, cooperation, and enthusiastic support in making this book a reality. Thanks to Susan Ireland for introducing me to the *Complete Idiot's* series, and Andrée Abecassis, an agent and friend. Also, I appreciate the contributions of my knowledgeable technical editor, Tony Palacios, the epitome of a tobacconist.

Extra special thanks to my cigar-loving wife Cyndi, who was so helpful and supportive during this process that I married her.

Special Thanks to the Technical Editor

The Complete Idiot's Guide to Cigars was reviewed by an expert in the field who not only checked the technical accuracy of everything you'll learn here, but also provided insight to help us ensure that this book tells you everything you need to know about cigars. Our special thanks are extended to Anthony Palacios.

Tony has more than 20 years experience in the retail tobacco business. He began as a stock clerk at Iwan Ries & Company (IRC), and was groomed by Stanley Levi, who built IRC into one of the largest and most prominent tobacconists in the country. Now in its 140th year, this multi-million dollar, family-owned business is run by fourth generation Charles S. Levi. Tony serves as vice president.

Tony has been intimately involved with the development and sales of the respected IRC house cigar brands and actively promoted the growth in cigar popularity long before the current cigar explosion. He has participated in and hosted numerous cigar events, and has total familiarity with today's wide range of cigar brands.

Part 1
Lighting Up, Kicking Back

Cigars: I can think of few things that have been the object of such passion. One thing is for certain: Very few people have no opinion about cigars!

Cigar smokers make a statement. It's a little contrarian—a little bit "on the edge." Enjoying a good cigar feels like a luxury; it's a treat to yourself that you savor slowly. A good cigar is a taste sensation unlike anything else, which is one reason it's so tough to describe the flavor of a cigar.

In Part 1, we'll explore how to get off on the right foot with cigars. By the time you're done, you'll know more than many cigar smokers—even the vets! We'll talk a little about how cigars are made, so you have enough ammunition to fire away at will. And you'll also learn the essentials—how to select, prepare, and smoke your cigar to get maximum enjoyment.

Chapter 1

If You Know Just a Little, Start Here

In This Chapter

➤ How to choose, light, and smoke your first cigar

➤ The best places to smoke a cigar

➤ How much should you pay for a cigar?

➤ The best cigar brands

➤ How to get the best deal on your smokes

I, like everyone else, started out as a cigar idiot.

I was 25 years old, and I had never smoked *anything* previously. It was the fall of 1982, and I was in Toronto attending a financial and banking conference. After dinner, each attendee was presented with a tubed H. Upmann Cuban cigar. I watched as others lit up and puffed merrily away. Intrigued, I slipped the cigar in my coat pocket.

I'd heard Cuban cigars were prized, and I knew they were illegal in the United States, and I'd never have the chance to try one back home. But I refused to smoke that cigar in public because I was afraid it would make me sick.

When the speeches were done, I retired to my room. I reached for a pack of paper matches (first mistake). Thank goodness, someone had the foresight to clip the cigar before handing it out, because I had no cutter (second mistake).

I struck the match and raised the flame to the cigar. At least I knew which end to light! I was lucky that I'd never smoked before, because my throat instantly closed, not allowing me to inhale the smoke, but simply to roll it around in my mouth and gently let the smoke drift out. Leaning back in my chair, I drew long, luxurious draughts of this magical cylinder.

I smoked it to the stub, which is what I do, to this day, with a really good cigar. I tasted flavors unlike anything I had ever experienced. Before I left Toronto, I bought a few Cuban cigars and drove home.

After I enjoyed all of those Cuban cigars, I searched for other cigars that offered a similar taste experience. I tried some mail-order offerings, but because I didn't know a thing about cigars, I didn't realize I'd bought some very inferior stogies. I threw most of them away and gave up on the whole idea. In retrospect, I realize that my enthusiasm for cigars waned because those I purchased through the mail were nothing like what I'd experienced with my first Cuban cigar.

Tobacco Leaves

"A woman is only a woman, but a good cigar is a smoke."

—Rudyard Kipling

I more or less gave up on cigars, figuring that anything made outside of Cuba was not worth smoking. I had neither the inclination nor the finances to acquire Havana stogies illegally, and I'd rather not smoke than smoke something bad. Several years after my disappointing mail-order experience, however, I rediscovered quality cigars, finding premium, handmade smokes from places like Honduras, Nicaragua, and the Dominican Republic. I discovered a local cigar merchant with a large supply of world-class non-Cuban stogies—and enough knowledge to help me make wise selections. This was during a time when non-Cuban cigars were coming into their own—every bit as good as their Cuban competitors. And I was turned on once again. My discovery and rediscovery of fine cigars was more luck than anything else. I would like to help you do better!

Like me, I hope you become passionate about a good cigar. Enjoying a smoke in the privacy of my home gives me time to kick back and contemplate the day—or maybe think about nothing at all. When I light up with my cigar-loving friends, we have a chance to talk, laugh, swap stories, and rate our smokes.

Fire Away!

To appreciate a good cigar, you don't need anything more than a good smoke and perhaps a few good friends with whom to enjoy the experience.

I'd like you to start enjoying cigars right now, while you're reading this book. A knowledge of cigars and tobacco definitely enhances your puffing pleasure, but you don't have to wait until you're an expert to grab a stogie and light up!

If I could tell you only one thing, it would be this: Smoking cigars, like enjoying wine, should be fun! There's a world of information and knowledge you can use to enhance your enjoyment, but you can also have great experiences with cigars no matter what "level" you're at. Discovering new brands and new flavors is an adventure, and with each new smoke, you'll add to your storehouse of knowledge.

So, how simple is it to get started? Here's all you need:

➤ A handmade cigar (about $3 to $10)

➤ A box of wooden matches or a disposable butane lighter (about $1)

➤ An inexpensive guillotine-style clipper (you can buy one from many cigar retailers for about $2, or you can have the dealer clip your cigar)

➤ An ashtray

➤ About 45 minutes to kick back and relax

Hey, that was pretty easy! In no time, you'll be smoking your favorite cigars like a pro.

A Basic Sampling

So, what cigar should you smoke? If you've already smoked a few (or more than a few) cigars, you may have some favorites. Most retailers will be able to present you with a selection of handmade smokes—the kind you should insist on buying.

It isn't snob appeal that should steer you to a handmade smoke. Later, we'll discuss in detail all the reasons you should buy handmade smokes, but for the moment, trust me that you'll get the best tobaccos, the best craftstmanship, *and the most enjoyable smoking* from a handmade cigar.

If you've never smoked premium handmade cigars, the selection at a well-stocked shop can be a little intimidating. If you're just starting out and you want to try a few different cigars, think about buying three sizes: a short, thick cigar (commonly called a *robusto*); a mid-sized cigar (a *corona* size—about five inches long); and a longer, larger cigar such as a *double corona* (about seven inches long).

This selection will give you a little variety and the chance to test out the smoking qualities of three cigars—each with a different feel and taste.

What brands should you select? You want to start off with mild, well-made cigars; they'll give you a good smoke and they're the easiest for a beginner to appreciate. In Chapter 6, I talk about how you can progress from mild to wild.

Cigar Speak
Cigars are classified by their length and girth. Certain combinations of length and girth are standard, and many of these have special names. Three examples are the **robusto** (short and thick); the **mid-sized corona** (moderately slim and in the middle of the cigar-length spectrum); and the **double corona**—sometimes called a **Churchill** (which is long and relatively thick).

Nationally available brands that combine quality and mildness are Macanudo, Don Diego, Temple Hall, Cuesta Rey, Baccarrat, Montesino, and Royal Jamaica. Most of these are also a good value—about $2 to $9. If you can't find *any* of these brands, ask the retailer for some recommendations.

In Chapter 20, you'll find a sample rating sheet with room for a lot of detail. Feel free to use all or part of it when you're starting out on your adventure.

Until you have a *humidor,* (a place in which to store your cigars and keep them moist and flavorful), you can keep a handful of stogies in a plastic storage container. (Buy a new one at the grocery store; don't use one that has stored food because it may give your cigars a funny taste.) You can also use a tight-sealing bag or box.

Lighting Up: It's a Gas

Getting started with cigars is pretty easy, and one simple trick can greatly improve your smoking pleasure: When you light up (using only wooden matches or a butane lighter;

I'll explain why in Chapter 3), hold the cigar gently in your mouth and turn it slowly as you let the flame kiss the end of the cigar.

Draw in air using slow, gentle puffs. If you're chugging away like a steam locomotive at full-throttle, you're pulling too much air in and the cigar will get hot. It takes a few seconds to light your cigar using this gentle puffing, turning technique.

Check the end to make sure that the entire tip is glowing orange. If there's a part that isn't glowing, return the cigar to your mouth and hold the flame to that section for just a second. Then take the flame away to avoid catching the wrapper on fire. If the wrapper does catch on fire, blow out the flame and let the cigar "settle down" for a moment before you start enjoying it!

Check the tip again for an even light. If it needs just a little more help, blow lightly on it to fan the glowing tip. Then let your cigar rest for a few seconds before you take that first luxurious puff.

Following this technique allows your cigar to get off to a good start; you've done everything possible to ensure that the cigar will burn evenly. Your cigar will burn, unattended, for about three to five minutes.

Cigars are meant to be sipped and savored, but not inhaled. The key to enjoying cigar smoke is to draw the smoke in, let it swirl around your mouth, savor it like fine wine, and release it gently from your mouth.

For some smokers, it's a mark of power and confidence to jam a big cigar between their molars and puff jauntily away. A better way to enjoy the full flavor and experience of a cigar is to "sip" it by pulling in a deep and satisfying draught while placing the stogie to your lips—not between your teeth.

Let your cigar rest for 30 seconds to a minute between puffs. Your smoke will be cooler, and because it's not crammed in your mouth, people will be able to understand you when you talk.

Unlike cigarettes, which will burn down to the filter if left unpuffed, cigar tobacco is too moist to burn without oxygen (provided by you). Most cigarettes also contain chemical additives that promote burning, while tobacco in handmade cigars contains no additives. (As with all rules, this one has an exception: A few brands are accented with a light flavor base and do contain additives.) If your cigar goes out, gently knock the excess ash off the tip and re-light it using the same technique as when you started.

Luck of "The Draw"

You know a cigar is handmade if one end is completely sealed and has to be clipped off in order to draw any air through the cigar. Not surprisingly, drawing air through the cigar is called, appropriately, *the draw*, and it is one of the most important aspects of smoking and enjoying a cigar.

Clipping a cigar is almost an art form in itself, and you have many options for how to clip a cigar. Chapter 3 talks about how to clip your cigar. Most places that sell cigars will clip them for you, which is a good option until you purchase a cutter.

Hot Tip
Don't let your cigar go out for more than a half hour. If you do, the accumulated tar and nicotine at the tip will make it bitter tasting when you relight. Allow enough time when you first light up (about 45 minutes) to ensure that you can enjoy your cigar from start to finish.

Hot Tip
Let the ash fall off your cigar naturally as you smoke. A good cigar can accumulate at least a half inch of ash at the tip before it falls off easily when you tap the cigar against the edge of your ashtray. If it doesn't drop off when you tap it, keep smoking, wait a while, and try again.

Cigar Speak
A **cutter** is a device used to remove the sealed tip of a cigar, which allows you to draw air through the cigar. Numerous types and several styles of cutters are available.

Hot Tip
A great deal of skill goes into combining leaves inside a cigar and rolling it by hand so you can draw in just the right amount of air. Too much draw and the cigar burns too fast. Too little and you can't get a nice puff. Top cigar makers carefully check the construction of finished products, which I discuss in Chapter 11.

Hot Tip
Never chew or chomp a premium cigar; instead, you should hold it in your hand or place it in an ashtray. Smoking stimulates saliva, so if you hold the cigar in your mouth, it will start to get soggy, clogging the air hole and ruining the draw.

Hot Tip
A smoked cigar butt sitting in an ashtray begins to smell very unpleasant after about an hour. If you're smoking at home, do yourself and those around you a favor by getting rid of the remains promptly. The best places: Toss it in the garden (flowers love ash and tobacco) or (ahem) flush it.

Of course, you can't test the draw by clipping the end and putting it in your mouth before you light up! Instead, your best bet is to buy well-known brands from manufacturers who take pride in turning out tens of thousands of perfectly crafted cigars. (Later in the chapter, you'll find a list of your best-bet brands.) Your odds are very good that cigars from these makers will be well made and reliable. Sometimes even the best makers let a bad cigar slip past their quality control, however, so don't be discouraged if you experience an occasional dud.

If you buy a cigar from a retailer, light it up right there, and discover that you're having a problem drawing air through the cigar (and you'll know after a puff or two), tell the retailer. Many times, the merchant will replace your cigar free of charge. For a retailer who wants your continued patronage, this courtesy is a very small cost of doing business.

Where Can You Smoke?

Right from your first cigar, you'll start to develop reasons why you like cigars. Your combination of reasons will be unique to you! You'll probably begin to discover times or places when having a cigar seems especially appropriate.

As you puff your way through the exciting world of cigars, keep in mind that unless you smoke outside in a strong breeze, or you live alone, or light up in your own home with no spouse or kids or roommates around, you'll be sharing your passion for cigars with others—and sometimes they'd rather you didn't. Remember that part of smoking is being considerate.

It's best to smoke a cigar inside, out of the breezes that can make your stogie burn hot and fast. If, however, your best chance to smoke is on your porch, out on the golf course, or while taking a walk, by all means go ahead and enjoy! You can smoke in the car, but it's a challenge to drive and properly savor a cigar at the same time.

If nobody minds you smoking at home, you're in good shape. If, however, you're not ready to jump over that hurdle, several indoor options are still open to you:

➤ Visit one of the growing number of cigar bars.

➤ Track down a cigar-friendly restaurant or pub.

➤ Enjoy your cigar right where you bought it; many smoke shops offer seating for customers.

You can frequently track down smoke shops and cigar bars by thumbing through the Yellow Pages. In Chapter 2, I talk about the different kinds of places where you can buy and smoke cigars.

Anatomy of a Cigar

When it comes to cigars, especially now that cigars are trendy, it helps to have a little knowledge right from the start. Understanding what contributes to a good cigar is delightfully complex, but we'll start off easy. The cigar itself is pretty simple. The following illustration sums it up.

Hot Tip
A high-quality, properly aged cigar will smell nicer to others than a cheap stogie, and it usually leaves less residual smell in curtains and fabrics. You may improve your chances of smoking in the house if you buy premium smokes.

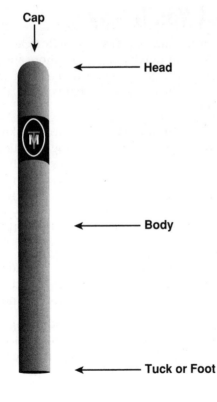

The anatomy of a cigar.

Cap

Head

Body

Tuck or Foot

I give a lot more detail when I discuss how a cigar is constructed in Chapters 9 and 10, but for now, here are the basics:

➤ **Filler** Long leaves of tobacco or cut up pieces of tobacco that comprise the bulk of the cigar and deliver most of the flavor.

➤ **Binder** Tough, coarse tobacco that holds the whole thing together.

➤ **Wrapper** A silky leaf of tobacco that makes your cigar look and feel attractive.

➤ **Cap** or **head** Offers a nice appearance and, if applied properly, feels good in your mouth and prevents the wrapper from unraveling.

➤ **Foot** The business end of the cigar—the end that you light.

Cigars are "simple" in the same way that automobiles are simple. You have a body, an engine, and some wheels. You get in, turn the key, push the gas pedal, and it goes. Of course, some complex functions are taking place, but you simply need to know to turn the key and push the gas pedal. Cigar smoking is similar.

Grab Your Wallet: What You'll Pay

What can you expect to fork over for the simple pleasure of a fine cigar? A lot of what you pay depends on where you make your purchase. (I'll talk more about the different places to purchase cigars in Chapter 2.) The good news is that a lot of great smokes are out there if you know what to look for. The bad news is that you can also find some mediocre smokes at some very high prices.

Hot Tip
What's the most important thing to remember when you buy a cigar? Buy it and try it. Regardless of the brand or price, if you like it, you win. If you're a budding aficionado, however, don't buy too many cigars at one time because what you like may change as you learn more.

In a cigar bar or restaurant, expect the kind of markup on cigars that you'd expect on wine or liquor—about two to three times more than you'd pay at a shop. It's tough to find a decent cigar in a bar or restaurant for less than $8. You can drop as much as $25 for a really fine cigar, but chalk it up to the cost of not bringing your own. Add it to the $38 bottle of wine you can find at the wine shop for $10.99!

In a well-stocked smoke shop, or at a liquor retailer with a decent humidor, you can probably find a nice handmade cigar (one of the smaller sizes) for around $2.50.

With today's cigar craze, demand is huge and supply is tight, and that means higher prices. Price doesn't always indicate quality, but until you have the knowledge to make a fully educated decision, try to stick with name brands and accept the going rate, which will probably average $5 to $8 for a medium-sized cigar.

Larger, longer cigars, like Churchills, cost more because they're harder to make and they use more tobacco. Smaller cigars, like Robustos or petite coronas, will cost less than larger cigars in the same line.

Today, you can find cigars at $25 each and higher, while some boxes of 25 may cost anywhere from $800 to $1,000. You don't have to spend anywhere near this much to get a great smoke, but if your budget allows you to experiment with some of these pricey stogies, go ahead. Remember: You can find some super smokes for $3 or $4, with boxes of 25 costing $70 to $100.

Hot Tip
If you want to buy a box (and you should, if you can find a box of a cigar that you like), expect to pay anywhere from $70 to $250 for a box of 25 super-premium, handmade cigars, depending on size and brand.

If you're trying a particular brand for the first time (and you don't have an unlimited budget), buy a smaller, less expensive cigar. The taste and quality of a smaller cigar will be representative of larger cigars in the same line; if you don't like the cigar, you've wasted a lot less money when you drop it in the ashtray!

I recommend selecting established, well-known brands. A lot of new handmade brands are coming on the market, but the reality is that their quality is not up to snuff. Some good new brands are popping up, but often the makers simply don't have access to good leaf. Your best bet for a great smoke is to find an established brand with a track record of quality and consistency.

By now you might be asking: "What are the well-known brands?" Well, hold on a minute and I'll give you a cheat sheet to start you off. In Appendix A, I've listed more extensive descriptions of many of these brands. This listing should help in your selection and give you something to compare against your perceptions.

What's in a Name?

Here's a listing, in alphabetical order, of cigar brands that have been around a while and whose makers have an established reputation for quality construction and tobacco. To help make your hunt easier, I've only included private-label or store brands that are sold through numerous retail outlets.

Because Cuban cigars aren't legally available in the U.S., I haven't included any of them in this list. Most Cuban brands have a non-Cuban counterpart—in name only; not even the smallest amount of Cuban tobacco is allowed in cigars legally exported to the United States.

➤ Arturo Fuente, Ashton, Avo Uvezian
➤ Baccarat, Bances, Bauza, Belinda, Bering, Butera
➤ Canaria D'Oro, Juan Clemente, Credo, Cuba Aliados, Cuesta Rey
➤ Davidoff, Diana Silvius, Don Diego, Don Juan, Don Tomas, Dunhill
➤ El Rey del Mundo, El Sublimado
➤ Fonseca

➤ Griffin's

➤ Henry Clay, Thomas Hinds, H. Upmann, Hoyo de Monterrey

➤ Joya de Nicaragua, Jose Llopis

➤ Licenciados, La Unica

➤ Macanudo, Montesino, Montecruz

➤ Nat Sherman

➤ Onyx, Oscar

➤ PG (Paul Garmirian), Partagas, Petrus, Pleiades, Por Larranaga, Primo del Rey, Punch, Punch Gran Cru

➤ Ramon Allones, Romeo y Julieta, Royal Jamaica

➤ Santa Clara, Santa Damiana, Sosa, Savinelli

➤ Te Amo, Temple Hall, Troya

➤ Zino

If you like a good deal, your head will turn when a cigar retailer shows you a great-looking no-name cigar that's half the price of the name brands. And you just may have found a great deal!

Many shop retailers and direct-mail sellers offer unbranded, handmade premium cigars. There's usually no cigar band on these smokes. Sometimes these are sold in bundles of 10 or 25, and often singly, as well. There are two kinds of no-name smokes:

Cigar Speak
The **band** is a colorful strip of paper applied around the cigar, usually near the head, that identifies the maker. It's the only mark a cigar manufacturer can use to identify individual cigars as his product.

➤ *Seconds* are cigars that have been rejected by a major manufacturer because they have flaws that make them unacceptable to sell as branded "firsts." A maker of super-premium stogies might reject a cigar for something as picky as a color flaw or spots on the wrapper. Sometimes a cigar will have a soft spot—maybe the roller had a bad day—and will be rejected. You will learn later more about why soft spots are not acceptable in premium cigars, and how they affect your smoke.

➤ *Bundles* are usually cigars that were made to sell as no-name smokes, but they can also be stogies that a retailer got at a special price. A manufacturer, for example, might have had an overrun on a certain size, or perhaps ran out of boxes. Typically, you'll see a group of 25 cigars called "Dominican Bundle" or "Honduran Bundle" indicating the country of origin. Bundles can be a one-time deal, or the retailer might have an ongoing order for these no-name smokes.

Why should you bother with unbranded cigars? Because if you get lucky you can get a great deal on a great smoke! For about half the price of a branded, banded cigar, you can get a cigar that's almost as good. Despite visual flaws or soft spots, many un-branded cigars usually feature the same tobacco and the same quality construction as branded cigars. (Be aware, however, that a no-name cigar might have a major flaw such as being rolled so tightly that you can't draw air through it. You take your chances with a no-name cigar.)

If you can buy a no-name stogie for around half the price of a name brand, get one, fire it up, and see what you think. What have you got to lose? If you like it and you can live with its flaws, buy a few more; because it's a reject, it may be the first, last, and only time that you'll find that particular cigar!

> **Cigar Speak**
> Sometimes cigars are sold in bundles of 10 or 25, rather than in a box. These are called **bundled cigars**. Bundling cigars and wrapping them in plastic saves money, so you'll usually find that less expensive smokes, or "seconds," are bundled. Most first-line name-brand cigars come in boxes, not bundles, but bundled cigars can be a good deal.

> ### Cigar Esoterica
> An issue of *The American Druggist* digest of 1908 cited a scientific study that the desire for tobacco could be overcome by rinsing the mouth with silver nitrate—a poisonous chemical more commonly used to develop black and white photographs and plate silverware. Would *you* want to smoke after using that mouthwash?

Retailers who are extremely well-connected with manufacturers may sell their own brand of cigars made by one of the major manufacturers. These cigars can range from dirt cheap to pricey, but they'll generally be less expensive than major brands because the retailer buys a regular allotment and the boxes, labels, and advertising all cost less for these cigars. If you're budget-conscious, or you just want to find a good "everyday" smoke at a very reasonable price, check out these options. Because you don't have a brand name to go by, the only way to know whether you like a particular cigar carried by a retailer is to try one.

> **Blowing Smoke**
> It's becoming hard to find cheap, no-name seconds (rejects from major manufacturers). A lot of these cigars are now bought by merchants, banded, given a fancy name, and sold at the same price as high-quality firsts.

The Least You Need to Know

➤ Enjoying and experimenting with cigars should be fun.

➤ For an even, cool smoke, puff slowly and gently on your cigar, giving it time to rest between puffs.

➤ Be considerate of those around you when you smoke.

➤ To be assured of the best consistency and quality, stick with established name brands.

➤ Feel free to try a "no-name" cigar if it's a good deal and you can afford to toss it if you don't like it.

Sniiif

Where There's Smoke, There's Fire

These days, it seems as if everybody is selling cigars. Although such a variety and selection is wonderful, the number of people offering smokes means you have to be a good consumer. New brands pop up every day, but a romantic-sounding Spanish name doesn't mean the cigar is a good one. While not just anyone can roll a cigar, it's surprising how many try.

As you keep reading, you'll see how much skill goes into making a fine cigar and growing a good cigar tobacco leaf. Even if a cigar looks good, you have no guarantee of the quality of tobaccos used to make it. And a lot of inferior leaf is being rushed into production to capitalize on the cigar craze. In this chapter, I offer some pointers about how to be a good consumer: what to look for, and what to be wary of. Ultimately, the best guide will be your own taste. What you like is what you should buy.

Desperately Seeking Cigars

It's not difficult to find cigars today, but it can be a trick to find good ones. I feel ambivalent about the exploding popularity of (preferably *not* exploding) cigars. On one hand, it's great to see an industry I know and respect enjoying new levels of prestige, success, and prosperity. On the other hand, I see a lot of inferior product coming on the market because of the rush to cash in on the popularity of cigars.

A lot of new cigar smokers have probably never tasted a really good cigar. At the same time, a lot of veteran cigar smokers are hopping mad because they can't find any of their favorite brands.

The scarcity of premium cigars has reached almost alarming levels. Cigar retailers are fighting for every box they can get, and in many instances, two or three customers are on the waiting list, ready to snap up every cigar that arrives.

Hot Tip

If you hope to find the most reliable and consistent source for premium cigars—a place that will give your order priority when the cigars you want are available—build a relationship with at least one retailer and become a loyal customer.

This scarcity will probably continue for at least the next couple years, because the backlog of good cigars is depleted, and each year only a limited amount of premium cigar leaf can be grown and properly aged. You can't just fire up the cigar assembly line and crank out more product at a moment's notice; a fine cigar requires years to complete. (We'll explore this fascinating process in Part 2.)

It seems as if everybody today sells what are marketed as premium, handmade cigars. These cigars might be made by hand, but that doesn't mean they're good. Part of the fun as you learn more about cigars will be discovering which retailers give you the best odds of finding a good smoke at a good price.

It's easy to buy cigars. You go to a place that sells them, either ask for advice or just grab a handful, and then go with the flow. If you find a good tobacconist and work with someone who really knows cigars and tobacco, it can be very easy to find great cigars. That's why I want you to have as much information as possible.

Don't expect a lot of guidance at a cigar bar or club, cigar-friendly restaurant, hotel lobby counter, or liquor store. Most of these places have only just begun carrying cigars, and they are seldom staffed with people who know much about the subject.

Tobacconist or "Seegar Seller"?

Your mission, should you choose to accept it, is to find a retailer—or several retailers—with connections. Your best bet is to find a smoke shop. You can usually tell a tobacconist (or smoke shop) from a "seegar seller" because a tobacconist sells a variety of tobacco products, including pipes, pipe tobacco, premium cigarettes, cigarillos, and, of course, premium cigars.

There's one main reason why smoke shops should be at the top of your list when you begin looking for a good smoke: They're more likely to have what you're looking for, and have more of it.

Smoke shops that have been in business awhile have better connections. Many shop owners are members of trade associations that provide the shop owners with direct and regular contact with leading manufacturers. Sometimes, the owners get special pricing and products from manufacturers.

Smoke-shop owners tend to buy a larger volume and variety of products, which ties them more closely to companies that distribute premium smoking-related products. All this puts a smoke shop closer to being first in line to receive whatever primo cigars are available. When good smokes are as scarce as they are now, you want every advantage you can get.

At an established tobacconist, you're more likely to find assistants who can give you valuable guidance in selecting cigars and smoking accessories. These shops are in business for the long run, and many of their owners believe that paying for and training a good staff is a great investment in customer relations.

I apply a very strict standard to anyone selling cigars, and smoke shops generally come closest to meeting my criteria for a good shop. A store should offer a wide variety of good, premium, and super-premium cigars. In addition, the staff must display at least a limited knowledge of the products being sold.

> **Cigar Speak**
> Several things distinguish a **tobacconist** from a mere cigar retailer. The tobacconist has a wide selection of brands and sizes; proper humidification for the stock; a strong working knowledge of cigars, tobacco, and brands; and a selection of smoking-related accessories such as cutters, lighters, and humidors.

> **Blowing Smoke**
> Even if you're a beginning cigar smoker, never accept a snooty, know-it-all attitude from a smoke-shop clerk, manager, or owner. The attitude is most likely covering up a lack of knowledge about the products.

Many newer cigar stores have developed a "clubby" approach, offering overstuffed chairs, glorious-looking humidors, a limited bar, and possibly even long-term cigar storage in humidified lockers.

A cigar store/club can be a fun place to enjoy a cigar. You have to be careful when seeking guidance in your cigar selection, however, because many of these establishments are primarily capitalizing on the cigar craze. Many I've visited are staffed by people with limited industry contacts, a very spotty selection, and little or no knowledge of cigars.

Spirited Sales—Liquor Stores and Cigar Bars

A relatively new phenomenon is the *cigar bar*. Cigar bars are places that sell a limited selection of cigars; have a nicely stocked bar, comfy chairs, and cozy nooks; and sometimes offer small appetizers.

You might periodically feel like stopping into one of these atmospheric bars and having a cigar. If you don't have your own stogie with you, just walk in, pick a cigar, step to the register, close your eyes, and open your wallet. Then, sink back in that leather couch, fire up, and set aside your cares.

Cigar Speak
A **cigar bar** is a place with comfortable seating and/or tables where you can make individual selections of cigars, and then accompany them with drinks.

Hot Tip
A tie between an upscale liquor store and premium cigars makes a lot of sense: Spirits and cigars go extremely well together. Check out local wine and spirits merchants as a potential stogie source.

One of the most common alternative places to find cigars today is the liquor store. In most cases, large chains and liquor superstores have the volume, buying power, and finances to build humidors and retail premium cigars. Some liquor retailers even had the foresight to begin selling cigars a couple of years before the "craze" hit.

Some liquor stores have set up smoke shops as a store within a store, and may have a reasonably knowledgeable manager and possibly even an informed assistant or two on staff. These are your best bets for finding good smokes and valuable guidance.

These stores also often have facilities for properly storing and humidifying the stock—whether it's a cedar-lined room or just a tightly sealed humidified display case. In addition, owners have established good contacts with suppliers, which means they're more likely to be closer to the top of the "pecking order" to receive premium cigars when they're available.

Although I've seldom seen a liquor store cigar shop that's on a par with a venerable smoke shop, many liquor stores are able to get decent supplies of good product. They understand the market for premium wines and spirits, and they apply the same principles to cigars.

Pasta or Cuban Corona?—Cigars at Restaurants

When I began smoking cigars, premium smokes were found in a smoke shop or the occasional club, and cheap smokes were sold at the drug store. Today, it seems like everyone is selling handmade cigars!

As with newly established cigar "clubs" and cigar bars, most restaurants that offer cigars should be viewed as places to pick up a single cigar from time to time. If you find yourself in a restaurant that sells cigars and you don't have your own, you have a great chance to make amends, buy a cigar, and enjoy it after a pleasant meal.

The nice thing about buying a stogie at a cigar-friendly bar or restaurant is that the staff will clip it for you and you can light up and start enjoying! It's a great way to ease into the world of blue smoke.

If you smoke a cigar or two a month, or find yourself in the occasional mood to do so, cigar-friendly restaurants are a great way to go. These places get terribly expensive if you buy from them on a regular basis, however, and because of the "Pecking Order Principle," they're not likely to get first choice of available cigars.

Many fine restaurants and bars have extensive wine and spirit selections, often with cellared rare vintages. With cigars, however, the offerings are different—often very slim. True, a few old, established restaurants have been selling cigars to customers for decades, but even if these establishments are high enough on the pecking order to obtain a respectable supply of premium product, the price is going to be high.

Although only a few restaurants and bars actually sell cigars, there are many cigar-friendly restaurants and bars throughout the United States. A cigar-friendly establishment welcomes you to bring your own and fire up after a hearty meal or with a smooth drink.

Cigars: In the Mail, on the Net

You can buy anything through catalogs and direct mail—including cigars. Cigar retailers have conducted very healthy mail-order businesses for years. Because this is the age of electronics, you can now buy cigars through the Internet, too.

A few years ago, when name-brand premium cigars were abundant, I would have suggested you supplement your visits to local cigar retailers by exploring the world of direct mail. It's trickier today because of the shortage of premium smokes.

Ordering by mail today can be a little frustrating, because often the cigars you select in the catalog will be gone by the time you contact the merchant. Some direct mailers have so little stock that they've resorted to selling machine-made and low-grade no-name cigars they would never have dreamed of carrying a few years ago.

> **Blowing Smoke**
> Many cigar bars and restaurants can't get cigars, so they're buying their product from retailers and marking them up for sale. These aren't places where you can expect to find a good deal on a cigar!

> **Hot Tip**
> Most restaurants charge you a steep corkage fee if you bring your own wine. But almost all cigar-friendly bars and restaurants—even if they sell cigars—will allow you to bring and smoke your own cigars. I almost always bring my own.

> **Blowing Smoke**
> One of my strongest pieces of advice for someone just learning about smokes is: "Buy only what you can touch, see, and smell." Until you understand enough to know the exact brand or characteristics you want, you'll benefit from being able to buy cigars in person.

Your best bet is to buy cigars in person. If, however, you live someplace where it's difficult to find a good supply of cigars locally, or you just want to see what's out there, I heartily encourage you to explore direct mail.

Hot Tip

A reputable mail-order merchant will make every effort to sell only the finest, freshest cigars, and you may have great luck in finding a smoke not available locally! Some merchants will gladly take back cigars and refund your money if you find the quality unacceptable on the first cigar or two. Ask before you buy.

Tobacco Leaves

"I vow and believe that the cigar has been one of the greatest creature comforts of my life—a kind companion, a gentle stimulant, an amiable anodyne, a cementer of friendship."

—William Thackeray

A number of top-notch retailers conduct large mail-order businesses, and many have toll-free numbers and catalogs. By asking knowledgeable cigar-smoking friends, surfing the Internet, or checking cigar magazines, you should be able to track down any number of retailers who offer cigars by mail.

When ordering by phone, the easiest approach is to tell the merchant the type of handmade cigar you want—size, shape, mild or full-bodied—and let the merchant tell you what's available. With the spotty supply of cigars, you could spend all day making a "wish list" only to find the retailer is out of stock on everything you want!

If you live in a city or town without a good retailer, or you just want to expand your options for finding premium cigars, explore the Net by firing up your search engine and searching for *cigars*. You'll find Internet cigar chat rooms and bulletin boards, as well as cigar bulletin boards on services such as America Online and CompuServe.

A number of smoke shops I know participate in cigar bulletin board activities, and many will ship cigars to you. Because I have "cigar" in the profile section of my online address, I get quite a few e-mails from people selling cigars—most of them telling me they have a great deal for me.

I've never bought cigars through the Internet, so I don't profess to know whether or not it's a good source of supply. Use the same caution in checking out an Internet cigar vendor as you would for any business offering products through the Net.

Lead Me to Your Humidor

Unless you buy cigars by direct mail or through the Net, you'll have the chance to check out the actual product. Handmade cigars are delicate creatures. Just because a cigar arrived at a retailer in good condition doesn't mean it will stay that way!

Throughout the book I'll talk about specific things to look for when you buy cigars. For right now, let's take a tour of the different storage conditions you're likely to find when you visit your local cigar retailer.

Unless you're in the Caribbean, where the humidity level is naturally perfect, a good rule of thumb is to never buy a premium cigar from a retailer of any kind if the cigar isn't kept in a humidified environment. At times you can tell immediately whether a cigar has been stored improperly; at other times, you'll need to do a little detective work.

Most retailers have one of two common humidors—or both. Individual cigars and open boxes are frequently displayed in sealed glass cases, which are kept at the perfect humidity level by water-soaked chunks of florist's foam (yes, the stuff works nicely), bricks of special absorbent clay, or other humidifying elements. These elements are usually hidden, but feel free to ask the retailer how he keeps the cigars in the display case moist and fresh.

Decide for yourself whether a cigar is fresh by applying the *pinch test*. If you're gentle, a retailer won't object. *Lightly* "pinch" the cigar between your thumb and index finger. It should feel firm, but not hard. If it feels like a piece of wood, or if you feel a soft, spongy spot, choose a different cigar from the same box and try again.

The pinch test is the easiest way to tell whether the retailer is properly humidifying the cigars. Glass cases are good for displaying cigars, but they aren't ideal for long-term storage because they're constantly being opened and closed as customers make selections. Consequently, it's tough to maintain proper conditions.

In smaller smoke shops, or those with limited display space, individual cigars are frequently displayed in glass cases, while unopened boxes are kept in a humidified room. You may not be able to check out this room for yourself, but you can judge by the condition of the individually displayed cigars.

An increasingly common option is for retailers to display boxed and individual cigars in walk-in, cedar-lined humidors, which have strict temperature and humidity controls. Ideally, these rooms also have a ventilation system or at least a fan to keep air circulating. Air movement helps keep mold from developing.

Usually, these rooms are kept moist using room-sized humidifiers. A conscientious retailer will continually monitor the temperature and humidity in the humidor. You may even see gauges. If so, sneak a peek at them: They should register close to 70 percent relative humidity and 70 degrees Fahrenheit.

Cigar Speak
The **pinch test** is an easy way to check the construction of your cigar. *Lightly* "pinch" the cigar between your thumb and index finger. It should feel firm, but not hard. If it feels like a piece of wood, or if you feel a spongy spot, choose a different cigar.

Hot Tip
Most restaurants and cigar bars keep only a limited supply of cigars because they plan on customers buying only one or two at a time. You'll usually find only a small glass case in these establishments because they're not doing big volume.

Blowing Smoke
If many displayed cigars have split wrappers, the retailer may store his stock in an under-humidified room. Moving cigars from a dry room to a humid display case will cause wrappers to split. If the retailer allows customers to mishandle the cigars, which can also cause wrappers to break, the retailer is still at fault. In any case, just say "no" to this retailer.

Blowing Smoke

Never buy cigars from a retailer who keeps them in refrigerated conditions! This used to be a fairly common practice, although fewer retailers are now using this method. Some people believe that refrigeration keeps cigars fresh, but refrigerators actually dry out a cigar. You won't find a savvy retailer using this technique.

Cigar Speak

Many once-common Spanish terms used to describe Havana cigar sizes and lengths have all but vanished. Among them: *coquetta* (flirt), *Puritano* (Puritan), *delicioso* (delicious), *breva* (pressed figs), *cazadora* (huntress), and *favortano* (favorite).

Some of these rooms are very spacious; others are cramped. The size of a humidor doesn't matter as long as the temperature and humidity are controlled. If customers are allowed to walk in and out of a humidor, it's tougher to keep a small room properly humidified because moisture is continually escaping.

You'll know if the humidor is the right climate for cigars because if you stand in one for any length of time—especially if you're wearing anything heavier than a pair of shorts and a short-sleeved shirt—you will start to get pretty uncomfortable after five or ten minutes. The right temperature for a cigar is not the best temperature for humans, but right now, your cigar's comfort is more important than your own!

Some retailers have large humidors, but they don't allow customers inside. You stand outside and make your selection of individual smokes by viewing displayed cigars through a glass window or a sliding glass door. Sometimes retailers do this because the humidor is too small to accommodate many customers. Other times, it's because the retailer is concerned that proper humidity won't be maintained as customers constantly enter and exit the humidor.

These are both very good reasons to keep customers out, but not being able to go into the humidor *does* make selecting the perfect cigar a little more difficult. Ask your sales assistant to bring out a full (opened) box of the brand and size you want so that you can pick out the best-looking cigar of the bunch. Remember the pinch test!

Not only are you more likely to find the nicest cigar, but picking out a cigar from the box is fun. Later, I talk about all the things you can look for to help you identify the perfect cigar, and why these things are important.

When to Walk Away

Right now, as you're starting on your cigar adventure, it's enough to know the following guidelines:

➤ If the cigar wrapper is cracked, *choose another.*

➤ If there's a whitish mold on the cigar, *choose another.*

➤ If the wrapper has green blotches all over it, *choose another.*

➤ If it's rock-hard or has spongy spots when you lightly pinch it, *choose another.*

➤ If it has little holes the size of a pinhead, or little "trails" running through it, *run like heck*!

Little holes in a cigar or little trails carved out in the cigar are signs of a tobacco beetle infestation. Later, we'll talk more about what this means. For now, unless you enjoy the prospect of smoking bugs, your best bet is to avoid making another selection from this box.

Whenever you buy an unopened box of cigars, no matter whether it's stored in a back room or right there in the humidor, ask the retailer to open the box so that you can inspect the cigars before purchasing them. You want to look for the same things you'd look for in a single cigar.

Until you start building more knowledge about cigars, though, stick to buying individual cigars. Buying a box of handmade cigars, like buying a case of wine, is a significant investment. You want to be sure what you're looking for before you take the plunge.

The Least You Need to Know

➤ Make friends with a local tobacconist to have the best chance of finding the cigars you want in today's tight market.

➤ Cigar bars and restaurants are fine for individual cigar selections, but stick with a full-service retailer for better selection and better prices.

➤ Make sure your retailer maintains proper humidity and temperature conditions for the cigars.

➤ Walk away from a retailer selling moldy cigars or stogies with signs of tobacco beetles.

Chapter 3

Bite a Hot Dog, but Clip Your Cigar

In This Chapter

➤ How to prepare your cigar with the right cut

➤ Selecting the best tool to "light your fire"

➤ Why you should give your cigar a rest in the ashtray

It's time to discover all the tools at your disposal to enjoy your cigar experience—from preparing your prize, to the proper way to light, smoke, and transport your cigars around the block or around the world. Lighters and cutters may seem like minor aspects of the cigar experience. After all, it's the *cigar* you're smoking, right? Not completely.

If you don't have the right tools to get your stogie off to a good start, you're a lot less likely to have the best smoking experience possible. Also, part of enjoying a cigar is the ritual—a subtle art that's lost on many smokers. The tools and gadgets that accompany cigar smoking provide part of the experience, so be prepared to enjoy!

The Cutting Edge

There's a fine and practiced art to preparing your cigar for smoking. Fortunately, it isn't rocket science, and if you have the right information, it's easy! The first step is choosing how to prepare the head of your cigar. All premium handmade cigars come with a cap of tobacco (cut from the same leaf as the tobacco used for the cigar wrapper) that requires either cutting or puncturing.

How you prepare the head of your cigar will determine whether you end up with a smooth, nice-feeling stogie or a wet, sloppy, shredding mess. If this sounds frightening, it should. A sloppy cut is the fastest way to ruin even the best cigar.

The goal of your cut is to "open" the cigar just enough to create a thick and satisfying draw (which I discussed in Chapter 1), but also to leave the cigar as intact as possible. You should feel a slight resistance when you puff, but you shouldn't have to work hard to draw through the cigar.

Assuming that your cigar isn't too tightly rolled, which is another problem entirely, nipping off or puncturing the cap will do the trick. One thing to remember when considering any cutter: The sharpness of the blade is everything.

Any type of cut with a dull blade will tend to mash the head, which could cause the delicate cap to fray, the wrapper to unwind, and bits of the filler tobacco to dislodge into your mouth. With that overriding rule in mind, let's take a look at all the alternatives you have for creating an air hole.

The "V"-Cut

A common and longtime favorite is the *v-cut*, which does exactly what the name implies. It's a top-to-bottom slice that creates a wedge through the head of the cigar. The v-cut goes deeper into the body of the cigar than any other type of cut, yet leaves the two sides fully rounded. By going deeper, it opens more surface area of the filler, creating a large and lush draw.

Cigar Speak
A **v-cut** is a top-to-bottom slice that creates a v-shaped wedge through the head of the cigar.

You'll find hand-held v-cutters everywhere—from simple stainless steel cutters to cutters with antler, rosewood, or gold handles to gold- or silver-plated cutters. Generally, hand-held v-cutters not only include a v-cutter, but one hole on either side to create a straight cut. They all work pretty much the same—with a spring-loaded lever and a pad for your thumb.

A v-cutter.

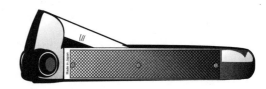

Cigar with a v-cut.

Here's how the v-cutter works: An indentation receives the head of the cigar, and holding the cigar in one hand and the cutter in your other hand, press down on the lever and the point of the triangular blade slices through the head of your cigar. Usually the sides of the cutter include two different-sized indentations for making a straight cut. When you use the cutter this way, the sides of the blade snick off the head of the cigar.

This all sounds wonderful, but v-cutters have one significant problem. I have seen and experimented with hundreds of these cutters, and while they're often temptingly beautiful, I've never seen one with a sufficiently sharp blade. Smokers' drawers around the world must be filled with used and discarded v-cutters! One recommended brand is the Boston cigar cutter, which has very sharp blades.

It's difficult to sharpen the blade of a v-cutter, even when it's new, because of the triangular shape. And it's impossible to re-sharpen the blade, because you'd have to break the cutter to get a file onto the blade. Consequently, I recommend against the hand-held v-cutters. Some smokers swear by them, but all the v-cuts I've seen involve some degree of crushing the head—exactly what you don't want.

As with all rules, this one has an exception: the large and heavy table v-cutter. To use this tool, you cut the cigar not by pressing your thumb on a lever, but by applying pressure to a lever that looks similar to an automobile stick shift. Of course, there's no guarantee that the blade will be sharp, but most table models I've seen have a very sharp blade that can be replaced with new blades ordered from the manufacturers.

The two drawbacks to the table model v-cutter are lack of portability and cost. The best ones will run you $350 or more. Granted, they usually sport nice wood and are very effective, but they're impossible to cart around. You can find tabletop v-cutters for as little as $50, but make sure you test the sharpness of the blade and smoothness of the mechanism by cutting a cigar or two before you buy the cutter. Many smoke shops have table v-cutters, however, so if you crave a v-cut, make your cuts at the store.

> **Cigar Speak**
> A **pinhole cutter** and a **cigar drill** are cutters that create a small hole in the head of the cigar to create an air hole through which you draw smoke.

Prices on hand-held v-cutters really depend on the materials used; a simple cutter may cost $20, while a fancy one could run several hundred dollars. In the end, you'll probably have a cutter that eventually ends up sitting, forgotten, in your bottom drawer.

The "Pinhole" Cut

The *pinhole cutter*, or *cigar drill*, is somewhat popular. Of all cutters, this one makes the most minor intrusion on the cigar. Usually, it's a simple device that looks like a cone with a small threaded screw protruding from one end. You place the cone over the head of the cigar, and then turn the screw. A sharp point enters the cigar head, drilling into the body about a half inch. A cigar drill may be a simple drill that requires you to have a steady hand when inserting it into the cap of the cigar.

A typical cigar drill, which makes a pinhole cut.

This type of cut leaves the head of your cigar almost entirely intact, and for those smokers (like me) who love the pleasing rounded mouth feel of the cigar head, this alternative is very tempting. By puncturing the head, you leave the cap virtually intact, minimizing the chances that it will unravel.

There are two drawbacks to this type of cutter. The first is that you have to hold the cigar with one hand, and pull the cone against the head of the cigar using your thumb and forefinger. Then, you have to deftly turn the screw with the fingers of your free hand. This leads to a lot of frustrating fumbling.

The second drawback is that these types of cutters usually make far too small an air hole for an adequate draw. If you can't get enough air through the cigar, you'll turn blue instead of contentedly puffing blue smoke. My advice is to avoid this cutter.

The "Puncture" Cut

A relatively recent entry onto the market is a *puncture cutter* that creates a sufficiently large hole to give you a satisfying draw. This cutter is very simple in concept: It's a very sharp blade rolled into a circle approximately the thickness of a pencil. You simply press the cutter into the middle of the cigar head and lightly twist, applying gentle pressure until the blade is inserted to the stop point—about $1/4$ inch.

A puncture cutter.

When you gently twist it out, you remove a small plug of tobacco. It's like drilling for a core sample of earth. I've found that with a sharp blade, this type of cutter combines the best of all worlds: It gives you a sufficient draw and preserves the rounded edges of your cigar head. Perhaps I'm very fussy, but I love rolling that smooth cigar around my lips, and it's easy to "sip" at the cigar. The puncture cut is my favorite cut.

Several manufacturers make this type of cutter, and most have blades that can be sharpened or cheaply replaced by the maker. One cutter on the market is made from a Remington .44 magnum bullet and sells for under $15. This tool is called a .44 Magnum cutter. You can order replacement blades for a few dollars. I don't use this cutter to make a statement, although it certainly is an attention-getter at the security gates of most airports I visit. I'm always prepared to show the guards what it is, and it always gets a good chuckle from them. (And they've always let me keep it!)

> **Cigar Speak**
> A **puncture cutter** is a type of cutter that, when inserted into the head of a cigar, removes a plug approximately $1/4$ inch across, creating a large air hole while still preserving the smooth, rounded head of the cigar.

The puncture cutter does have drawbacks, but the problems are more related to the cigar itself than the cutter. If the cigar is dry, even the slight pressure the puncture cutter requires will cause the end of the cigar to split. This won't happen with a properly humidified cigar, but being delicate creatures, cigars will sometimes just dry out. I always have an alternative cutter to use in case the cigar has become too dry and I don't want to wait to rehumidify it.

The other "problem" is that this cutter won't work on a cigar that has a pointed cap, such as a pyramid. If you want to do a puncture cut on thinner cigars, look for a puncture cutter such as Davidoff makes, which has three different hole-size options in one cutter. You might become a fan of the puncture cut, but you should also consider the most versatile of all cuts: the straight cut.

The Straight or Guillotine Cut

Cigar Speak
The **straight** or **guillotine cut** is the most common of all cuts. It lops off the head of a cigar in a straight, clean line, allowing air to be drawn through the cigar. A straight cut can be made using a cutter with one blade or two blades.

The *straight*, or *guillotine*, cut is by far the most popular. It's the easiest to make, works on all but the very thickest cigars, and opens up almost the entire end of the cigar to draw. The straight cutter is available from hundreds of different manufacturers—and in a few variations on the theme of a single blade that slices down through the head of the cigar.

With some exceptions, the guillotine cutter has a large hole that can handle a very thick cigar. A blade slides up and down in a track. You place the head of the cigar in the hole, and press down on the blade to cut the cigar.

A single-bladed "straight" or "guillotine" cutter.

If you have a guillotine cutter with a sharp blade, and you line up the cigar so that the cut runs perpendicular to the cigar and not at an angle, you can hardly go wrong. You'll have plenty of draw, and the cut will be so clean that you won't find yourself spitting out bits of filler or wrapper as you smoke. The use of a straight cutter is as much about technique as anything.

I've seen smokers lop off up to an inch of their cigar, which is unnecessary and wasteful. The goal is to slice off the least amount of the cigar possible in order to open up the end.

Most smokers will slice off about $1/8$ inch of the head, which will remove most of the "flag" or "cap" of tobacco. Some smokers do this because the flag (a loose piece of tobacco applied with natural glue as the finishing touch to the cigar) has a tendency to come off while you smoke. If this happens, just peel off the strand of tobacco that's left and smoke on. In Chapter 10, we'll talk about this delicate, but important, snippet of tobacco.

A cigar with a straight cut.

Some smokers use the guillotine cutter to "shave off" only as little as possible of the head—just enough to expose the filler inside and create draw, but not enough to destroy the flag. By doing this, you end up leaving the cigar head slightly rounded—something I enjoy.

If the head of the cigar is very flat, this "shaving" is a real challenge and requires a steady hand to remove just the very end of the cap. With cigars that have a relatively pointed head, making a straight cut is easy and requires a guillotine cutter. You simply clip off approximately $1/8$ to $1/4$ inch—just enough to create a draw.

Cigar Speak
The head of a premium cigar is covered by a **flag** of tobacco, which is carefully applied at the end of the cigar-rolling process. If applied properly, the flag is smooth, feels good in your mouth, and helps prevents the wrapper from unraveling.

Two Blades: Better Than One?

There are variations to the straight cutter. Several manufacturers, notably Davidoff, offer a *double-bladed cutter*. You insert the cigar into the cutter hole and apply pressure with your thumb and index finger to two separate blades. The theory is that two sharp blades coming from both directions will make a cleaner cut.

A double-bladed guillotine cutter.

If you've ever worked with wood, you'll see the logic behind this theory. When you use a saw, it enters the wood cleanly, but often at the very end of the cut, the pressure of the saw causes the wood to splinter. The same is true with the single-blade guillotine, which enters the top of the head and then pushes the cigar against the other end of the cutter.

If your blade is dull, this final action can lead to the tail end of your cut being ragged. With a sharp blade (preferably one made from hardened English Sheffield steel, which maintains a surgical edge for years), the cut is so clean that it's like cutting butter with a hot knife.

A problem with inexpensive double-bladed cutters is that there's considerable "play" in the blades, and the result is that instead of lining up perfectly at the end of the cut, they're so far out of alignment that they meet in the middle of the cigar head and pinch off the last bit.

Does this ragged finalé bother you? Let your tongue explore the cigar as you smoke to determine whether this edge is a problem for you. As insignificant as an imperfectly cut cigar might seem, a lot of veteran smokers despise the sensation of a ragged edge—and I'm one of them. The rule of thumb is that if you want to use a double-bladed guillotine cutter, buy a good one such as Davidoff's, and be prepared to spend $50 to $60 for two very sharp blades encased in a plastic housing.

The Scissors Decision

Another straight-cut option is the *scissors cutter*, which looks like a barber's scissors with two curved blades at the end. The advantage of this cutter is that it opens wide enough to accommodate any size cigar: from the narrowest to the largest ring gauge you'll find. The very finest cutters have very sharp blades, but you should test the cutter's sharpness before plunking down up to $100 for one of these things.

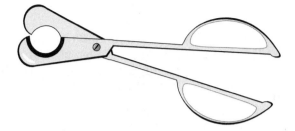

A scissors cutter.

My personal problem with a scissors cutter is that I find it difficult to control just how much of the head I snip. There's no way to steady this cutter, and there's no way to consistently shave off just the cap. If you feel comfortable with the scissors cutter and you find a sharp one, however, it's certainly a reasonable choice.

> **Cigar Speak**
> A scissors cutter looks like a pair of scissors but has special blades for cutting a cigar. It delivers a straight cut.

The Price of a Good Cut

What should you expect to pay for a guillotine cutter? Looks can be very deceptive. A complimentary cutter you get from the tobacconist or the cutter you pay $3 for might serve you in an emergency, but the blades are usually dull and your cut will be rough.

When you're getting started, it's just fine to use one of these, but don't expect more than a few good cuts from a cheap guillotine cutter. The PG (Paul Garmirian) cutter is a very modest-looking guillotine housed in plastic for less than $15, but the guide track is dead-on and the blade is the sharpest steel available. It's short on looks, but delivers hundreds of surgically sharp cuts.

You can also buy very nice cutters, plated in gold, for several hundred dollars. If the blade is razor-sharp and you have the budget, it's a nice extravagance. Remember that part of the enjoyment of a cigar is the ritual, and there is *nothing* like the feel of preparing your cigar with a gorgeous gold- or silver-plated cutter.

However, if the blade is dull, it can't perform the one function it's supposed to perform. Before purchasing any cutter—especially if you intend to buy an expensive one—test it out on a cigar. Buy a cigar from your retailer and try the cutter!

Speaking of razor-sharp edges, I'll let you in on a secret: I buy a large packet of cardboard-encased single-edge razor blades from the hardware store and drop them in every brief-case and suitcase I own. You can buy a huge pack of these blades for a song. When I find I've forgotten my cutter, I can rummage around for one of these razors, place the cigar on a plate or hold it carefully, and slice off the tip. This cutter isn't stylish, and you have to be very careful to steady the cigar on a solid surface, but it's a darned sharp cut that works well in an emergency!

Antique Cutters

Finally, a word about antique cigar cutters. Many are nothing short of amazing contraptions, such as a table-mounted miniature guillotine with a weighted blade that plunges from a height to whack the cigar. Don't keep something like this around if you have kids or if you're prone to having one brandy too many on a Friday night!

Other antique cutters are ornate and beautiful. By all means, collect these if you find them attractive, but stick with simple, new cutters to get a perfect cut. Age, rust, and wear dulls the blades. Frankly, I doubt most of these ever made a decent cut!

C'mon Baby, Light My Fire

You've given your stogie the perfect cut, and you're ready to fire up. Not so fast! Lighting implements come in thousands of styles, colors, and shapes, ranging from the humble paper match to a $2,500 gold and diamond-encrusted lighter. What you use to light up is a function of your personal taste (and your budget!), but you need to remember a couple of basic guidelines when selecting "fire."

Paper's No Match for Cigars

You don't want your light to contain any chemical flavors because your cigar will pick them up. For this reason, avoid paper matches, which have sulfur on the match head; the sulfur also impregnates the stem of the match to keep the match burning.

Blowing Smoke
You don't have to let the flame touch your cigar to light it! You can easily light your cigar by holding the flame $1/4$ to $1/2$ inch from the cigar. By drawing in gentle, slow puffs of air, the cigar will heat up and light without direct contact with the match.

If you're craving a cigar and all you have is a book of paper matches, go ahead, but remember one trick: Don't let the flame directly touch the cigar. Your cigar will pick up a slight chemical taste, and you may notice it at least for your first few puffs—not a great way to start. Not only do paper matches have sulfur in the head to get them started (you must let this burn off), but they are infused with chemicals to keep the paper burning. From start to finish, they'll impart a chemical taste if they touch your cigar.

You'll probably need several matches to accomplish this no-contact task of lighting up, but it's worth the effort in order to avoid a chemical taste. If at all possible, however, avoid paper matches.

Lighter Fluid: Cigar Arson?

For the same reason I suggest you stay away from a paper matches, I recommend that you avoid any lighter that uses lighter fluid—as opposed to one that uses a gas like butane. Lighter fluid also burns with a slight chemical taste.

When using a lighter fueled by fluid, think back to the time Uncle Harry used lighter fluid to fire up the barbecue, but put the steaks on before the fluid had completely burned off. Remember that flavor? Lighter fluid imparts a distinct and very unpleasant taste to your cigar.

I'd tell you to avoid fluid-fueled lighters, but this is easier said than done! Many interesting, collectible, and attractive lighters are fueled by lighter fluid. Zippo lighters, for example, are extremely popular and are also fluid-fueled.

Zippo recommends that cigar smokers use the same basic lighting technique that I suggested for paper matches: Keep the flame out of direct contact with the cigar during the lighting process. You then have to decide whether you notice any residual lighter fluid taste.

Blowing Smoke
If you're partial to a particular fluid-filled lighter, you'll just have to experiment to determine whether you notice any aftertaste when using it. Even if you do notice a small chemical taste in your first few puffs, your delight in using a particular lighter may outweigh this initial unpleasantness. Likewise, you might not notice any aftertaste at all.

Wood Is Good

An excellent choice for lighting cigars is the wooden match. Most, but not all, have no chemical additives to enhance burning. To use wooden matches, strike the match and then let the initial flare-up die down.

When the initial flare-up subsides, you'll know that the flame is now feeding on the wood, not the head of the match. To be on the safe side, hold the flame away from the cigar when lighting—just as I suggest for paper matches.

It's a Gas

In the opinion of many aficionados, the butane-fueled lighter is the best device for lighting cigars. Butane is a colorless, odorless gas that's injected into the lighter and reconstitutes as a liquid under pressure; when you "snick" the striker, the butane comes out as a gas once again.

You can use the classic lighting technique of holding the flame at a distance from the cigar, but because the flame is feeding off a gas with no odor or taste, it doesn't really matter whether you allow the flame to directly touch the cigar.

Butane lighters come in a wide range of styles and prices—from 75-cent disposables to expensive and elegant one-of-a-kinds costing thousands of dollars. The easy availability of butane-fueled lighters means there's no excuse for not having and using one. You can find an attractive, refillable lighter for under $20 that will give you years of service.

Technology enables manufacturers to continue developing interesting variations on lighters. You can now buy electronic lighters that use a super-hot coil, rather than flame, to light the cigar. This new lighter is a fine alternative to traditional tools, as long as you move the pinpoint dot of heat around the tip of your cigar to ensure full and even lighting.

Another version of a standard lighter uses butane to generate something that looks like the flame of a welding torch. This alternative is fine, also, because it uses butane. Use caution in lighting your cigar, and keep the super-hot flame at a slight distance from the head or it could singe the wrapper—or even set it burning at its own pace!

The keys to a good light are generally to avoid lighter fluid, to not let the flame touch the cigar if you have any doubt whether it contains chemicals, and to find something that enhances your aesthetic experience and "lights your fire."

Ashtrays: Give Your Cigar a Break

Unless you're a king who flicks his ashes on the floor for others to clean up, you need an ashtray, right? But an ashtray doesn't only contain your ash; if the tray is specifically designed for cigars, it also provides a "resting place" for your cigar.

A cigar needs to be treated gently, and savored. You can't puff too frequently, or the excess oxygen will make the cigar burn fast and hot, releasing bitter tars and oils. Keeping your cigar at a "slow burn" minimizes the heat at the "business end" of the cigar and helps ensure that certain volatile chemicals aren't released. So, you ask, what does this have to do with an ashtray?

An ashtray made for cigars enables you to give your hard-working cigar a much-needed rest as you puff your way to the finish line. Holding a cigar (and if you're an animated speaker, waving it around for 45 minutes) can get pretty tiresome, so the ashtray gives you, and your cigar, a break.

Not just any ashtray will do for your cigar. There are many variations on a theme, but the basic cigar ashtray has a sufficiently long indentation to cradle your cigar and prevent it from tipping into the bowl of the tray or teetering backwards onto the table or floor. A classic cigar ashtray has a "trough" that's several inches long, with a bowl at one end to receive the ash.

This tray is functional and elegant—especially in crystal. The only disadvantage of this long trough is that as your cigar becomes shorter with smoking, you're forced to lay the butt of the cigar directly on the glass. Without complete air flow, the head is more likely to remain soggy from whatever saliva remains on it.

To properly support even a very long cigar, you really only need a trough that's an inch or so long. To be sure, a shorter trough doesn't provide quite as much stability at the start of your cigar, but it works better as your smoke progresses because it allows air flow at the head of the cigar.

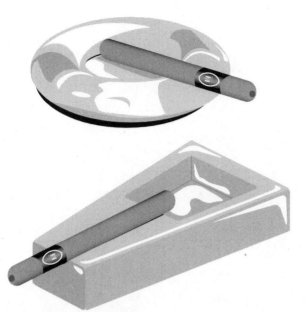

Typical ashtrays specially made to cradle cigars.

The Least You Need to Know

➤ Whatever cutter you select, it has to be razor sharp to avoid ruining the tip of your cigar.

➤ *Don't* light your cigar with paper matches or lighters that use fluid.

➤ *Do* light your cigar with wooden matches or a butane-fueled lighter.

➤ Give your cigar a chance to rest by using an ashtray made for cigars.

Ya Gotta Speak Da Language

Now that you've got a grip on which end of the cigar is up, and you're giving some thought to where to find smokes, the next question's gotta be: "What the heck am I looking for?" Well, believe me, this is where the fun really begins.

You're now able to walk into a cigar shop and start looking around. If you're assisted by someone with some cigar expertise who has smoked the cigars on display, you can glean a lot of information. You shouldn't count on finding a knowledgeable assistant, however, so it helps to know what to look for and what questions to ask.

Basic Cigar Speak—Talking the Talk

Starting with this chapter, you're going to run into some unfamiliar terms that are used to describe cigars and cigar making. *Cigar speak* is a different language. Don't let the words throw you a curve; once you get the hang of a few basics, the words aren't really intimidating.

Let's begin with some basic cigar speak—the words you need to know to start having fun with cigars. Later, we'll talk in greater detail about what these terms mean. Here's the "short list" of words you see, along with a clear and easy explanation of each:

➤ **Handmade cigar**   When you see a cigar that says "made by hand," you can generally figure that the tobacco leaves were picked, sorted, and bundled by an individual, not a machine. The cigar itself was fashioned by a skilled cigar roller using a few simple tools.

➤ **Machine-made cigar**   Most or all of the cigar was made by a machine, and many of the processing stages such as picking the leaves, grinding up the filler tobacco, and rolling the cigar were completed by machine.

➤ **Premium or super-premium cigar**   This is the cigar you're going to buy because it's made by hand and it's a brand that's consistent from one cigar to the next and from box to box. Because you can't taste-test a cigar before you buy, selecting a premium cigar is one way to improve your odds of getting a great product every time.

➤ **Short filler**   The middle of a short-filler cigar is filled with scraps of tobacco, so if you see this phrase on a box, you know it's machine-made.

➤ **Long filler**   Long-filler cigars are filled with long leaves of tobacco deftly gathered together by a roller. A long-filler cigar is almost always handmade, and all premium handmade cigars are long-filler cigars.

➤ **Ring gauge**   This is a way to measure the thickness of your cigar. Cigar thickness (diameter) is measured in $1/64$-inch increments, so a 32-ring cigar is $32/64$ inch, or one-half inch. A 64-ring cigar (too big to smoke effectively) would be one inch in diameter.

➤ **Length**   The length of your cigar is measured in inches or millimeters. I'll use inches in my discussion of cigar lengths, and you can convert to millimeters if you like!

➤ **Shape**   For all practical purposes, the shape of a cigar is the length balanced with a particular ring gauge. Some standard combinations of length and ring gauge exist—such as *corona* or *robusto*.

➤ **Color**   The only part of your cigar's tobacco that you can see (without cutting it open) is the wrapper. *Color* refers to the shade of the leaf used to wrap your cigar, which can range from light green to almost jet black.

➤ **Strength or body**   The relative *strength* or *body* of your cigar, from mild to full-bodied, is one of the most important things to know and also one of the most challenging. You can't tell how "strong" a cigar is by where it was made. Right now, it's enough to know that if you're starting out, start with mild and work your way up.

➤ **Blending** Most cigars are *blended*, which means manufacturers use tobaccos from all over the world to achieve the desired balance of flavor and strength. Like blended whiskey, you never know what tobaccos are used; you have to let your taste be the guide.

The Box Score

Cigar speak is useful when talking to people about various cigars, and also when you're jotting down your personal opinions about a cigar you've just smoked. One of the first places to start is surveying the boxes your cigars are displayed in.

Most of the time, a retailer will display individual cigars for purchase in the original box. Use the information on the box to learn more about the cigar you're considering. Put on your detective cap, and let's check out the clues.

Is It a Premium Smoke?

Brand name is the most obvious clue provided by a box, but there are many other clues. The most critical thing to look for is whether the box is stamped "Handmade" or—in Spanish—"*Hecho a Mano.*" A box almost always tells you whether the cigars are hand-made.

A box label conveying the romance, brand name, and origin of a fine cigar.

While the stamping "Handmade" is a mark of pride, it doesn't assure quality. It's an art to roll a great cigar, but learning to roll a passable cigar isn't too difficult.

Even if a cigar is handmade, it might have been assembled hastily or carelessly. If you don't see "Handmade" or "Hecho a Mano," you almost certainly don't have a handmade product. Keep in mind, however, that this is just one of many clues you'll use to find a really good smoke!

Branded a "Winner"

A critical clue in reading a box is who made the cigar. I'm not a slave to labels, but when you're starting out, you have a better chance of finding a good cigar by sticking to the established brands listed in Chapter 1.

You can stick with winning brands, but sometimes it's a trick to find these established premium brands in today's market. Shops often sell out of these brands as quickly as they come in. Often, the cigars are snapped up by regular customers before they ever make it to the shelf. Take heart: You can find good cigars if you know how and where to look.

> **Cigar Esoterica**
>
> Most wooden cigar boxes made today are Spanish cedar. An old government report noted that a century ago, cigar box materials included poplar, red gum, elm, cypress, oak, mahogany, and maple, plus the more esoteric tupelo and balm of Gilead.

> **Blowing Smoke**
> The past couple years have seen an explosion of new cigar brands, and many I've smoked are expensive, harsh, and poorly constructed because they use inferior or under-aged tobacco—stuff that no manufacturer would put in a flagship brand. If you stray from the old, established brands to try some new, exotic brand, *caveat emptor*.

The spotty supply of name-brand cigars, as well as the growing number of new cigar retailers who don't have the clout to get them, has spawned a lot of new handmade cigar brands. It's easy to find new cigars, but beware: They may be nothing more than cigars slapped together using tobacco rejected by the big boys.

So many new brand names have cropped up in the past two years that it's almost impossible to keep up. The upside is that you might stumble upon a good cigar that isn't an established brand. After you have tried some of the major brands, you'll have a benchmark for a good cigar, and you then can experiment with all sorts of new names.

Is Wood Always Good?

Cigars nestled in cedar boxes might seem like a slam-dunk winner. Cedar boxing connotes quality, aging, and craftsmanship. It's true that many of the finest brands—Davidoff, PG, and Avo Uvezian, to name a few—come in cedar boxes. It's also true that many fine brands come in boxes completely covered in paper—A. Fuente, Te Amo, Don Diego, H. Upmann, Partagas, and Macanudo, to name a few.

In cigar speak, cedar is good, but don't assume that a cedar box means a good stogie. The cedar used for making cigar boxes is relatively cheap—too low a grade for use in furniture, guitars, humidors, and whatever else Spanish cedar is used in. A wooden box isn't a guarantee of quality.

Cigar Speak
Premium cigars come **packed** in two ways: square pack and round pack. All handmade cigars are round when they're made, and a round pack preserves this shape. Certain cigars are pressed so tightly into a box that they assume a slightly square shape from the **box pressure**. If done properly, a square-shaped cigar will taste fine and draw properly.

Boxed In: Feeling the Pressure

You can also use the box to size up how your cigars have been packed. Two basic types of packing are used: *round pack* and *square pack*. Your basic rule of thumb: Square pack is usually found with less expensive and machine-made cigars, while most premium handmade cigars are round pack. Some cigars, such as the Padron Anniversario series, feature a packing method that renders the cigars almost square—a throwback to the "old days" when many cigars were square-packed.

With square pack, the cigars are essentially pressed into a box so tightly that they conform to the square box. This *box pressure*, as it's called, doesn't make a difference with a short-filler cigar, but it can crush the filler leaves of a handmade cigar and seriously damage its "draw." It can also crush delicate wrappers.

Blowing Smoke
A hundred years ago, a significant percentage of cigars—including premium Havanas—were squished into boxes to save shipping space. Today, you'll find few premium cigars packed this way because it's too damaging to what has become a very expensive product.

Round-pack cigars are boxed in such way as to preserve the natural round shape of the handmade product. A round cigar is no guarantee of a good smoke or a good draw, but it's a visual sign that you're on the right track.

I've had some very enjoyable cigars that were boxed under pressure and were as square as a nerd at a cocktail party. If you take a pass on square cigars, you'll be missing out on some great ones. Don't disregard a square cigar.

A number of cigar brands, or certain cigars within a line, arrive individually wrapped in cedar or tubed in glass or metal. The cedar wrapping, if it's touching the cigar, may impart an additional pleasant cedar essence, but it won't protect the cigar.

Tubes provide no assurance of a quality cigar, but they are a great protection against the rigors of shipping. It's also a great way to transport individual cigars for a few hours while you anticipate a great cigar after a meal.

Don't Let a Machine Make Your Cigar

Don't expect either a great smoke or great tobacco from a machine-made cigar; this product will get you through only until you have the chance to kick back in an easy chair and smoke a true premium product. Machine-made cigars are cheap; if you outlay no more than a couple dollars, you'll probably get what you paid for. Machines do a great job of cranking out a consistent product with just the right firmness, no soft spots, and never a hard draw.

"Machine-made" and "short-filler" cigars are almost one and the same, because you generally can't have one without the other! Humans can't sprinkle little shreds of cigar leaf into a cigar shape and roll it. Neither can machines deftly combine and roll long leaves of tobacco into a cylinder that burns evenly. The cigar roller's art is in his hands, and it takes an expert "feel" to use just enough long leaf, compress it just so, and ensure a good draw and even burn.

Because handmade cigars are just that—handmade—you'll occasionally find a loser among even the best cigars. They may be rolled too tightly for a good draw, have a spongy spot you might have overlooked, or burn unevenly because the filler wasn't rolled "just so." This is the price of buying a handmade product, but you'll find that with the best brands, such mistakes are rare.

Occasionally a machine-made cigar will make a nice dog-walk cigar, or a good smoke for when the wind is blowing on the golf course. Premium and super-premium cigars are always handmade, however, and you should look for these when you want to ensure that you get a good smoke.

Your initial detective work and knowledge of cigar speak will clue you in to a machine-made cigar. The box will frequently say whether the cigars are machine- or handmade. If, however, the box doesn't specifically read "handmade" or "machine-made," other dead giveaway phrases to a machine-made cigar are "short-filler" and "contains all natural tobacco product." *All-natural tobacco product* means you're getting some part of the tobacco plant, but you don't know which part.

Sleuthing further, look at the binder of the cigar. Handmade cigars use a binder made from an intact, tough, natural leaf; many machine-made cigars, on the other hand, use a binder made of ground-up tobacco bits that are then processed with a natural "glue" and pressed into long sheets cut to size by—you guessed it—a machine.

Now look at the tip, or head, of the cigar. If the cigar has a plastic tip attached to the head, it's machine-made. No premium handmade cigar has a plastic tip.

Even without a tip, the head of the cigar will clue you in to how the cigar was made. The heads of almost all machine-made cigars are pre-punched with a hole. The machines punch the hole and roll the wrapper leaf into the hole to hold everything together. If you clipped such a cigar as you'd clip a long-filler cigar, little shreds of tobacco would dislodge in your mouth the entire time you smoked. I can't think of a handmade cigar with a pre-punched head, although a few might exist.

Tobacco Leaves

"What is it comes through the deepening dusk, Something sweeter than jasmine scent, Sweeter than rose and violet blent, More potent in power than orange or musk? The scent of a good cigar."

—"The Scent of a Good Cigar," Kate A. Carrington

Shorted Out—Turn On to Long Filler

Machine-made, short-filler cigars allow manufacturers to use every scrap of discarded tobacco—including veins and stems, which taste strong and bitter, partially because they have more nicotine than the leaves. Short-filler cigars not only use scraps, but because they are cheap smokes generally enjoyed by stogie-chompers, they frequently use inferior tobacco that didn't make the grade for premium smokes. An exception to the machine-made rule is the Cuban cigar, which we'll discuss in a minute.

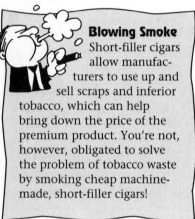

Hot Tip
Many short-filler cigars are flavored with cherry, anise, rum, and other glycerin-based agents. This might sound like an interesting change of pace, but the flavoring usually exists to cover up really bad tobacco. If you don't want to take my word for it, try a few.

Blowing Smoke
Short-filler cigars allow manufacturers to use up and sell scraps and inferior tobacco, which can help bring down the price of the premium product. You're not, however, obligated to solve the problem of tobacco waste by smoking cheap machine-made, short-filler cigars!

Blowing Smoke
If a well-meaning friend gives you a Cuban cigar, it's most likely to be short filler, dried out from a long journey in someone's suitcase. Dried-out short-filler stogies may still be smokable, although they burn hot. Dried-out long-filler cigars are a different story: At best, they have to be carefully rehumidified; at worst, they're a total loss.

With the growing appreciation of quality in everything from single malt scotch to cigars, the short-filler cigar, assembled by machine, would seem to be a dying breed. Most new and younger smokers would rather spend $12 and have one great cigar than use the same $12 for 25 crummy cigars. The times call for moderation—and appreciation of the finer things. Never choose a quantity of machine-made cigars over a few excellent handmade cigars.

While short-filler cigars are in a different league than premium handmade stogies, in a few rare instances a major manufacturer will offer a machine-made short-filler cigar using such exceptional tobacco scraps that you end up with a great everyday cigar at a super cheap price.

A couple interesting machine-made cigars are available. One is A. Fuente fumas, which are made with the scraps of aged tobacco used in $12 super premium handmades. Another is the F.D. Grave Munniemaker line, which includes some cigars that use all Connecticut leaf (generally used only for wrappers); the leaves deliver an interesting, almost beefy-flavored smoke.

Finally, many of the smaller sizes of Cuban cigars are machine-made with short filler. Whereas a Romeo y Julietta Churchill will be handmade, the petite coronas are made by machine. Many of the smaller-tubed Cuban products are machine made and are quite a bit cheaper than handmade Cubans. These cigars are one way to enjoy Cuban tobacco on a budget.

Where Was Your Cigar Born?

Most cigar boxes include the cigar's country of origin. Any imported cigar also carries a tax stamp on the box, which tells you where it came from.

So how much attention should you pay to where your cigar came from? Wine labels carry a great deal of information, including the country and usually the region of origin—very helpful information. With almost all cigars made outside of Cuba, however, the country of origin means very little these days.

Country of origin used to mean more. Honduran tobacco tends to be stronger than many tobaccos, and the Honduran government used to forbid products from other countries to be imported, so cigar makers had to work with what they had.

Jamaican and Canary Island cigars were synonymous with mildness, but no major brand has been made in Jamaica since the Royal Jamaica factory was destroyed in hurricane Hugo and production moved to the Dominican Republic.

Many veteran cigar smokers still associate the Dominican Republic with mild smokes. This perception no longer holds water because some of the most full-bodied non-Cuban cigars—Avo Uvezian, PG, and Arturo Fuente Don Carlos, for example—are all made in the Dominican Republic.

This said, some broad generalizations still hold true for many premium cigars. Cigars made in Cuba, Honduras, and Mexico tend to be more full-bodied. Cigars that come from the Dominican Republic and Nicaragua tend to be milder.

The Least You Need to Know

➤ Select handmade cigars, and avoid machine-made cigars.

➤ Use the cigar box to determine the brand, whether the cigar is machine- or hand-made, and the country of origin.

➤ Buy cigars that have been packed carefully, not squished together.

➤ Don't make assumptions about whether the cigar is mild or strong based on where it came from.

What You See Is What You Get

You've gleaned as much information as you can by scanning the shelves of cigars, and you're ready to make your choice. And what a selection you have! The most obvious visual characteristics of cigars are the color, the thickness, and the length.

Let's start by figuring out what these important elements mean, and how they combine to create what you see, hold, and puff. Remember, there are three basic parts to your cigar:

➤ The *filler* is the tobacco rolled inside your cigar, comprising the bulk of your smoke.

➤ The *binder* is the tobacco leaf used to hold the whole affair together in a nice, neat cylinder.

➤ The *wrapper* is the smooth, attractive tobacco leaf used to "dress up" your cigar for presentation.

Because you can't see inside a cigar to the binder and filler, the color and appearance of the cigar wrapper is your only visual clue when selecting a cigar. Ranging from green and yellow, through rich orange, tan, brown, and black, the color provides an indication of what to expect in taste.

Brown Is the Color of My True Love's Cigar

That may be a loose interpretation of a famous line from a poem, but it's true. Within that relatively narrow color spectrum (brown), however, is a rainbow of variations.

Hot Tip
Avoid the oft-repeated mistake of assuming that a darker wrapper signals a strong cigar—even if somebody told you so. Although it's true that darker wrappers generally impart a fuller, often slightly sweeter taste, they may be wrapped around a very light, mild binder and filler.

As with red versus white wine, the lighter a wrapper, the milder the taste. A lighter color wrapper will contribute less to the overall flavor of a cigar than a dark wrapper. Although a wrapper accounts for less than 20 percent of a cigar's overall flavor, it's a cigar's single most important visual element. Color does not necessarily indicate the kind of tobacco leaf used, and it certainly doesn't indicate whether the cigar is mild or full-bodied.

A light wrapper means nothing. Many very full-bodied cigars come with light-colored wrappers. Let's take a look at what you're likely to encounter when you make your selection. Although cigars can fall into at least 50 formal classifications of color, they all are part of six common categories:

➤ Double claro, candela, jade, or American Market Selection (AMS)

➤ Natural or claro

➤ Colorado claro or English Market Selection (EMS)

➤ Colorado

➤ Maduro or Spanish Market Selection (SMS)

➤ Double maduro, oscuro, or maduro maduro

Most cigars with maduro or natural wrappers will be labeled as such, but you'll seldom find packaging that describes the specific wrapper color. This is where you get to be the expert, and make your own decision regarding color. My Descriptive Guide to Cigars (Appendix A) often describes wrapper color, which will let you compare your own evaluation against mine.

Double Claro, Candela, Jade, or American Market Selection (AMS) Wrappers

For years, this was the favorite wrapper of American smokers. It's *flue cured*, which means that after the tobacco leaf is picked in the field, it's artificially heated in barns rather than allowed to naturally cure in the warm breeze. This heating process seals in some of the chlorophyll, which lends the light green hue.

This style of wrapper has always been resoundingly shunned by the rest of the world. Today, even in America, it's hard to find a candela wrapper on anything but an inexpensive cigar. This category fell out of favor because flue curing arrests the natural maturation of the leaf at a very early stage, so candela wrappers are the most flavorless and bland wrappers.

Natural or Claro Wrappers

This wrapper is light brown, and it is the most common color you'll find on premium cigars—both Cuban and non-Cuban. The tobacco leaf used for these wrappers is fully matured and has been allowed to dry naturally and slowly in large, open barns.

The tobacco plants yielding these smooth, flawless natural wrappers have been grown under cheesecloth to protect the color and appearance. Exposure to sunlight tends to darken the leaf. Shade growing, perfectly timed harvesting, and careful air curing results in a silky, tan wrapper.

A claro wrapper has a light, delicate, but distinctively smooth flavor. Like all quality wrappers that have been properly shipped and humidified, it should ideally have an oily sheen and silky appearance.

Hot Tip
Look for wrappers that have an oily sheen, which shows the cigar has been perfectly humidified and that the leaf is exceptional. This glistening is a nice bonus. But even if the wrapper is dull looking, provided that it passes the "pinch test" (see Chapter 2) and has some spring, it's fine.

Blowing Smoke
Ideally, a wrap-per should be one color, and free of blemishes or a greenish tinge. But with the current increase in cigar smoking and the resulting shortage of wrappers, you may have to accept a wrapper—even on a super premium smoke—that's less than visually perfect.

Good examples of natural wrappers are found on Ashton (renowned for its fine wrappers), Don Diego, and Macanudo. A generally fine example of the Cuban-grown claro wrapper on a Havana cigar is found on the Cohiba, noted for its silky coffee-and-cream texture and appearance.

Colorado Claro or English Market Selection (EMS)

This wrapper is slightly darker than a claro; the Spanish term *colorado* (red) describes the slight dark reddish hue. Some Connecticut leaf falls into this category, depending on the curing process. Most Sumatran and Ecuadorian wrapper leaf would fall into this category, as would the Cameroon leaf (discussed in Chapter 10). The Cameroon is an exceptionally rare leaf—and one of my favorites.

The Cameroon leaf has tiny bumps and a wonderful oily sheen. As it burns, the ash displays small white bumps against a backdrop of fine gray ash. An aesthetic delight!

You'll find good examples of this wrapper on Dominican-made Partagas cigar, and the A. Fuente Hemingway series.

Colorado claro leaf imparts more flavor to the cigar than a natural wrapper; this characteristic is particularly noticeable with the Cameroon wrapper. I have trouble finding a term to describe the Cameroon wrapper, but "nut-like" and "slightly spiced" is perhaps the closest I can come to accurately assessing its flavor.

The wrappers on Davidoff cigars are colorado claro at its best. It's a Connecticut shade-grown wrapper (see Chapter 10), but one of the darkest and richest of this variety you'll find. Other cigars featuring a fine colorado claro wrapper include the Dominican-made Montecruz sun-grown and H. Upmann, Honduran-made Hoyo de Monterrey and El Rey del Mundo, and Tampa-made La Gloria Cubana.

Colorado Wrappers

This wrapper is perhaps the connoisseur's delight. This oily, reddish leaf is a joy to behold. This leaf isn't a special variety; it is usually grown in Connecticut, but is also found in varieties grown in the Dominican Republic and Cuba. This is a leaf that the gods of tobacco selected to have exceptional color and flavor—and one that an expert grower knows how to nurture.

The colorado leaf is very aromatic due to its high oil content, and it has a smooth mouth feel. I'm not sure I've seen a satisfying description of the colorado wrapper flavor, but I am familiar with the visual and gustatory pleasures it delivers. You'll frequently find such wrappers on the PG and Avo cigars.

Maduro Wrappers

This wrapper is distinctly dark brown and quite different from the natural and colorado wrappers. The long process used to create a maduro wrapper concentrates the flavor and creates a sweet, pronounced taste—favored by connoisseurs because of its fullness and richness. The dark color of a maduro wrapper is caused by two factors:

➤ The leaf is left on the tobacco plant for as long as possible before being harvested. After the leaf is picked, it's allowed to air-dry in barns.

➤ The tobacco usually undergoes a process in which it's treated with heat (and sometimes pressure) to draw out the oils and "cook" the tobacco. The oils are then allowed to retreat back into the cigar. This process can be repeated several times, each time making the leaf darker.

Because of the time required to process the leaf, and also the more limited demand, maduro cigars are generally difficult to find—particularly in today's market, where demand exceeds supply and cigar makers are trying to supply as many stogies as possible to anxious smokers.

If you do come across a brand you like with a maduro wrapper, consider snapping up as many as your budget will allow. You never know when you'll see them again.

A fine maduro leaf should be very dark, oily, and shiny. The process places considerable demand on the leaf, so by nature, maduro leaves must be tougher and thicker. They generally come from a slightly different variety of tobacco, and they are also the lower leaves. Owing to the type of leaf, you can expect small veins and bumps on the wrapper.

The process and leaf combine to create a distinctive, spicy-sweet character—both in the smoking and on your tongue. Few smokers would argue that the maduro leaf lends an exceptional amount of flavor to the cigar—the most of any wrapper.

> **Hot Tip**
> The maduro wrapper isn't nearly as silky and smooth as a fine natural wrapper. It should still, however, be neatly wrapped around the cigar and free of large, prominent veins.

I very much enjoy a fine cigar with an equally fine maduro wrapper. The rich, spicy flavor of a maduro wrapper makes it something best enjoyed by a more seasoned smoker seeking different, fuller flavor.

Just as you might begin drinking light wines and move on to fuller varieties, the passion that begins with lighter cigars often grows to encompass something bolder as you, the connoisseur, expand your palette. Fortunately, you can try bolder cigars without moving away from a brand you enjoy: Many cigar makers produce the same cigar with both natural and maduro wrappers. Good examples, albeit challenging to find, are Ashton and Punch Gran Cru maduro-wrapped cigars.

Double Maduro, Oscuro, or Maduro Maduro Wrappers

If it's possible to get darker than maduro, this is the wrapper. Almost jet black in color, it has been subjected to even more extensive processing than maduro wrappers. It imparts a very rich, pronounced, spicy flavor. As with the maduro wrapper, expect a bumpy, somewhat veiny appearance.

Few cigars feature the option of a double maduro wrapper. Punch makes an oscuro-wrapped robusto, and the JR Ultimate cigar offers several shapes with the option of an oscuro wrapper.

> **Cigar Speak**
> The thickness, or girth, of a cigar is expressed in 64ths of an inch. This is called the **ring gauge**, which is the thickness if you placed a ring around the cigar. A 64-ring cigar would be an inch in diameter. A 32-ring would be a half inch. Most cigars fall into the range of 38 ring and 50 ring.

Size Does Matter

Ring gauge is the $1/64$ of an inch question! There are fat cigars and there are thin cigars, and all of them are measured by ring gauge.

You'll hear terms such as "38-ring gauge cigar" (thin) or "50-ring gauge cigar" (fat). After you understand what ring gauge means, you'll be able to easily make a size choice.

Various ring gauges, or thick-nesses, of com-monly found cigars.

38 Ring

32 Ring

44 Ring

50 Ring

47 Ring

52 Ring

Hot Tip

A general rule of thumb is that the coolness of your smoke has more to do with the ring gauge than the length. The "fatter" the cigar, the greater the exposure to air and the cooler the smoke. For most connoisseurs, an ideal ring size for coolness and "mouth feel" ranges between 46 and 52—approximately $^3/_4$ inch.

Ring gauge is nothing more than a measurement, in $^1/_{64}$ inch increments, of a cigar's circumference. (Remember your high school geometry class?) A 64-ring gauge cigar is $^{64}/_{64}$ inch in circumference, or exactly one inch. That's a huge cigar—one you would have trouble fitting into your mouth. A 32-ring cigar is $^{32}/_{64}$ of an inch, or a half inch in circumference—very slim.

Most standard cigars fall between a 32- and 52-ring size. *Ring size* has to do with how much of the cigar's burning tip is exposed to air, and also how comfortable it feels in your mouth. A fatter cigar smokes cooler and slower because more of the filler is exposed to air. Your mouth is only so big, however, and a really fat cigar is tough to get your teeth around!

A lot of what you prefer in a ring gauge depends on what feels comfortable to you, and also how you smoke your cigar. You should always "sip" your premium cigar, as opposed to jamming it between your teeth and puffing away like a locomotive.

Sipping your cigar will also keep the head of your cigar relatively dry. Holding it in your mouth for prolonged periods will cause you to salivate excessively, which will make your smoke soggy and produce bitter, tarry juice that will mar the quality of your smoke.

The Size That's Right for You

By "sipping" a cigar, a smaller person can enjoy a large ring size. But there's also a benefit to matching a ring gauge to your height, weight, face shape, and what feels comfortable between your fingers.

There are no hard and fast rules here; if how you look with your cigar matters to you, then buy a few different sized cigars that you like, take them home, and check yourself out in the mirror.

Ring size also has to do with appearance. A dainty woman puffing a 50-ring Churchill will make a statement—but not exactly a dainty one. In contrast, she can sip at the large cigar, never taking it fully into her mouth, which presents a much more ladylike appearance (if that, indeed, is what she's striving for).

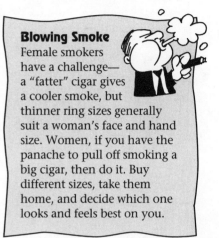

Blowing Smoke
Female smokers have a challenge— a "fatter" cigar gives a cooler smoke, but thinner ring sizes generally suit a woman's face and hand size. Women, if you have the panache to pull off smoking a big cigar, then do it. Buy different sizes, take them home, and decide which one looks and feels best on you.

Although it has more to do with "mouth feel" and comfort in my hand than any concern for my appearance, the range of cigars that feels most comfortable for me is about a 48 ring and, in length, is up to a double corona (about $6^{1}/_{2}$ inches).

I like the generous burning area of a 50-ring cigar, but any thicker than a 50 ring doesn't sit well between my fingers, and or feel good in my mouth. I'll smoke a 42 ring, but something like a 38-ring Lancero feels too long and thin for my liking.

By exploring and smoking a variety of stogies, you'll naturally find the ring gauges and lengths that feel best to you.

Eenie, Meenie... Popular Lengths and Shapes

Most brands offer a choice of several popular lengths, and your selection should primarily be your personal preference (or what's available). Various lengths are paired with ring gauges that provide optimal smoking qualities and appearance, and this pairing has led to a group of more-or-less standardized cigar shapes.

Because cigars are such a tradition-filled product, you'll find that most popular sizes have developed standard names. Often, a size was named after a famous smoker who favored it, such as "Rothschild" or "Churchill." Similarly, the shape can dictate the name, such as "Pyramid" or "Torpedo."

The classic midrange size is the corona, which is generally between five and six inches long and has a ring gauge of about 40. The classic "short and fat" cigar is the

Blowing Smoke
Although ring gauge—the cigar's thickness—can dramatically affect a cigar's smoking attributes, length has little influence. A longer cigar will smoke cooler if you're a "hot" smoker and puff too much, but if you allow the cigar to properly rest between puffs, and you're smoking a well-made cigar, any length cigar will smoke cool and pleasant.

Hot Tip
Many brands use their own special names to describe various lengths, usually for marketing reasons but sometimes because the cigar features a unique blend. This naming can get pretty confusing. After you get familiar with your favorite cigar shapes as measured in inches (length) and ring gauge (thickness), you can virtually ignore the shape names.

"Rothschild" or "Robusto," which averages $4^1/_2$ inches in length and has about a 48-ring gauge. The largest standard size is the "Churchill," which is approximately seven to eight inches long with a ring gauge of 48 to 50.

A cigar's length and shape carries with it certain traditional connotations, which you may or may not care about. Large cigars such as the Churchill, "Presidente," "gigante," or "director" signal bigness, prestige, power, and confidence. A slim cigar such as a "Lancero" or "panatela" have been associated with sophistication and elegance. What kind of mood are you in?

You can easily choose the size you want simply by going into a retailer, eyeballing the selection, and picking what looks good to you. However, it's helpful to know the basic shapes and lengths so you can "talk cigar" with your friends, and you'll be better prepared to describe to a retailer the kind of cigar you want.

You might ask, "Why not just have one standard length and a few basic ring gauges?" That would be easier, but not nearly as much fun. You can also select different shaped and sized cigars to suit the amount of time you have to smoke, as well as how you feel. Some smokers pick one favorite length and never vary from it. Although double coronas and Robustos dominate my personal humidor, I have a mix of different shapes and sizes because I enjoy the variety.

The following are the standard shapes you're likely to encounter, along with average lengths and ring gauges. To help you select the right cigar for the right occasion, I've also provided average smoking time, which will vary depending on how fast you puff and whether you're outdoors on a windy day or inside.

Specific brands will usually employ their own names for these shapes. Armed with your knowledge of average lengths and ring gauge ranges, you'll be able to figure out how they match up to the standard shapes. Starting with the largest, here's the lineup.

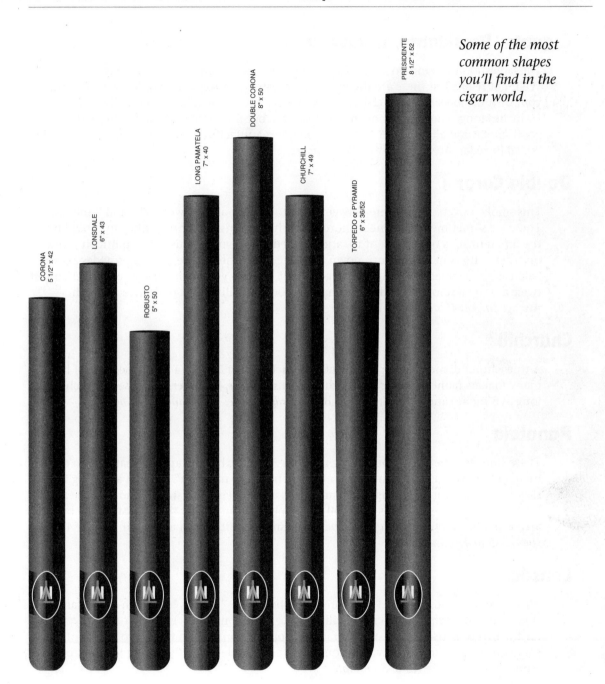

PRESIDENTE
8 1/2" x 52

DOUBLE CORONA
8" x 50

LONG PAMATELA
7" x 40

CHURCHILL
7" x 49

TORPEDO or PYRAMID
6" x 36/52

LONSDALE
6" x 43

CORONA
5 1/2" x 42

ROBUSTO
5" x 50

Some of the most common shapes you'll find in the cigar world.

Gigante, Presidente, Immensa

The largest of the standard sizes, *gigante* in cigar speak means "almost too big to smoke." Well, not really, but these are the perfect celebratory smoke when you're crowned king of your own Caribbean republic! They range from 52 to 64 ring, and are usually about 8 to 10 inches long. They are almost novelty stogies, but if they're well-made, they can be a good smoke and a fun gift. A number of major manufacturers make these available singly, boxed in cedar. *Average smoke: 1 to 1^1/$_2$ hours.*

Double Corona

This smoke hovers somewhere between a 49 to 52 ring and between 7^1/$_2$ and 8 inches. These are sometimes misnamed Churchills, which stems from the confusion caused by the different sizes of cigars sent to, and smoked by, the notoriously cheap British prime minister, who could never turn down a freebie. I feel the double corona provides a great balance between length and ring gauge, and it is also a good value because you get almost twice as long a smoke as with a corona, but you generally don't pay twice as much. *Average smoke: 45 minutes to an hour.*

Churchill

A true Churchill measures approximately 7 inches with a 47 or 48 ring. Because of how many makers named products after the famous smoker, however, you'll see Churchills as long as 8 inches and as short as 6 inches. *Average smoke: 45 minutes to an hour.*

Panatela

These smokes have a ring gauge ranging from 34 to 39, but are approximately 6 to 6^1/$_2$ inches long, which cuts a slim, elegant line. The "long panatela" is about a 36 ring but may be up to 7^1/$_2$ inches long. The panatela is a relatively hard size to find because a thin, long cigar is extremely difficult to roll, and smokers don't favor them because the burn area is small, which tends to make the cigars smoke hotter than a large ring cigar. *Average smoke: 35 to 45 minutes.*

Lonsdale

This extremely common and popular size is about 6 to 7 inches long with a standard 42 ring, although each manufacturer will produce variations. The cigar was originally made for the Earl of Lonsdale. Most manufacturers offer a Lonsdale in their assortment of standard sizes, although they'll seldom call it a Lonsdale—usually opting for their own name. *Average smoke: 45 to 50 minutes.*

Corona Grandes

This cigar is similar to a Lonsdale in length, about 6 to $6^{1}/_{2}$ inches, but sports a slightly larger ring of about 44 to 46. The corona grandes provides another optimal combination of length and ring gauge. *Average smoke: 45 minutes.*

Corona Extra, Corona Royale

Yet another variation on the corona, the extra or royale falls somewhere between the classic corona length and the corona grandes— about $5^{3}/_{4}$ inches with a 44 or 46 ring. *Average smoke: 40 minutes.*

Corona

The benchmark middle-of-the-road size for all cigar measurement, the classic corona is $5^{1}/_{2}$ inches long by 42 ring. Most manufacturers offer a corona, but you'll seldom find it called a corona as makers opt for their own romantic or descriptive names. *Average smoke: 30 to 45 minutes.*

Cigar Speak
The word **corona**, which is the mid-sized and most commonly made cigar, comes from the Spanish description of the "prime cut" upper leaves of the tobacco plant used to make filler. It literally means "fine" and was originally applied to premium Havana cigars in a variety of sizes.

Petite Corona

This cigar usually features the classic 40 to 42 ring of a corona, but is closer to $4^{1}/_{2}$ to 5 inches long for a shorter smoke. *Average smoke: 25 minutes.*

Robusto, Rothschild

Originally called a *Rothschild* after the Baron de Rothschild, who favored these stubby wonders, this cigar's classic size is $4^{1}/_{2}$ inches by 50 ring. You can find variations, of course, but the robusto is distinguished from all other smokes by its wide ring gauge relative to its short length. This has become a very popular size, and for good reason: The wide ring gauge delivers a cool smoke, it doesn't take a major commitment of time to smoke, and because there's less tobacco, it's generally one of the more affordable ways to sample a particular brand without taking out a bank loan. Watch out for the Macanudo Rothschild, which may have the Rothschild name, but it's actually a Lonsdale! Only Macanudo knows why it named a Lonsdale a Rothschild! *Average smoke: 25 to 40 minutes.*

Belvedere, Ascot, Demitasse

These are more or less catch-all names for very small, generally thin cigars with rings of 30 to 36 and lengths of 3 to 5 inches. These are not machine-made cigarillos, but actual handmade smokes. Because of the small size, they're tough to make by hand, but a well-made demitasse delivers a short, very satisfying smoke. They have to be savored slowly to avoid overheating! *Average smoke: 15 to 20 minutes.*

Daring to Be Different

Smokes with unusual shapes have certain characteristics that may lend a unique twist to the smoking experience.

Belicoso, Petite Belicoso

This cigar is noted for its refined, pointed head, which is challenging for the roller to properly fashion. The regular belicoso is about a 48 ring by 6 inches, while the petite version in about a 40 ring by 5 inches. *Average smoke: 30 to 50 minutes.*

Culebra

This cigar is fascinating anddifficult to make and, consequently, hard to find. It's three cigars, each about 34 ring and 5 to 6 inches long, intertwined. To smoke it, you have to unwind the cigars very carefully, and if they're not perfectly humidified, they'll crack. Each cigar will remain somewhat twisted and gnarled, but it's a fun smoke and a great way to share with two other cigar-smoking friends. It's definitely a novelty, but a nice change of pace. *Average smoke: 30 minutes.*

Pyramid

This cigar is tough to describe by ring size, because the tip is usually about a 52 ring, graduating down to a pointed 42 ring at the head. Pyramids are usually about 6 to 7 inches long. The idea behind this shape is to give you the largest possible burn area, while giving you a very manageable head. They're extremely difficult to make because the filler leaves have to be deftly rolled to avoid constricting the draw at the head, so this task is usually left to a maker's most experienced rollers. You'll find few pyramids, and even fewer ones with a good draw, but if you do, they're a real treat. *Average smoke: 45 minutes to an hour.*

Torpedo

This is a peculiar-looking shape, rather than a size. It's tapered at the head, relatively flat at the end, with a bulge in the middle.

It got its name because it looks like a torpedo. It's an old-style cigar shape, and was more frequently encountered 100 years ago than today. The torpedo shape is challenging to hand roll, and it doesn't lend any particularly interesting smoking attributes to the cigar, which is probably why you seldom find these cigars. *Average smoke: Varies, depending on the size.*

Perfecto

A perfecto is another old-time shape, seldom encountered today. It's similar to a torpedo because it has an odd-looking bulge, but unlike the torpedo, it's pointed at both ends. Once one of the most popular shapes, you'll seldom find a perfecto these days. It's usually about the size of a corona, with similar smoking length.

The Least You Need to Know

➤ A smooth, shiny wrapper is your most obvious clue to a good cigar.

➤ Light wrappers don't always mean a mild cigar, and dark wrappers don't always mean a strong cigar.

➤ Thickness is measured by $1/64$ inch, called *ring gauge*.

➤ Ring gauge and length are combined to create standard sizes and shapes.

➤ Choose a size and shape you like.

Part 2
Cigar Trek—In Search of Perfection

As you continue your journey through the world of cigars, you'll be confronted with a lot of choices—and a lot of information (and mis-information). A friend might tell you about the strong cigar that made him sick. Do you avoid that brand? Someone might tell you he can get you some primo Cuban cigars, but the stogies cost $35 apiece. Do you jump at the chance or take a pass?

As you've already learned, you have precious little information to work with. Relax! This is the time to let your taste buds take over and feed you loads of information. From deciding whether a cigar is too mild, too strong, or just right, to deciding whether a cigar tastes good enough to warrant a big price tag, Part 2 helps you interpret what your tongue is saying.

What's Inside Your Cigar?

In This Chapter

➤ Why almost all cigars feature a blend of tobaccos from all over the world

➤ How to work your way up from mild to "wild," full-bodied smokes

➤ Why you want to try a full-bodied cigar

➤ Telling a "strong" cigar from a bad cigar

➤ Determining whether where a cigar is made indicates its strength

A lot of what gives a particular brand of cigar its unique taste is what's inside—stuff you can't see, and a blend of tobaccos you can't figure out from looking at the box! Discovering what you like is a process of experimenting, but you can use a lot of information to understand better what you're tasting.

How Your Cigar Is Orchestrated

Most non-Cuban cigars are blended, often using tobaccos from around the world to create a harmonious product. The process is a lot like a symphony orchestra, comprised of the finest international musicians, playing different instruments to create a stirring performance. The manufacturer is the conductor, and in the hands of a relatively few individuals lies the skill to successfully manage this complex process.

Hot Tip

The Cuban tradition is to use the leaf from only one country—in this case, Cuba. This tradition emerged before the days of Fidel Castro—back when most cigar leaf was grown in Cuba. After Castro, however, the cigar dons left the country and tobacco became a common crop in many countries. Today's cigar makers have access to tobacco from all over the world.

Blowing Smoke

Several manufacturers produce completely separate lines of cigars—with notably different tastes. Don't let the line differences confuse or intimidate you; instead, look for the full name to guide you. For instance, Punch and Punch Gran Cru are both Punch cigars, but they are different lines with very different tastes. Different sizes of cigars within each line, however, generally taste about the same.

Every country, and regions within each country, has unique-tasting tobacco with distinct characteristics. Even the same seed, planted in different countries, will taste very different (I'll talk about this in much greater detail in Chapter 13).

The skilled manufacturer knows how to acquire, test, and compare these tobaccos, blending them in just the right proportions to create a "signature" taste that's consistent year in and year out. Manufacturers reveal very little about the combination of tobaccos used in their cigars. It's enough to know that when you buy one of their brands, you know to expect a very similar tasting product.

Cigars of different sizes, but within the same line, are generally blended to taste the same whether you smoke a chubby robusto or a large double corona. Brands such as A. Fuente and Davidoff have particular sizes that sport unique blends, but this is rare. (These special blends are covered in Appendix A.)

To nail down just the right burn characteristics, the cigar maker may make slight adjustments to a blend based on length, but the goal is for the different lengths to taste more or less the same.

Numerous cigar-savvy books and magazines have claimed that cigars of the same brand and line taste different. Most manufacturers would disagree. If you were to compare two different lengths of cigars from the same line, you might notice subtle differences, but those differences typically are not because of a blending change by the manufacturer. Although there are exceptions, most manufacturers keep the mix the same throughout lines.

I'm giving you a basic rule you can take to the humidor with you: Most brands employ basically the same blend of tobacco, regardless of length. You'll find that the corona of one brand will taste pretty much the same as the Lonsdale or Churchill of the same brand. There will be subtle differences because of the length and ring gauge, and as you read on, you'll start to understand why the tastes differ. At this point, it's enough to remember that most makers use the same blend in all the different sizes of cigars they make, so the taste will be very similar.

From Mild to Wild: Work Your Way Up

One of the most important jobs a cigar maker has when blending cigars is to give the product a certain "body" or "strength." Many factors influence what makes a finished cigar tobacco mild or strong; we'll explore all these variables later in this chapter.

A full-bodied cigar isn't strong or harsh, but a "heavy" smoke may be a little more challenging for a beginner to appreciate. "Heavy" usually means the leaf has higher tar and nicotine content, and until you learn to appreciate these flavors, you're better off sticking with a milder cigar.

Remember that you can no longer tell by country of origin whether a cigar is full-bodied or mild. Even within a given country, growers are able to nurture tobacco plants that yield anything from a very mild to a very full-bodied tasting leaf.

Initially, stick with milder cigars such as Macanudo, Montesino, Baccarat, and others that I review in my descriptive guide in Appendix A. When you're shopping for milder smokes, you can really benefit from the guidance of a sales assistant who has tried the various cigars.

> **Hot Tip**
> What makes a cigar mild or full-bodied? In a nutshell, the major attribute of a "heavy" cigar, believe it or not, is a higher tar and nicotine content. While tar and nicotine are detrimental to inhale, they also lend fullness, roundness, and richness to the smoke. These attributes are all positive, which is a good enough reason to puff and savor—but never inhale—a cigar.

If you can't get this kind of guidance, your best bet is to experiment! Like me, you may start out loving a really full-bodied cigar such as a Punch, Avo, or PG.

> **Cigar Esoterica**
> A story goes that in the early days of Cuban cigar making, one manufacturer developed a soft, spongy cigar that became the rage. It was called *panatela*—which means *sponge* in Spanish. Somehow, the word endured, but now describes a classically long and thin (and not spongy) cigar.

If you haven't smoked many cigars, I don't suggest you begin your adventure with a cigar that you know is full-bodied. But, hey, I was a complete cigar idiot, and I came out just fine.

"Pumping Up" to a Full-Bodied Smoke

A heavier, more full-bodied cigar is sometimes called *Cuban-style* because even though there are some mild Havanas, the traditional Cuban preference has been for a robust

Blowing Smoke
There is nothing wimpy about enjoying a light-bodied cigar! You may discover that "mild" is all you really like, and there are many excellent, mild smokes available. The benefit of being able to enjoy a range of strengths, from mild to wild, is that you have more freedom to select certain styles of cigars for various occasions.

cigar. Somewhere on your journey toward the wild side of cigars, you may decide to get off, finding a full-bodied cigar simply doesn't suit your taste. This preference could change as time passes, but you have to listen to your taste buds and appreciate what you do and don't like.

If you've ever experimented with wines or spirits, you may have tried a strong, peaty single malt scotch or a red wine loaded with oak and tongue-curling tannin. You may have decided you just don't want to go there even if the experts rave about them! The same is true with cigars—let your taste be your ultimate guide.

A Saturday-morning smoke, for example, may be a perfect opportunity to enjoy a very mild petite corona. As the grand finale of a rich, heavy meal with several wine courses, a full-bodied cigar will send a loud and clear message to your heavily assaulted taste buds, whereas they might not even notice a mild cigar.

As you smoke more and richer cigars, your taste becomes acclimated to the higher tar and nicotine content of full-bodied stogies. In my extensive tastings and samplings with those who enjoy spirits such as scotch whisky or brandy, a similar transformation takes place. Beginners opt for light, mild, lower-proof spirits; the higher alcohol content and complexity overwhelms their senses. With time and tasting experience, they become used to higher proofs and are also able to identify the subtleties of older spirits.

Like alcohol, tar and nicotine provide the double-edged sword of use and potential abuse. Moderate use and enjoyment may help minimize the health risks that are associated with excessive drinking or smoking. For a more complete discussion of moderation, see Chapter 22.

Is This a Strong Cigar?

Even though you'll hear the term "strong" used to describe a full-bodied or "heavy" cigar, many connoisseurs cringe at the term. I know I do. To many aficionados, a "strong" cigar is a harsh, undesirable cigar. "Strong" means that for any number of reasons, the stogie grabs you by the throat and shakes you around a bit.

When a smoker claims, "That cigar was just too strong for me," it could be that it was too full-bodied for his or her liking. It could also mean that it simply was not a good cigar. In many instances, a "strong" cigar will make even a veteran smoker queasy.

A cigar may be strong, or harsh, because the nicotine and tar content is excessive. It could be that the tobacco isn't of good quality. The biggest failing in cigars, assuming that the basic tobacco is of good quality and it's well made, is that the leaf was improperly or insufficiently cured, processed, and aged. This process is a true art—one we'll spend quite a bit of time on as we continue our cigar adventure together.

Right now, it's enough to know that young tobacco—no matter how good the basic leaf is—will make you feel ill if you smoke it before it's fully aged. The nicotine content of young tobacco is exceptionally high, and it contains a great many naturally formed compounds that do not taste pleasant when burned. During the aging process, these either disappear or fall to acceptable levels.

If you've been literally nauseated by a "strong" cigar that also has the reputation of being a full-bodied cigar, don't swear off all "heavy" cigars because of that one bad experience. To help avoid getting bad cigars, try the very best cigar you can find as you move up the "relative strength" ladder. You're far more likely to find a properly aged, properly made cigar, which at least lets you make an accurate decision regarding whether you like fuller-bodied smokes.

> **Hot Tip**
> Try not to be confused by the difference between a "strong" cigar, which may not be a good thing, and cigars of varying "strength," which is one way to describe the gradations from mild to wild. A cigar maker will not be particularly pleased if you tell him you think he makes a really nice, strong cigar. It may seem like a semantic argument, but trust me on this one.

If you think I'm advocating that you at least *try* to work your way to heavier smokes, you're right. Many, if not most, aficionados end up enjoying heavier cigars; these cigars are the pinnacle that lets you look down and appreciate the various stages of the climb. And just because you enjoy a "heavy" cigar doesn't mean you can't appreciate a variety of smokes.

Finding a Heavenly Body

As cigar making in non-Cuban nations has matured over the past three decades, the country of manufacture means less and less. Not only do these countries have access to tobaccos from all over the world, but makers in these countries have expanded their lines to include a variety of different styles.

It used to be that specific countries produced mild or strong cigars. For example, the Dominican Republic once was associated with producing mild cigars, while Honduras was known for rich, full-bodied cigars. There are only a few major cigar makers in the world, and they have access to tobaccos grown anywhere—whether mild or full-bodied.

Some of the world's most full-bodied cigars now come from the Dominican Republic. Not only is this full-bodied tobacco grown there, but it can be brought in from other countries. Today, there are very mild cigars made in Honduras, as well as very full-bodied smokes.

In Chapter 13, we'll talk about how the country in which a tobacco is *grown* influences the taste of a tobacco. However, the advent of blended cigars makes the country of origin unimportant. A cigar made in Honduras may include tobacco from all around the world. So don't get hung up on where a cigar is made. Yes, this makes your job in selecting cigars a bit tougher, but you'll soon have the knowledge needed to make your selection regardless of where a cigar was born.

Honduras

Honduran tobacco tends to be heavier because of the growing conditions. Up until a few years ago, the Honduran government would not allow any outside products to be used in cigars assembled in Honduras. Even the wood and materials used for the boxes had to come from Honduras.

> **Blowing Smoke**
> Honduran and Cuban cigars are commonly regarded as the "strongest" cigars available, which is still somewhat true. The traditional Cuban style, and the one adopted by many of the dons (the owners of cigar brands and plantations) who left Cuba for Honduras in the late 1950s, is full-bodied and heavy.

That situation has changed, and Honduras, like most cigar-making countries, has a system that allows foreign tobacco products to be imported and used in constructing cigars. Not only is it possible to grow a mild leaf in Honduras, but it's also possible to import mild leaf from other countries. Today, you could make a mild cigar in Honduras by combining mild varieties of Honduran tobacco with mild leaf from other countries.

There's also the issue of "style" to be considered. I don't know if it was coincidence or plan, but when the great Cuban cigar dons left Cuba as Fidel Castro came to power, they tended to disperse to countries that produced tobacco consistent with their individual styles. The Cuban Hoyo de Monterrey, Punch, and H. Upmann were (and still are) among the most full-bodied Cuban cigars available.

The dons who made those cigars all went to Honduras, and they duplicated the full-bodied style of their Cuban cigars. The climate and soil conditions of Honduras contribute to full-bodied tobacco, and so does the particular seed that was brought to these countries by the Cuban dons. In addition, those makers sought to replicate the character and strength of the cigars they produced in Cuba, and the tradition continues today. Consequently, the Honduran Hoyo and Punch are among the most full-bodied non-Havana cigars you'll find.

Mexico

Mexican cigars also have a reputation for being relatively full-bodied. The hot climate, the soil, and the lack of rainfall tends to make the tobacco grown a bit stronger. Tough growing conditions do interesting things to tobacco plants in terms of concentrating flavor, tar, and nicotine in the leaf. Sun-grown Mexican leaf, which is even darker and more intense, yields a relatively heavy smoke.

Dominican Republic

The Dominican Republic, Jamaica, and the Canary Islands have historically had the reputation of producing milder cigars. The reasons include climate, rainfall, and sun—all of which affect the strength and flavor of tobacco. But you might as well toss out these old guidelines because they mean nothing today. The world has changed. Japanese brand cars are assembled in the United States and use parts from all over the world. The same is true with cigars made in the U.S., Dominican Republic, Honduras, Nicaragua, and Mexico.

Hot Tip
You'd be hard-pressed to find a cigar that doesn't use some Mexican leaf. The toughest, tastiest binders come from Mexico, and the strong, almost harsh and ruddy flavor of Mexican leaf lends a very interesting quality to a cigar. Some smokers prefer all-Mexican leaf cigars, but these cigars can be a bit rough and no-nonsense—somewhat like Mexico itself!

If I had to make a broad generalization, I'd say that the best cigar tobacco in the world is coming from the Dominican Republic, and the majority of the finest cigars are being made there. I'd also tell you that some of the world's mildest cigars come from the Dominican Republic, but also some of the world's most full-bodied smokes. You just can't judge much about a cigar based on where it's assembled, and that's especially true for the Dominican Republic, which has taken the place of Cuba as the world's premier cigar-manufacturing nation.

Strength Is Relative

To help you figure out which brands are mild and which are wild, I've developed a "relative strength guide." It works a bit like a thermometer: Start with the mildest cigars at the top and work your way down to the heartiest, most robust cigars available.

The guide reflects my personal taste, but most experienced cigar smokers would generally agree with my assessment. You can work your way along the scale, experimenting and gradually progressing to the more full-bodied smokes.

I've only listed major, established brands. Many new cigar names are popping up, but few of them have consistent nationwide distribution. I've also found the quality of these newer brands to be spotty because the supply of tobacco is inconsistent. You may not be able to find all of the brands listed in this strength guide, but you're sure to find representative brands in each category.

The relative-strength guide.

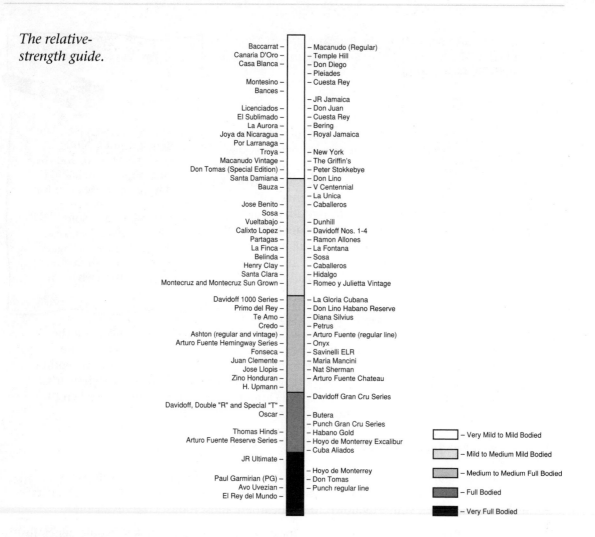

Baccarrat –	– Macanudo (Regular)
Canaria D'Oro –	– Temple Hill
Casa Blanca –	– Don Diego
	– Pleiades
Montesino –	– Cuesta Rey
Bances –	
	– JR Jamaica
Licenciados –	– Don Juan
El Sublimado –	– Cuesta Rey
La Aurora –	– Bering
Joya da Nicaragua –	– Royal Jamaica
Por Larranaga –	
Troya –	– New York
Macanudo Vintage –	– The Griffin's
Don Tomas (Special Edition) –	– Peter Stokkebye
Santa Damiana –	– Don Lino
Bauza –	– V Centennial
	– La Unica
Jose Benito –	– Caballeros
Sosa –	
Vueltabajo –	– Dunhill
Calixto Lopez –	– Davidoff Nos. 1-4
Partagas –	– Ramon Allones
La Finca –	– La Fontana
Belinda –	– Sosa
Henry Clay –	– Caballeros
Santa Clara –	– Hidalgo
Montecruz and Montecruz Sun Grown –	– Romeo y Julietta Vintage
Davidoff 1000 Series –	– La Gloria Cubana
Primo del Rey –	– Don Lino Habano Reserve
Te Amo –	– Diana Silvius
Credo –	– Petrus
Ashton (regular and vintage) –	– Arturo Fuente (regular line)
Arturo Fuente Hemingway Series –	– Onyx
Fonseca –	– Savinelli ELR
Juan Clemente –	– Maria Mancini
Jose Llopis –	– Nat Sherman
Zino Honduran –	– Arturo Fuente Chateau
H. Upmann –	
	– Davidoff Gran Cru Series
Davidoff, Double "R" and Special "T" –	
Oscar –	– Butera
	– Punch Gran Cru Series
Thomas Hinds –	– Habano Gold
Arturo Fuente Reserve Series –	– Hoyo de Monterrey Excalibur
	– Cuba Aliados
JR Ultimate –	
	– Hoyo de Monterrey
Paul Garmirian (PG) –	– Don Tomas
Avo Uvezian –	– Punch regular line
El Rey del Mundo –	

☐	– Very Mild to Mild Bodied
☐	– Mild to Medium Mild Bodied
☐	– Medium to Medium Full Bodied
☐	– Full Bodied
☐	– Very Full Bodied

The Least You Need to Know

➤ Most cigars use a blend of tobaccos from all over the world.

➤ If you're just starting out, try mild smokes.

➤ A cigar that makes you sick may have badly cured tobacco.

➤ Don't assume a cigar is strong because of where it's made.

Chapter 7

Havana Cigars: Straight Up, Cuban Style

In This Chapter

➤ Why Cuba doesn't blend tobaccos

➤ The full-bodied Havana smoke

➤ How Cuban seed got around the world

➤ Are Cuban cigars the best?

➤ The government and Havana stogies

➤ Separating real from phony Havanas

When manufacturers blend their cigars to achieve a full-bodied, rich cigar, you might wonder, "What are they aiming for?" More often than not, they're creating a cigar in the classic Cuban or Spanish style. A Cuban- or Havana-style cigar (the terms are interchangeable, since virtually all Cuban cigars are manufactured in or around Havana) is hearty, powerful but not overpowering, and smooth as silk. A good comparison is dark French Roast coffee or espresso.

In Chapters 7 and 8, I'm going way out on a limb. I'm going to tell you why Cuban cigars and tobaccos are great, but I'm also going to say things that most cigar connoisseurs acknowledge but few books or magazines say: Cuban cigars aren't what they used to be. For many reasons, they are not the best smokes, nor are they the best value. While I'd love to do like everyone else and perpetuate the myth that Cuban stogies are always wonderful, and worth every premium penny you pay for them, I can't do that. I'm going to tell it to you straight, and if you can obtain enough Cuban cigars to sample, you'll be able to make your own decisions.

The traditional Cuban-style cigar is the benchmark for all cigars. I've been lucky enough to have smoked Cubans when they were the best. Every cigar maker strives for the Cuban style of making rich, flavorful cigars. To create a cigar that's both rich and smooth is a true test of the cigar maker's art, which is why I said earlier that you'll never quite scale the "Mt. Everest" of cigardom until you can appreciate a perfectly made, full-bodied cigar. How did this Cuban style evolve?

We Don't Blend No Stinkin' Cigars!

Cuban cigars are unique for two main reasons. First, the tobacco itself is unlike anything grown anywhere else in the world. (Later in this chapter I'll discuss why.) Second, Cuban cigars have never been blended; they contain only Cuban tobacco.

Cuba has several growing regions, each with different soil, minerals, and water that produce leaf with different characteristics. Cuban cigars might contain tobacco blended from many of these regions, but they won't contain tobacco grown outside Cuba. The tradition of unblended cigars goes back to when Cuba was the preeminent cigar-growing nation. The tobacco was so superior to anything else grown that to use leaf from other nations would diminish the quality of a premium Havana cigar. Today, this is no longer true.

Blowing Smoke
A great Cuban cigar is a unique taste treat, but if you live in the U.S., remember these simple rules: It's illegal for any Cuban product to be sold in the U.S.; it's illegal to sell or buy a product containing anything made in Cuba; and it's illegal to import Cuban products into the U.S.—even a few cigars for personal consumption.

If you've had the pleasure of sampling really top-notch Cuban cigars, and comparing them to the finest products from the Dominican Republic, Honduras, or other nations, you'd see for yourself that in the 30 years since the U.S. outlawed Cuban products, the rest of the world has come a long way in catching up with the quality of Cuban tobacco.

In fact, Cuban cigars might even benefit from blending in tobacco from around the world—particularly when a drought destroys a crop or there's a shortage of a certain type leaf! Cuban cigars rely solely on Cuban leaf, which leaves few options if the crops fail to come in perfectly and abundantly.

Once or twice per decade, rainfall and temperature come together to nurture a perfect crop. Between these perfect years are several good years—and usually a few bad ones. The quality of the crop affects the blend of filler tobaccos available after aging, making Cuban cigars rather volatile in flavor and quality. But that's the price of not blending tobaccos.

In reality, nothing tastes like top-quality, aged Cuban leaf grown under ideal conditions. Nowhere else in the world has the exact growing conditions needed to create the taste of Cuban leaf. However, "different" isn't necessarily "better." Many connoisseurs say Cuban leaf is the best, bar none. Certainly, no other tobacco has the mystique of Cuban cigar leaf. How much less attractive would a Cuban cigar be if it also contained tobacco from other nations—in an undetermined quantity, no less! And how much more appealing would any non-Cuban cigar be if it could claim to have even a pinch of Havana leaf?

Cuba has naturally been protective of its fine tobacco, and for more than a century the country has had strict laws against importing non-Cuban tobacco. That tradition remains to this day.

Cuba probably could import tobaccos—the U.S. is virtually the only country with trade restrictions against that island nation—but it steadfastly refuses. Like wine makers who live and die by the particular crop and vintage grown on their slopes, the Cubans rely on their homegrown crop to make their cigars.

Full Body: In the Spanish Style

We'll talk later about exactly what makes Cuban tobacco so different, and so prized. One of the key characteristics of the finest *flor de Habana* (flower of Havana) is that it is mildly peppery and spicy, full-bodied, yet incredibly smooth. This is the taste and style to which Spanish smokers have been accustomed for more than 300 years.

As with their wrapper preferences (remember the hearty maduro, or Spanish Market Selection that I discussed in Chapter 5?), Spanish markets traditionally prefer a more full-bodied style of cigar. That's why the concept of a "Cuban-style" cigar is synonymous with *full-bodied.*

The first word many smokers associate with the style and flavor of Cuban cigars is *strong.* But a good cigar, no matter how strong (my preferred words are *heavy* or *full-bodied*), should still be smooth and not harsh. Good Cuban cigars are smooth, which is why I was able to enjoy a Havana stogie, even though it was the first cigar I ever smoked.

To say that all Cuban cigars are full-bodied, however, is an extreme over-generalization. Over the centuries, Cuba has manufactured a variety of cigar styles to appeal to the tastes of the world's smokers. For example, a few years ago, boxes of pre-Castro Cuban Dunhill cigars were sold at auction. They were encased in candela wrappers (bright green, flavorless leaves that have been rapidly heat-cured rather than air-cured). Even though they were Cubans, they probably tasted bland because they were made for American smokers who, at that time, preferred bland smokes. Cuba has always made a variety of cigars with the export market in mind.

> **Cigar Speak**
> **Cohiba,** the word used to name Cuba's best and most famous brand of cigar—which was created for Fidel Castro—is taken from the term for tobacco used by natives of the Caribbean hundreds of years ago. When Christopher Columbus first arrived in the Caribbean in 1492, he heard the native Caribs speak of **cojoba,** the powdered tobacco leaves in their pipes.

Even today, certain Cuban cigars are considerably milder than others, although the overall Cuban and Spanish preference is for a hearty style. These days, the world's cigar preference has caught up with the traditional Cuban style of a more full-bodied smoke. Many of the world's great Cuban and non-Cuban smokes are very hearty. How did the Cuban style find its way into cigars made outside Havana?

How Cuban Seed Traveled Around the World

In the 1950s, cigar manufacturing was a thriving, established industry in Cuba. The Havana smoke was unquestionably the world's finest. Thousands of Americans made the short boat trip from Florida to Cuba to enjoy the clubs, cabarets, fine rum, and cigars of Havana. American dollars flowed into the Cuban economy from both tourism and industry.

Like many Caribbean nations in that era, however, Cuba was ruled by an iron-fisted dictator. Fulgencio Batista had firm control of the country and toured his beautiful, dirt-poor land in his favorite cars. Although there were many social and political nuances, the bottom line was that under Batista's rule, the rich got richer, and the poor got poorer.

A young cigar-smoking upstart, dismissed by Batista as a local rabble-rouser, began to rally the peasants throughout the countryside. The young man's name was Fidel Castro, and the rest of the story, as they say, is history.

When Castro came to power, he nationalized all Cuban industry and appropriated money and property from Cuba's elite ruling class. Some were imprisoned for crimes against the people. Most of Cuba's cigar manufacturers were successful and wealthy, and it didn't take a brain surgeon to see the writing on the wall.

Most of the cigar manufacturers fled Cuba with few possessions, although wealthy Cubans with foresight had considerable assets stashed offshore. One of the most important assets taken by the escaping Cuban cigar manufacturers was the latest hybrid varieties of Cuban tobacco seed.

Tobacco plants can easily grow four feet tall and nearly as wide from leaf tip to leaf tip. The plant, however, springs from a seed that's no bigger than a coarse grain of sand! Imagine how easy it was, then, for cigar makers to leave Cuba with entire tobacco fields in their pockets.

Blowing Smoke

Many non-Cuban brands claim to be made with 100 percent Cuban seed—which is simply a good way to work the word *Cuban* into the sales pitch! Much of the tobacco used in non-Havana premium cigars is grown from Cuban seed, which is the generic name for the plants whose ancestors came from Cuba. Cuban seed tobacco has been propagated outside Cuba for nearly a century.

Although Cuban seed had been propagated outside Cuba for many years (without the knowledge of the Cuban tobacco *padrons*, or tobacco "godfathers"), Cuban seed tobacco grown elsewhere was generally disappointing. When Castro entered the scene, the tobacco plantation owners took their best and latest hybrid seed with them. They also took something more valuable than the seed: their knowledge.

Some of the displaced Cuban manufacturers settled with their families in Florida (specifically, Miami and Tampa), overseeing the reestablishment of their businesses in various Caribbean nations. Others chose to settle in Caribbean and Central American nations to be closer to the fields and the manufacturing.

Cigar Esoterica

When Cuban tobacco growers left their homeland, they chose Honduras as one of the most promising spots for cultivation because they felt it most closely approximated Cuba's climate. Makers of some of the heaviest Cuban smokes, such as Punch and Hoyo de Monterrey, set new roots in Honduras, where those brands are still made and are still among the most full-bodied smokes available.

The cigar *padrons*, sometimes on their own and sometimes aided by American corporations, began to re-create what they had left behind in Cuba. Their task was gargantuan. Tropical nations like Panama, Nicaragua, the Dominican Republic, Costa Rica, and Honduras had soil, terrain, and climate similar to Cuba's. However, there were no established tobacco fields in these nations.

To prepare soil to produce a great crop of wine grapes can take decades, even if the basic soil is perfect for wine growing. The same is true for tobacco, which is a tough and hearty plant, but which requires a very careful balance of nutrients and moisture to produce high-quality cigar leaf.

There was no one to make cigars in these new countries: All the Cuban cigar rollers were peasants and most remained in Cuba. Most of the skilled tobacco farmers and factory managers also remained in Cuba.

The transplanted Cuban manufacturers had to prepare and cultivate fields, as well as build barns, warehouses, and factories. They had to train farmers how to plant, grow, and nurture cigar leaf tobacco, which requires special care. They had to select people from primarily agricultural backgrounds and teach them to make cigars from start to finish!

Cigar Speak
Climate is a critical part of growing good cigar leaf, and even slight differences in temperature and rainfall will give the same type of tobacco plant a different flavor. The Caribbean, with so many micro-climates, often has several variations within one country. It's impossible to replicate the growing conditions from one country to the next.

The path from exile to success was a long one. In the years following the Cuban trade embargo of 1962, cigars made outside Cuba were generally poor. Soils were similar to Cuban soil, but different enough that it took years to find the right combination of fertilizers, minerals, and moisture.

Climates and soils in these other tropical nations were different enough from Cuba that Cuban seed plants grew, but lost flavor and character. The plants were hybridized and the soils given specific minerals and nutrients to mimic Cuban soil. This process required years of work, however. Today's great smokes from these nations show that the Cuban makers were successful in transplanting both the crop and the cigar-making culture.

Are Cuban Cigars the Best?

Many connoisseurs say that without a doubt, Cuban cigars are the best. Living in the U.S., where they're illegal, I haven't had as many opportunities to smoke Cuban cigars as I would like, but over the years, I've enjoyed many great Cuban smokes.

The debate over which country produces the best cigars is the same one that takes place among wine lovers. Is a California Napa Valley Cabernet Sauvignon or Sonoma Valley Zinfandel *better* than a French red wine from the Burgundy or Bordeaux regions? Excellent wines come from all these regions, but they are distinctly different.

What you think depends on your taste, but you could make strong arguments for both sides. Ultimately, why try to figure out which is best if you enjoy them all, for different reasons, at different times, and with different meals?

When Cuba was virtually the only country producing truly premium cigar leaf, Havana cigars were decidedly the best. But today, with manufacturers who've spent four decades perfecting tobacco cultivation in nations such as Honduras, the Dominican Republic, and Nicaragua, some great leaf is being grown outside Cuba.

Cuban officials still say they produce the best cigars, and that they're wonderfully consistent and well-made. Well, it just isn't true. As you'll read in the next chapter, a Havana cigar isn't always a handmade cigar—or even a good cigar!

Can a Government Make a Good Cigar?

When Castro assumed power in Cuba, all tobacco growing and cigar production was nationalized and placed under the control of the state. The Ministry of Agriculture oversees the growing of tobacco, the Ministry of Industry oversees production, and a state-run monopoly called *Cubatabaco* handles product marketing and sales.

The government is in charge of maintaining the style, quality, and consistency of the individual brands. Cuba's tobacco fields are mostly owned and worked by individuals, but the farmers' only customer is the government, and they must sell their tobacco at fixed prices.

Cigar Esoterica

The tradition of Cuban farmers having to sell their tobacco at fixed prices to the government isn't anything new to that country. In the early 1700s, the Spanish monarchy (Cuba was a colony of Spain) introduced **Estanco**, literally *monopoly*, that bought all farmers' tobacco at a price set by the government—not by the market.

For the most part, aficionados agree that over the years the government has done a decent job of maintaining the quality and individual style of the finest Cuban cigars.

For instance, most Cuban Partagas cigars are known for rich, spicy flavor and dark, shiny wrappers. This reputation still holds true. Cohiba cigars are noted for excellent craftsmanship and a creamy taste with just a hint of spice. Sancho Panza has always been a relatively bland smoke with a slightly salty taste, which has been preserved. Hoyo de Monterrey cigars are noted for luscious wrappers and a pleasant but pronounced peppery "bite."

It's tough enough to make several brands under one roof, but the Cubans go one step further. Unlike non-Cuban manufacturers, who usually make all the shapes and sizes of one brand in one factory, some Cuban factories make one particular shape for several different brands—each incorporating a different blend of tobacco. How do they keep it all straight? The advantage of this tradition is that it gives rollers the chance to become highly skilled at making certain shapes.

Cuban cigars have some significant problems with quality and consistency, which I talk about in Chapter 8. Under state control, the number of Havana brands has dwindled from several hundred to about 20. Many of the famed "flagship" Cuban brands were kept, and the smaller brands disappeared when the government took over. To my knowledge, the only new brand introduced by Cubatabaco has been Cohiba.

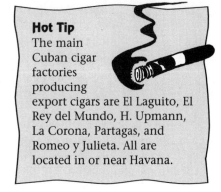

Hot Tip
The main Cuban cigar factories producing export cigars are El Laguito, El Rey del Mundo, H. Upmann, La Corona, Partagas, and Romeo y Julieta. All are located in or near Havana.

Many regular smokers of Havanas say that certain factories do a better job of making particular cigars than others. Boxes are stamped with a code that indicates both the factory where the cigars were made, and the date they were made.

Tracking down specific cigars using these codes, and knowing which factories do the best work, is just a little too esoteric for me. And as you'll discover in the next chapter, no matter how much detective work you do, Havana stogies carry no guarantees.

The Name Game

Once upon a time, Cuban brands such as H. Upmann, Partagas, and Punch were exclusively Cuban. When the manufacturers and owners of these brands fled Cuba in 1959, they reestablished them in new countries. Cuba, not recognizing any trademarks or registration rights, simply appropriated the brand names and carried on.

Davidoff used to make a Dominican and a Cuban line of cigars. A few years ago, however, the Swiss company said it was dissatisfied with the quality of Cuban manufacturing, and didn't appreciate how Cuba was pressuring the company to turn over its operations to the government.

Davidoff moved all manufacturing to the Dominican Republic and stopped using Cuban tobacco. The Cuban government, wanting to continue the cigar, tried to appropriate the name and continue selling a cigar named Davidoff, but was pressured into dropping the idea.

Dunhill also stopped producing cigars in Cuba, primarily because, like Davidoff, the company felt it was being pressured by the Cubans to relinquish control of the brands, the names, and the quality control. These were the only non-Cuban cigar companies selling a branded product made in Cuba, and with that country's track record of poor cooperation with outside companies, will probably be the last for some time to come.

Cigar Esoterica

In a world increasingly conscious of global trademark violations, Cuba may be in for some tough times. In several countries, courts have ruled that Cuba does not own certain brand names, but has simply appropriated those names. Under such a ruling, France banned the sale of Montecristo, H. Upmann, and Por Larrañaga cigars. Until Cuba settles infringement suits, finding Cuban cigars could get increasingly difficult.

In many cases, the labels and cigar bands of Cuban and non-Cuban brands are almost identical. Recently, the situation has become even a bit more confusing as non-Cuban makers have introduced to the U.S. market handmade smokes with the Cohiba, Romeo y Julieta, and Saint Luis Rey names.

This name game can get pretty confusing for smokers—particularly folks outside the U.S., where non-Havana cigars have been growing in popularity and availability in recent years. In Toronto or London, for example, it's possible to have two almost-identical boxes of Partagas cigars sitting side-by-side: one Cuban, and the other from the Dominican Republic.

If Cuban cigars are ever cleared for export to the United States, there will not only be brand confusion, but some significant legal wrangling over trademark violations and patent protection. A lot of the cigar-making families who left Cuba and took their brand names with them live part-time or full-time in the United States.

Large non-Cuban corporations own many of the worldwide rights to brand names such as Partagas, Por Larañaga, Punch, and even the Cubans' own brand, Cohiba! They probably won't welcome competition from a Cuban product with debatable rights (at least, under U.S. law) to the trademark. If the trademarks are ever challenged, watch for a *very* interesting battle.

Regardless of how Cubatabaco and government officials feel, their game face is to sneer at the prospect of entering the U.S. market. They have more worldwide demand than they can now supply, they argue, so the U.S. is unimportant.

All of this name-exchanging might have your head spinning, so I've compiled a list of leading Cuban brands that are also available in non-Cuban versions. You can whip out this list as a first step the next time someone offers a "can't-miss" deal on what is being touted as a Cuban cigar.

➤ Belinda
➤ Cohiba
➤ El Rey Del Mundo
➤ Fonseca
➤ La Gloria Cubana
➤ Rafael Gonzales
➤ Hoyo De Monterrey
➤ Montecristo
➤ Partagas
➤ Por Larrañaga
➤ Punch
➤ Quinterro
➤ Ramon Allones
➤ Romeo y Julieta
➤ Saint Luis Rey
➤ Sancho Panza
➤ Troya
➤ H. Upmann

Leading Cuban brands that to my knowledge have no equivalent include the following:

➤ Bolivar
➤ Cifuentes
➤ Diplomaticos
➤ La Esception Jose Gener
➤ La Flor de Cano
➤ Los Statos
➤ Juan Lopez

So, are you confused? Keep reading, and I'll tell you what to look for on the band and box to determine whether or not your cigar is a Cuban product—or simply carries a wonderful Cuban brand name!

Faking You Out: Know Your Cubans

As a modern cigar lover, your most pressing concern is to be able to tell the difference between a Cuban and non-Cuban cigar, if you're fortunate enough to come face-to-face with something you think (or you're told) is Cuban. Be aware that lots of fake Cubans are being sold. Some fakes are actually good cigars, but if they're priced astronomically because they're being passed off as Cuban, you're being taken.

Hot Tip

On Cuban cigars, the terms "Made in Cuba" and "Made in Havana" are considered interchangeable because virtually all Cuban cigars for export are made in factories in or around Havana. For more than a century, a "Cuban" cigar and a "Havana" cigar have been synonymous.

Blowing Smoke

Boxes of pre-1959 Cuban cigars are quite different and varied. They're also legal to buy and sell in the U.S., because they were made before the embargo. A few authentic boxes, filled with well-preserved cigars, are still floating around, but it's unlikely you'll run across one. If someone tries to sell you a box of Cuban cigars and says that they were made before 1959, be suspicious.

But let's be positive. Assuming you have the chance to acquire some Havanas through a reputable retailer somewhere in the world (outside the U.S.), you can look for a few clues to ensure that what you have is truly a Cuban product. If you have the cigar in front of you, you can use some simple methods to distinguish Cuban cigars from their non-Cuban (and unrelated) counterparts.

Cigar bands on all Cuban cigars will say *Habana*, *Cuba*, *Made in Havana*, or *Hecho en Cuba* (that's "Made in Cuba" in Spanish). Tubes containing individual Cuban cigars (many smaller Havanas come in metal tubes) also carry the country of origin.

All Cuban cigar boxes carry the Cubatabaco name, and a logo of a stylized tobacco leaf. If you buy from an authorized Cubatabaco retailer, he or she should have plenty of posters and window stickers touting that fact, and you can compare logos.

You're also protected by purchasing your Cuban cigars at an authorized Cubatabaco products dealer (outside the U.S., of course). The Cuban government is quite aggressive about prosecuting in court anyone found to be faking Cuban cigars and using the Cubatabaco stamp. No legitimate retailer would ever try to pass off fakes.

Like the cigar bands, all Cuban boxes are stamped *Made in Havana, Cuba*, *La Habana, Cuba*, *Hecho en Cuba*, or *Made in Cuba*. That stamp can be faked, but can be a helpful clue in your search.

Finally, the box will include a large Cuban tax stamp—an ornate stamp that has been used since 1912. The intricacy of the stamping is almost like currency, making it challenging but not impossible to duplicate or photocopy.

The tax stamp is wrapped around one corner of the box, sealing the lid to the bottom of the box, which can only be opened by breaking the seal. If you're buying an unopened box, make sure the tax stamp is intact. The Cuban tax stamp is glued very tightly to the box, and it's tough to peel off.

Check the printing on the stamp to make sure all the details are extremely crisp. Even if someone could peel off a tax stamp, piece it together and photocopy it, the copy won't be as crisp as the original.

If you really want to play detective—not a bad idea considering you're about to buy a box of cigars that probably costs several hundred dollars—whip out a pocket magnifying glass and check for a clean and even application of the light olive green ink on the slightly grayish-white paper of the tax stamp.

Some people find used Cuban cigar boxes and fill them with fakes. If the box has been opened, figure that the contents might be fakes and know what you're getting into.

You might run across mail order or Internet merchants who weasel-word their sales pitches to imply that they're selling Cuban stogies. They may be selling non-Cuban brands with the same name as Cubans, or they may be selling outright fakes.

In the case of Internet vendors based outside the U.S., they may be legitimately selling Cuban smokes, but they can't legally ship them to anyone in the U.S. If they ship by mail, it's a violation of U.S. Postal regulations.

A legitimate foreign-based retailer might not care about getting caught because he or she doesn't have stores in the U.S. or pay U.S. taxes. If such a retailer is willing to ship Cuban cigars to the States, the cigars would probably arrive with no invoice, and no other paperwork identifying the retailer.

At worst, you'll pay for smokes that never arrive because you were dealing with a scam artist, or the smokes will be shipped but they'll be discovered and confiscated. At best, however, you might come home from work to find the real deal sitting on your doorstep, wrapped in brown paper!

Was My Cuban Cigar Made by Hand?

If you live in the U.S. and you receive a Cuban cigar from a friend, chances are good that it was tubed and machine-made. Many Cuban brands have some machine-made cigars and some handmade cigars. For example, the Partagas petit corona is made by hand, while the slightly smaller and tubed Partagas petit corona especiales is machine-made.

Hot Tip
If you want greater assurance that you're buying hand-made Cuban smokes, stick with larger sizes, which are generally made by hand, and check for the term *Hecho a Mano* ("made by hand") on the box or cigar band.

Many smaller Havanas are machine-made with short filler, and many of these come in metal tubes. The best and biggest Cuban cigars, using the best tobaccos and biggest leaves, are handmade. Larger or unusually shaped Cuban cigars (such as a pyramid) tend to be handmade because they're difficult for a machine to make. Larger sizes are preferred by serious cigar nuts, so it makes sense to concentrate on those sizes. Finally, there's the practical matter that with a larger cigar, the maker can get maximum use out of large, high-quality leaves.

Scraps and short leaves can easily be bundled into smaller smokes. I've told you to avoid machine-made cigars, but I'm going to break the rule when it comes to Havanas. You won't get as good a quality cigar with a machine-made Havana, but you will have the chance to sample Cuban tobacco at a lower cost than the fancy handmades.

The Least You Need to Know

➤ Havana cigars feature only Cuban tobacco.

➤ Cuban cigars are usually more full-bodied than smokes from most countries, but you can find mild Havana cigars.

➤ Non-Cuban cigars used to be inferior, but they have caught up and many are just as good as Cuban cigars.

➤ Many Cuban and non-Cuban brands have the same name; to distinguish true Cuban cigars, look for markings on the cigar bands and boxes that show they're from Cuba.

➤ There are a lot of fake Havanas, so be a good detective if you plan to buy Cuban smokes.

Chapter 8

The Myth and Magic of Havana Cigars

> ## In This Chapter
>
> ➤ The unique taste of Cuban tobacco
>
> ➤ Why Cuban cigars are illegal in the U.S.
>
> ➤ Why Havana has problems with quality control
>
> ➤ Cuban brands and shapes to look for

Now that you have a better understanding of Cuban cigars, it's time to look at what makes these things so magical. We'll separate the *myth* that Cuban cigars are always wonderful from the *fact* that they are not. Believe me, I don't intend to spoil the fun of Cuban smokes, because there's nothing like 'em. But, hey, you might as well know what's up!

Whenever I have the chance to nab a Havana stogie—one that looks good at a price I can afford—I do. If I had an opportunity to fill a humidor with Cuban smokes, I would. I'd never think about making room for those Cuban smokes by tossing out the hundreds of wonderful non-Cuban cigars aging in my humidor, patiently awaiting their turn. I'd be happy to give them some Cuban companions, though!

Cuban Cigar: Still Champion

Many factors contribute to the greatness and unique flavor of Cuban leaf: the climate, rainfall, soil, and underground streams that help irrigate the fields. As with wine, where vineyards even a few miles apart will give the same variety of grape a different taste, a slight variation in any of these factors will yield distinctly different-tasting tobacco crops. That's why, even though the Dominican Republic is part of the same mountain range that juts up from the blue Caribbean waters, the two nations have different growing conditions.

Even within Cuba—a tiny island no larger than New Hampshire—there are at least six districts that produce unique-tasting tobaccos. With this marked regional difference within one small island nation, you don't need to wonder why other nations cannot replicate the taste of cigar leaf grown in Cuba.

The Cubans take great pride in growing their tobacco and making their cigars. They have centuries of skill and practice behind them. You can debate whether or not Cuban tobacco is the world's best, but no aficionado would argue that it's unlike anything else. At its best, Cuban cigar leaf is the champion of all tobaccos.

In addition, Cuban cigars have a magical appeal. Maybe it's the rich history and tradition of Cuban cigar making. Perhaps the intrigue occurs because a fine Cuban cigar has always been a rare treat generally reserved for the wealthy—or those with influence among the growers or the Cuban government.

For American smokers, there's the allure of getting your hands on something extremely rare and illegal. A friend might give you a Havana cigar, and no matter how bad it is, you'll be appreciative because you know it's something special and coveted—and contraband.

So You Want to Be a Smuggler?

Since the 1962 U.S. embargo against Cuban products, it has been illegal to import anything made in Cuba. This law extends to products containing anything made in Cuba. Havana cigars, available worldwide, are not generally available in the world's largest cigar market: the United States.

Cigar Esoterica

When President Kennedy was preparing to sign the Cuban trade embargo into law, he instructed aide Pierre Salinger to acquire at least 1,000 of the President's favorite Cuban stogies (H. Upmann Petit Havanas) the previous night. Salinger found 1,200, and this bit of "insider information" enabled Kennedy to enjoy Havana smokes until his untimely death.

Before the embargo, it was common for cigars made in the U.S. and a few other countries to include at least some Havana leaf. And while today it would be legal for cigar makers in the Dominican Republic, Honduras, Panama, and other countries to import Havana leaf and use it in their cigars, they don't because they couldn't sell these cigars in the U.S.

The letter of the law governing Cuban products hasn't changed much since 1962, but since the embargo, U.S. Customs officials generally allowed people to bring a box or two of Cuban stogies into the country for personal use. Of course, if an official felt inclined to enforce the law, the smokes were confiscated by the Customs Service.

Under President Clinton's administration, U.S. Customs has actually cracked down harder on Cuban products. Even individual cigars are being confiscated. Although the risk is slight of arrest or detention related to bringing Cuban smokes into the U.S., it's certainly a disappointment to have a $500 box of stogies snatched away by a Customs official—under the trained nose of a tobacco-sniffing pooch.

Blowing Smoke
Some U.S. citizens who travel abroad and want to bring a few Cuban smokes home for their personal consumption get rid of the box and remove the cigar bands. Without the identifying box or band, there's no way for anyone to tell where a cigar was made.

Always remember that the sale of Cuban cigars is forbidden in the U.S., and strict penalties are enforced for merchants who sell Cuban products. Some of my friends who operate retail shops have, on occasion, had a surprise visit by government officials. Even retailers who used to hold a Cuban cigar or two to give to special customers have stopped because they prefer to remain in business!

My Cigar Just Exploded

Although smoking Cuban cigars is a pleasant option, the modern experience of smoking Cuban stogies has peaks of pleasure and valleys of great disappointment.

My most disappointing experience with a Cuban cigar had to be a Montecristo No. 1—one of my favorite handmade Havanas. The weather was chilly, I was out of the country, and I was looking forward to firing up that lovely No. 1, which is a generously sized Lonsdale. Shortly after I lit the cigar, I began to feel queasy. The tobacco was young—underage and probably rushed into production.

Soon after I got queasy, the cigar began to unravel like one of those Chinese paper flowers you place in a bowl of water. I soon had a black, smoldering, nauseating mess on my hands. This experience was nearly equaled by one with some lovely Cuban Hoyo de

Blowing Smoke
One hallmark of a good cigar is consistency from cigar to cigar and box to box. Premium cigars should have uniform wrapper color, smooth draw of air through the cigar, firm (never spongy) construction, slow, even burn rates, carefully aged tobaccos, and consistent flavor. Cuban stogies today have great variation of wrapper colors, and the construction ranges from good to totally unacceptable.

Monterrey coronas that were so tightly rolled I couldn't draw any air and had to throw them away, virtually unsmoked.

At the other end of the spectrum, I remember sipping *cafe con leche* (coffee with loads of milk, which is a preferred style in the Caribbean), and smoking an equally creamy Cohiba that I wished would burn forever. Those are the highs and lows of modern Havanas.

In Search of Consistency

Although Cubatabaco officials would like the world to believe that every one of their cigars are perfect, anyone who smokes Cuban cigars knows this isn't the case. Regardless of the quality of the tobacco, if the cigar is badly made or the tobaccos improperly aged, you'll have a smoking experience similar to my "low points" with the Montecristo or the Hoyos.

Overall, the biggest problem with Cuban cigars is quality control and consistency. No matter what the Cuban government says publicly, the U.S. trade embargo has had a huge negative impact on the country's economy, with the inability to sell cigars in the U.S. being one of many financial blows. I'd say the country is "dirt poor," but soil is one of Cuba's great assets!

With the need to generate revenues from exported cigars, there's a lot of pressure on Havana to produce cigars and sell them as quickly as possible. An old TV ad featured Orson Wells pronouncing: "We will sell no wine before its time." Making good wine is a slow and painstaking process, and so it is with cigars. At minimum, cigar-making requires more than a year from planting a tobacco seed to rolling the leaf.

Ideally, cigar leaf should be allowed to age longer, which can easily take three to five years. (We'll look at this amazing process in Chapter 15.) Without a doubt, this time-consuming process yields the best smokes. If you needed money in the worst way, would you be tempted to favor the shorter time frame? This is a problem for Cuba: The country doesn't have the financial resources to produce a perfect cigar.

If you smoke enough Cuban cigars, you'll find that a lot of *green* and just plain inferior tobacco is being used. Green tobacco is not literally green; it's leaf that hasn't had enough fermenting, which is an important process we'll talk about in Chapter 15. Green tobacco can make even the most experienced cigar smoker queasy because it's filled with bitter tars, nicotine, and ammonia, which it releases when lit. The cigar tastes bitter and harsh, and the released ammonia makes it stink big time.

Overall quality control is a major problem for Cuban manufacturers. Many Cuban rollers take great pride in their work and are very skilled. However, they don't have the same financial and career incentives as their counterparts in other Caribbean nations. Cuban rollers still make nearly twice as much salary as the average Cuban, but a lot of badly rolled products manage to find their way out of Cuba these days.

Whatever the reasons, cigars coming out of Cuba are very inconsistent. Before virtually giving up on buying Cuban cigars a few years ago, I was finding at least half the cigars in a box of 25 to be of inferior quality. Many of the cigars burned too fast, were rolled too tightly, or started to unravel when smoked—all fatal flaws in the construction of a cigar, but ones that are almost impossible to discover until you buy the stogie and start smoking. Today, the situation is even worse.

You can find good Cuban smokes in Mexico, Bermuda, and South America, but put on your detective hat and use every technique you now know to size up a good cigar—and watch out for fakes. Wherever you look, expect to pay big bucks for Cuban smokes.

Pricey Stuff

Not figuring in foreign currency exchange rates, you can easily pay $30 to $50 for a large, handmade Cuban stogie. Boxes of 25 can top $1,000. I'm not ashamed to admit that even if I knew all 25 cigars in that box were perfect, that price is out of my league. Besides, even if I were a high roller, I like to get my money's worth.

If I could be virtually certain that by spending $35 or so on one Havana, I'd have a great smoke, I'd do it in a heartbeat. But with Cuba's quality-control problems, I'm not confident that my investment would be rewarded with a great cigar—and the thought of dropping that half-smoked investment in the ashtray is almost too painful to contemplate!

Seriously though, if you can afford to take the risk that comes with buying Cuban cigars—and you have the opportunity—go for it!

> **Cigar Speak**
> Tobacco that has been insufficiently cured, processed, and aged is called **young** or **green tobacco**. Proper processing removes many chemical compounds that make tobacco harsh and strong. Smoking even the best tobaccos, without proper maturation and mellowing, will make you sick. The tobacco maker's art is to convert a green vegetable product into a rich, mellow cigar leaf.

> **Hot Tip**
> The best places to find a quality Cuban cigar are Geneva (Switzerland), London, and Munich. The finest Havanas go there because they bring the highest prices. The easiest places for Americans to find Cuban cigars are Canada and the Caribbean nations. Retailers in major Canadian cities carry a pretty good selection. Availability of handmade Cuban smokes in the Caribbean nations is spotty.

Have-a-Havana

In the old days, when stogies had names like "HavaHavana," "Uwanta Cigar," and "Paid in Full," it was easy to find Havana as well as American-made smokes containing Cuban filler. Now, the only way for most smokers to find Havana leaf is to buy a Havana cigar.

Cuba does export some of the cigar tobacco leaves it grows, and its two main customers are Spain and the United Kingdom. However, the majority of Havana leaf stays in Cuba, and all the best leaf stays there, to be turned into Havana smokes.

I assume that no matter how inconsistent, unpredictable, or expensive Cuban cigars have become, you'll want to try some Havanas if you have the chance. So I've compiled a brief summary of some of the most celebrated brands and shapes.

If you think selecting non-Cuban cigars is confusing, Cuban cigars take that confusion to another level! As I explained in Chapter 7, many leading Cuban brands offer both hand-made and machine-made cigars. To get more assurance of a handmade product, buy the larger sizes and look for "Hecho a Mano" on the band or box.

Various cigar sizes, even if they're the same brand, may have very different tastes and styles. Unlike blended cigars made outside of Cuba, which generally use similar blends no matter what size or shape they are, the taste of Cuban cigars varies considerably based on the size and shape. I wish I could give you a hard and fast rule for how and when this differs, but I can't! For example, the classic Montecristo No. 2, a pyramid, tastes quite different than a Montecristo No. 1.

Here's a random selection that might help you get started if and when you run across Cuban cigars. Rather than group the cigars by brand, which is unreliable because the blends are different and not all are handmade, I'm giving you specific cigars to watch for. The cigars I've listed are handmade unless I've noted otherwise.

➤ **Bolivar Belicosos Finos**   Featuring a delicately pointed head, this *figuardo* (shaped) 5$^1/_2$ inch by 52-ring cigar is one of the best Bolivars. Like most Bolivars, it's full-bodied.

➤ **Bolivar Champions Petit Corona** (machine-made)   For a machine-made, this 5 inch by 35-ring smoke is a decent cigar and gives you a taste of Havana leaf.

➤ **Cohiba Esplendido**   Cohiba cigars incorporate the best, most aged tobaccos in Cuba. In my experience, Cohibas are the most consistent in quality of any cigars because they are still the cigar of dignitaries (even though Fidel Castro no longer smokes). This brand is expensive, and the Churchill-sized Esplendido (7 inches by 47 ring) is one of the priciest. At its best, it packs a medium-full bodied flavor with a coffee-and-cream smoothness that's like great cappuccino.

➤ **Cohiba Robusto**   Like other Cohibas, the Robusto (4$^7/_8$ inches by 50 ring) under-goes an additional fermentation process that's standard in many premium non-Cuban cigars, but not common in the hastily made modern Havanas. This cigar offers a dense and smooth smoke.

➤ **Cohiba Lancero**   If you like a long, elegant panatela (7$^1/_2$ inches by 38 ring), this is your best bet in a Cuban cigar. Like most Cuban cigars, this stogie can be very harsh when you first buy it—a condition accentuated by the fact that it is very thin and burns fairly hot. If you buy several and find the first disappointing, set the rest aside for up to a year in your humidor. I've found that, given time, this cigar can really blossom.

➤ **El Rey del Mundo Tainos**   This Churchill-sized cigar (7 inches by 47 ring) is probably that line's best offering. It's one of the mildest Havanas.

➤ **El Rey del Mundo Coronas de Luxe**   This cigar is light and smooth. If you like a well-made cigar with decently aged tobaccos, this is a good choice. It's a medium-length smoke (5$\frac{1}{2}$ inches by 42 ring), and it is easy for the beginning cigar smoker to enjoy.

➤ **Fonseca Demitasse**   The Dominican-made Fonseca cigars are far more interesting than these light-bodied, somewhat bland Cuban smokes. I'd consider the demitasse (4$\frac{1}{2}$ inches by 36 ring) a nice, mild smoke. The best Cuban leaves go to the larger cigars of other brands.

➤ **H. Upmann No. 1**   Overall, I have little experience with Cuban Upmann's because I've found the consistency and quality disappointing. However, I've had a few good experiences with the No. 1—a classic Lonsdale of 6$\frac{1}{2}$ inches by 42 ring. It has a medium body. Machine-made, tubed Upmanns are one of the most commonly found Cuban cigars smuggled into the United States. They are a decent smoke and provide the thrill of smoking a Havana, but they're on a par with a cheap bundled Honduran cigar.

➤ **Hoyo de Monterrey Churchill**   This larger Hoyo is, of course, handmade, and apparently extra care is taken in the selection of tobaccos and the making of this cigar because it seems a bit more consistent than many other Cuban brands. This cigar (7 inches by 47 ring) is medium bodied, but with a lot of the peppery qualities that make Havana leaf special. The Hoyo Epicure No. 1 used to be a superb and robust cigar, but I haven't seen it in a long time and I don't believe it's being made any longer.

➤ **La Flor de Cano Short Churchill**   This brand is very difficult to find, especially in handmades. It's extremely mild, but it's probably the best of the line. The Short Churchill is actually a robusto at 5 inches by 50 ring.

➤ **La Gloria Cubana Tapados (Corona)**   I can't resist the charming young lady on the band, who calls alluringly to me. Oh, well. This is a very old Cuban brand, but it seems to have become inconsistent over time. The Tapados (5$\frac{1}{4}$ inches by 42 ring) is a classic corona with a medium-full flavor and hints of pepper.

➤ **Montecristo No. 1**   Montecristo is the biggest-selling Cuban cigar by a wide margin, and probably for good reason. It's a venerable name and seems to have maintained its charisma among Cuban cigar aficionados. The Cubans have continued to pay attention to the brand—probably because the consistency and quality seems higher than that of other Havanas. The No. 1 is a Lonsdale (6$\frac{1}{2}$ inches by 42 ring), and it's a very smooth, full-bodied smoke.

➤ **Montecristo No. 2**   This pyramid, or torpedo, is simply a fun cigar with everything you could want in a Cuban smoke. It's about 6 inches long with a 52 ring at the head. The head tapers to a delicate point at the foot. It's a flagship cigar that the Cuban makers, even in these days of spotty quality, seem to revel in making. If I could afford a box of Cuban cigars, this is one of the few brands I would purchase—with confidence that it would contain the best tobaccos and craftsmanship Cuba offers.

91

➤ **Partagas Lusitania**   Always one of my favorite Cuban smokes, the Cuban Partagas brand is, like many Cuban cigars, inconsistent these days. Still, a substantial (7^1/$_2$ inches by 49 ring) Lusitania (named after the famous ship sunk by German U-boats in World War I) can be an incredible cigar experience. Cuban rollers lavish all their skill on this cigar, which has long been one of the classic Havana smokes. The cigar tends to be somewhat dry, but it still has that earthy, full-bodied, Partagas explosion of flavor.

➤ **Partagas 8-9-8**   I love this Lonsdale, and I'm not usually a Lonsdale fan. It's packaged nicely and seems to be made very well by modern Cuban standards. The Dominican-made Partagas 8-9-8 cigar is also one of my favorites; it has the same earthy quality as its Cuban brother, although it is not so full-bodied and is far more consistent. Still, a good Cuban 8-9-8 (6 inches by 42 ring) is a treat.

➤ **Partagas Petit Corona** (machine-made)   I've had extremely good luck with the machine-made Partagas cigars, and I have no idea why that should be. Compared to the harsh-tasting machine-made Cuban Romeo y Julieta or H. Upmann stogies, the Partagas machine-mades are smooth and tasty. If you're on a budget and crave the taste of Havana leaf, your best bet in machine-mades are Partagas, and the Petit Corona (4^1/$_2$ inches by 42 ring), is one of the most interesting choices.

➤ **Por Larrañaga**   I feel compelled to mention this cigar—even though it's virtually a dead brand in Cuba—because it has such history associated with it. The brand was Rudyard Kipling's. I know little about it because it's virtually impossible to find. There is no particular size or shape I'd recommend. You just might want to try it if you find it.

➤ **Punch Double Coronas**   This large (7^1/$_2$ inches by 49 ring) cigar receives the attention of the expert rollers and tobacco graders because of its size and the prestige it has among cigar connoisseurs worldwide. You'll find some of the best filler tobaccos and wrappers in this medium-full bodied smoke.

➤ **Punch Punch**   This Corona Extra (5^1/$_2$ inches by 46 ring) is considered a classic. As one of the larger sizes, it receives special attention in manufacturing and tends to contain aged tobaccos.

➤ **Punch Machine Made**   These cigars are very common, usually tubed, and overall of pretty decent quality. If you're looking to try Cuban tobacco, this might be a reasonably economical choice, but it won't be on a par with the large, handmade stogies. Here again, I won't give you a size or shape; just sample what you can find.

➤ **Ramon Allones**   These cigars are generally full bodied and come in limited sizes that are tough to find. If you enjoy "heavy" smokes, give these a try—if you can find them. It's hard to recommend a particular size or shape, because these cigars are hard to find; you might want to sample whatever you can find.

➤ **Romeo y Julieta Fabulosos** (9$^{1}/_{2}$ inches by 47 ring) or **Clemenceaus** (7 inches by 47 ring)   This brand has a good, medium-full body. I'd stick with the large sizes because a lot of these are manufactured, and only the extraordinarily large cigars get special attention.

➤ **Saint Luis Rey**   I haven't had much personal experience with this brand, but it's supposedly very nice and probably worth a try. Production is limited, as are sizes, so it may be a challenge to find. Try any size you can find.

➤ **Sancho Panza**   I've found this brand to be somewhat harsh and salty, albeit mild. All you can do is try one, but from what I've heard, this brand is relatively far down the pecking order to receive the best Havana leaf, which is reserved for Partagas, Montecristo, and some other brands. I can't recommend any individual cigars from this line.

The Least You Need to Know

➤ Since 1962, it has been illegal to buy or sell Cuban smokes in the United States, or to bring them into the country.

➤ The quality and consistency of Cuban cigars is unpredictable, so be careful if and when you buy them.

➤ Many Cuban brands have both machine-made and handmade cigars in their lineups.

➤ Large Cuban cigars are more likely to be handmade, while smaller sizes and tubed cigars are more often machine-made.

Chapter 9

How the Cigar Becomes a Star

In This Chapter

➤ Preparing aged tobacco for manufacturing

➤ How cigars are made

➤ Why making cigars is an art

➤ How a roller makes a cigar look beautiful

By now, you're getting savvy about selecting, smoking, and appreciating a wide variety of cigars. I hope you've had the chance to puff at least a few cigars where everything came together: the taste was great; the cigar burned slowly and evenly, leaving behind a nice ash at the tip; the draw of air was perfect, and it didn't get bitter or tarry even at the very end. Perfection!

You knew it was good, but maybe you got to wondering *why* it was *that* good. What combination of factors in the growing, aging, and manufacturing contributed to that "wonder cylinder?" The next several chapters deal with how a cigar becomes a star. We'll start with the making of a fine cigar, which is critically important. After you've discovered what it takes to make a great cigar, we'll look at the time-consuming and artful process of growing, curing, and aging fine cigar leaf.

Don't Try This at Home: Creating a Cigar

In many parts of the world, including cities like Tampa and Miami, cigar-making is a cottage industry. The entire process of making a cigar—from preparing aged, cured leaves for rolling to applying the final cap of tobacco on the head—requires very simple equipment. Other than a few wooden and metal implements, the entire process of making cigars is "in the hands."

The experience of the people, not the equipment, makes for a perfectly constructed, rolled, and evenly burning cigar. Practice makes perfect, and the workers in a cigar factory—from leaf sorters to the top cigar rollers—perform their assigned tasks hundreds of times a day, every day.

Seeing thousands of tobacco leaves each day, sorters learn to grade leaves quickly by size, color, and quality. Creating up to 150 cigars per day, rollers can gather up just the right combination of leaves for the filler, use the perfect amount of pressure to bind them into a cigar shape, apply wrappers, and deftly roll the final product.

Just as you use all five senses when selecting and smoking a cigar, all the senses also come into play when making a cigar:

> ➤ **Touch** Tobacco leaves have to feel just right; pliable and silky, never brittle or soggy.

Blowing Smoke
From the time the leaves are picked from the tobacco plant to having a smokeable product takes about six months. At this point, the leaves can be used to make good cigars, but they're likely to be harsher than leaves allowed to "sleep" from one to five years.

> ➤ **Sight** Each type of leaf looks different, and the graders and sorters know just what to look for in each leaf.

> ➤ **Smell** Good cigar leaf has a subtle perfume.

> ➤ **Sound** The subtle rustle of the tobacco leaves tells you whether they're too dry and brittle for making cigars, and when they need to be moisturized before continuing the construction process.

> ➤ **Taste** Throughout the leaf-aging and cigar-making process, factory managers, graders, and owners taste-test aging tobacco for readiness. They're always smoking finished products, using their experienced palates to tell them if their blends are "on target."

Awaking the "Sleeping" Leaf

Tobacco leaves are brought to the factories from the aging warehouses in large, square bales, called *tercios*, that contain hundreds of individual leaves. In this state, the leaves look a lot like large and ancient spear heads: pointed at the tip, widening in the middle, and tapering almost to a point at the stem-end.

Fine scotch whisky or Cognac brandy is left to mellow in oak barrels, and that extra aging is reflected in smoothness and price. Similarly, almost all cigar tobacco is allowed to "sleep" in bales for at least several months, but a quality-conscious cigar maker will set aside the finest tobacco leaves and allow them to age and mature for up to seven years.

In the cigar factory, these bales of tobacco—which in factories outside Cuba may come from anywhere in the world—are opened and, for the first time in a long time, exposed to light.

> **Cigar Speak**
> **Tercio** is a burlap-wrapped bale (about the size of a hay bale) containing aged individual tobacco leaves. The tercio is used to protect and transport the tobacco, and also to store the tobacco during the aging process.

Bales filled with fine Olor cigar leaf "sleep" in a warehouse, ready to be made into cigars.

After "sleeping" in a warehouse, locked in bales of burlap and palm bark (we'll talk later about the art of baling tobacco for warehousing and aging), the leaves are almost like a solid block—because of the pressure.

These aged leaves are as fragile as they are valuable. Even though they've been resting in the humid tropical climate, they have lost much of their moisture. Clumsy handling at this point would "shatter" these dry, brittle leaves and render them useless for handmade cigars. At this point, they're much too delicate to endure the rigors of being bent, bunched, and shaped into a cigar.

Workers carefully open the bales and separate the leaves. The leaves need moisture, and fast, so they're transported to a special room with 95-percent humidity and given a "sauna bath." The leaves stay in this room for as long as 24 hours. Experienced workers continually feel the tobacco to decide when it's pliable enough to "work" into a cigar.

The dry, newly awakened tobacco leaves are wetted, gently shaken to remove excess moisture, and placed in a steamy room until they're pliable enough to be rolled into cigars.

Cigar Esoterica

Tobacco is like a sponge: left in dry conditions, it quickly turns hard and brittle. When exposed to humid air, it quickly absorbs the moisture and becomes silky and pliable. It's almost as if the leaf is alive again, even though it may have been picked years earlier. It's a miraculous thing to watch a leaf come alive after its long rest.

Remember that a cigar has three main elements: the filler, the binder, and the wrapper. All of these are made of different tobaccos. While the processing of cigar leaves is very similar, the tobaccos used for different parts of the cigar are kept strictly separated so that they can be combined later into perfect proportions.

When the tobacco leaves have been sufficiently awakened and revitalized after their long sleep, they're ready for a final sorting, grading, and color classification. Before being sent to the rollers, experienced graders sort the leaves.

Giving a Cigar "The Look"

Wrapper leaves are carefully examined and classified by color and quality. A few splotches or water spots on a filler or binder leaf won't matter, because you, the consumer, never see these. A nice-looking wrapper is critical to the visual appeal of a cigar, however, and great care is taken to check all wrapper leaves for a perfect appearance.

The final step in preparing the wrapper leaf for manufacturing is to split it in two. This step is important for a couple reasons. First, a whole-leaf is too unwieldy and large to roll, but a half-leaf is perfect. This is true for all parts of the cigar; filler, binder, and wrapper. If you carefully unravel a cigar wrapper, you'll find an almost perfect half-leaf, which has been trimmed at the head and tuck end.

Moistened leaves are divided in half, and then carefully sorted and stacked before being sent to the tobacco blender.

The second reason for splitting the leaf is because an ideal wrapper should be smooth. Having a prominent *bump* (the central leaf vein) spiraling down the cylinder would look and feel pretty lousy. (Before these leaves were set down for their long sleep, the main stem was removed, leaving a small "v" indentation at the base of the leaf. Leaving the rest of the central vein intact made the leaf easier to store and handle until it was ready to be halved.)

One of the most critical aspects of making a cigar is combining the filler leaf in just the right proportions. After filler leaves are inspected, revitalized, and sorted, they are sent to a room to be weighed and measured into perfect proportions for cigars. This is why *tercios* of tobacco are kept strictly separated!

The master blender who compiles these leaves follows exact proportions, but also relies on skill to determine when to make small changes in the blend. Different groups of tobacco may have slightly different characteristics. If there's a significant variation in a particular group of leaves, the master blender may talk with the factory head about making an adjustment. The goal is to achieve consistent flavor and quality.

A tobacco blender weighs leaves to match formulas for various cigars. The measured leaf is sent to the factory floor to be turned into cigars.

In Cuba, all the leaf used for filler, binders, and wrappers is Cuban, but it may come from different regions of Cuba, and it may also come from different varieties of tobacco plants. In Cuba, these different tobaccos require the same degree of care in blending.

Outside Cuba, *tercios* containing tobacco from many other countries may be shipped into the factory. In cigar fillers, for instance, a master blender may combine tobaccos from as many as six different countries to create the desired taste.

No matter where the tobacco comes from, each ingredient is carefully weighed and measured and portioned into small piles that will be taken into the rolling room and placed on the table of a cigar roller. The cigar is about to become a star.

The Art of Cigar Rolling

Cigar Speak
One way to make cigars is for some workers, called **bunchers**, to assemble the "guts" of the cigar. The bunchers then turn the cigar over to the more experienced **rollers**, who apply the wrappers. It's easier to be a buncher than a roller, so with this method, you need fewer master rollers. The other way is for one roller to make the entire cigar. Both methods produce fine cigars.

Every cigar factory has a unique character and appearance. In Havana's El Laguito, cigar makers sweat in the heat and roll stogies in the spacious but grimy parlor rooms of a former mansion. At the Fuente factory in Santiago, Dominican Republic, rollers work and listen to Japanese radios in a large, spotless, bustling, air-conditioned factory.

Wherever premium cigars are made, there's one prevailing goal: to make a quality cigar each and every time. In the factory, the cigar roller is the celebrity, and the "gallery" is the stage.

The *gallery* of a cigar factory is usually a very large, well-lit room with a high ceiling. Long rolling tables stretch from one side of the room to the other, almost like pews in a church. Attached to the table is a long shelf, on which are probably sitting some cigar molds. Each roller's position has a chair, and rollers work at the same place every day.

At regular intervals are tall metal contraptions sitting on the roller table shelves; these contraptions are called *cigar mold presses*. They look like book presses, with a metal frame supporting a large, threaded metal screw used to apply pressure to stacks of cigar molds. A few empty cigar molds are scattered around the factory, but many are filled and in the presses.

The gallery of a cigar factory. Cigar molds are stacked in front of the rollers.

The Roller at Center Stage

Cigar rollers are skilled artisans with mechanical precision. Their job requires considerable knowledge to properly combine just the right amount of tobacco and roll a perfect cylinder, and yet it's repetitious and potentially mind-numbing!

Like accurate machines, rollers create one cigar after another, all day long. An experienced roller can make 95 to 150 cigars a day, depending on the size and shape. Larger cigars, or cigars with special shapes such as the pyramid, take considerably longer to make than smaller cigars like robustos or coronas.

I've always thought that to overcome the boredom of a repetitious job, a good roller must love tobacco and enjoy the feel of handling the leaves and making a cigar. The task of rolling cigars is as much in the touch and the experience as in the mind. Engrossed in their work, rollers almost appear to meditate as they create cigars.

Cigar Esoterica

To help keep workers mentally stimulated, the tradition of the **lector**, or reader, evolved in Cuba years ago. The lector would sit at the front of the gallery and read books, poetry, or newspaper stories to the rollers. At some Cuban factories, the tradition of the lector continues. In many factories throughout the Caribbean, however, the lector has been replaced with native *salsa* music, blaring from portable radios.

Many bunchers and rollers puff on cigars while they work, leaving a sweet-smelling blue haze throughout the gallery. The usual tradition is to allow workers to smoke their own products at work, and to take home a set number of cigars each week for personal consumption.

When the rollers go on break, they banter with each other. It's a real fraternity. In the rolling room, however, it's all business. Apart from quality-control experts—often former top rollers—walking through the room and checking the rollers' work, there is little conversation. Rollers concentrate on their work, and because they're paid based on the number of cigars they make, they are intent on reaching their daily quotas.

If you want to be a *tabaquero*, or roller, you'll need at least two years as an apprentice roller before a quality manufacturer will let you create cigars on your own. It usually takes several more years for a roller to rise to the top and become skilled enough not only to meet aggressive quotas, but to roll the most perfect cigars. At most factories that produce several different grades of cigars, you find that newer rollers make smaller and lower grade cigars, while the top rollers are assigned to make the largest and most expensive cigars using the best tobacco.

Cigar Rolling: A Silky Touch with Steel Muscles

Great dexterity and (in the case of larger sizes) considerable strength is required to gather the leaves, press them into shape, and roll a cigar.

You'll find very few women working as rollers, in part because of the strength and endurance needed to crank out 100 or more cigars a day, and probably also for societal reasons. After the Cuban revolution, women were allowed to become rollers, but even at most Cuban factories, the majority of rollers still are male. Women do work in many cigar-related jobs, from sorting, bunching, and grading leaves to making boxes and applying cigar bands.

Being a roller is often a traditional family occupation. In Cuba, where cigars have been made for more than two centuries, several generations of rollers often work in the same factory. In other nations, where cigar-making has only been common for a few decades, sons are just now beginning to follow their fathers, learning the art of rolling.

Cigar Esoterica

In many Caribbean nations, being a roller for one of the major cigar manufacturers pays relatively well, carries considerable prestige and stability, and offers the chance to move up the ranks—perhaps from a novice *manojeador* (someone who bundles leaves) to a top roller creating the most difficult shapes, or even a factory manager making a very handsome living.

If you sit in the roller's chair, you'll see a flat, time-worn and tobacco-stained wooden table with a raised back to keep tobacco from falling onto the floor. Cigar molds are stacked around, and a couple of basic hand tools lay on the table. Most of the cigar-making process is done entirely with the hands.

When a tool is needed, it's most often the "tuck" (or, in Spanish, *chavetta*): a crescent-shaped piece of metal with a sharp, but not razor sharp, blade. The roller uses this tool to manipulate, or "tuck" the tobacco into place, and also to trim the leaves to proper size. The other basic roller's tool is a round steel punch with a wooden handle, used to cut quarter-sized pieces of wrapper leaf for the finishing touch: the cap or flag.

> **Cigar Speak**
> A **chavetta** or tuck is a specialized crescent-shaped knife that is one of the cigar-roller's only tools. It's used to cut the leaf, pack the filler into the cigar, and shape the stogie.

Imagine, then, that you're a master cigar roller, or *tabaquero*. You sit down at your table. You're assigned to make one of your company's most sought-after cigars, a large 6½-inch, 50-ring belicoso with a delicately tapered head. At either hand are neat piles of tobacco leaves—enough to create your daily quota of cigars. The cheerful, up-tempo sounds of Caribbean music fills the air, and you're ready to roll!

The Art of Filler Bunching

The first thing you'll make is the cigar's filler. You take a leaf from one pile, then the next, and then the next. You gather the pliable, dark brown leaves in one hand, bunching them together like a pleated fan.

A buncher gathers tobacco leaves to make the filler.

Hot Tip
The Cuban style of bunching filler tobacco leaves is called **book rolling**, where the various leaves are combined and folded in on themselves like pleats of a Japanese hand fan. You want to look for cigars that are book-rolled; if made correctly, they burn cool and even. If you look at the foot of a book-rolled cigar, the filler tobacco inside will look like a folded fan.

Hot Tip
The alternative to book rolling is **concentric rolling**, which is the prevailing technique used to create Philippine and Indonesian cigars. Instead of being bunched accordion-fashion, the leaves are rolled in a concentric manner. Because this has to be rolled more loosely to ensure proper draw, cigars with concentric-roll fillers tend to burn hotter and faster than book-rolled cigars.

Sometimes, you'll add in shorter leaves at the top or bottom of the cigar if the blend calls for a changing flavor as the cigar is smoked. Some makers blend certain cigars to start out mild and then become more robust as they're smoked, which requires an exact placement of certain leaf types in the cigar.

Deftly, you bunch the leaves of tobacco in your hand, adding a pre-measured quantity of leaves to make one cigar. You form the leaves into a cylinder that's a little longer than the 6-inch belicoso, and very close to the 50-ring gauge thickness of the finished cigar. If you let go of the leaves now, the cylinder would spring open and the cigar would be lost.

Bonding with Binders

Holding this bunch of tobacco tightly in one hand, you reach for a thick, dark, tough leaf that's called the *binder*. This leaf will replace your hand as the agent holding this springy filler together.

Gently, you rotate the cylinder and wrap the binder leaf around the filler, starting at the top of the cigar and spiraling downward. Of course, this process isn't just a matter of figuring out how to encase this springy mess in a tobacco leaf: You have to apply just enough pressure to create a perfect draw.

If the cigar maker wraps the binder around the filler leaves too tightly, you won't be able to draw enough air through the cylinder. If he fails to put enough pressure on the bunch, too much air will get through and the cigar will burn too hot. Finally, if he's careless as he gathers the filler tobaccos in his hand and applies the binder, the finished cigar will have spongy spots that will cause it to burn unevenly.

But you're a *tabaquero*, and even though the pressure is on to crank out your daily quota of cigars, you're good! This cylinder in your hand, called a "bunch," is beginning to look like a cigar, albeit with split ends. You might lay it on the table, still applying pressure on it with your hand, and use your tuck to shape the cigar and push the tobacco into place.

Even now, if you let go of the cylinder, it'll quickly start to unravel. While it looks pretty much like a cigar, the bunch is somewhat lumpy and not perfectly conical. It's time to apply some pressure to get that cigar to shape up.

Cigar Molds: Full-Court Pressure

Close at hand, you have an empty cigar mold just waiting to be filled. Cigar molds consist of two wooden halves. The bottom has about 20 troughs in the exact shape of the cigar being made, from the short robusto to the long presidente.

The base is thick and sturdy wood designed to withstand the pressure of the cigar press. The top of the mold is a mirror image of the bottom, and the two fit together to shape the cigars inside.

The roller places cigars in a cigar mold.

The mold in front of you is worn smooth around the corners, and is grayish brown from years of use, handling, and tar and nicotine stains. You place the bunch carefully into one of the troughs on the bottom of the mold. You're such a skilled roller, of course, that you created a perfectly sized bunch that fits snugly and perfectly into the belicoso-sized trough.

When you complete enough cigars to fill the mold, you join the top of the mold to the bottom, using pegs on the sides of the mold as a guide for lining up the two halves. It's a very snug fit, and the mold doesn't completely close. About a half inch of leaf on each cigar hangs out the front and back of the mold.

Blowing Smoke

If you don't think it's important to store your cigars at tropical humidity, bring home a cigar mold from the Caribbean. Unless you place the mold on a humidifier throughout the winter, this seemingly sturdy wooden mold will quickly split and warp in the dry air. It's dramatic proof of the damaging effect a dry climate has on tropical wood—and tobacco.

Stogies getting pressed into shape in a cigar mold.

You hand off the cigar mold to one of your co-workers so that you can return to rolling cigars. The mold is placed in the press, probably with several other molds from other rollers, and the handle of the press is cranked, pushing a metal plate down onto the cigar molds. It's cranked until the cigar molds are completely closed, which means there's just the right amount of pressure to form the cigars.

They'll sit in those molds under pressure for about an hour. Then the press is unscrewed and every mold is taken out and opened, and each cigar is turned slightly. The mold lids are replaced and the whole process repeated over and over until the entire cigar is pressed and perfectly round.

Finally, the cigars are removed from the molds. The several hours of pressure has made them round and firmed them up. They won't spring open now. No glue is used to keep the cigar together: The natural moisture and oils of the tobacco, combined with skillful rolling and pressure, are all that's needed.

The cigars are quickly given the "squeeze test" to see whether they contain any soggy spots—no sense in going any further if they have this flaw. Because you are a master *tabaquero*, your cigars are, of course, flawless!

It's time to apply the wrapper and finish the cigar. Sometimes, the roller who made the body of the cigar handles this task. Sometimes, the bodies of cigars are made by bunchers, and then taken to a roller who just applies the delicate wrapper leaves. Let's assume you work in a factory in which rollers make the entire cigar, so you're the one who gets to finish off this magnificent stogie.

Wrapping It All Up

The cigars are returned to you in dark, gnarled binders with ragged ends. They are pretty sorry looking. Before you is a pile of thin, silky, oily half-leaves of wrapper tobacco that will cover this ugly binder and make your cigar irresistible to any connoisseur.

You hold up a wrapper leaf. It's slightly wrinkled, but you can see it's a perfect, even reddish-brown or *colorado claro* color, without a speckle or spot on it. These leaves have been carefully sorted and graded many times before they reach your table. As the roller, your job is not to waste or destroy a single one of these very expensive leaves.

You lay the cigar on the table, and take a wrapper leaf from the pile. With your tuck or "chavetta," you trim the leaf to the exact size necessary to encase the cigar. You take a small piece of the scrap tobacco you've just trimmed and use your circular knife to cut a small round piece, setting it aside for later.

Laying the cigar on the top corner of the wrapper leaf, you carefully begin to wrap the leaf around the cigar in a spiral fashion, starting at the tuck end and working toward the head of the cigar.

The roller applies a wrapper to cigar, using a crescent-shaped knife (called a chavetta) and a guillotine.

With one hand you roll, and with the other you stretch the wrapper leaf so that it's perfectly smooth. You might use your tuck to smooth the wrapper as you roll the cigar. The leaf is silky and pliable under your hand, but you know that if you tug just a bit too hard, the leaf will tear and years of growing, hand sorting, and aging will be wasted.

But you *are* a master roller, and the cigar quickly takes shape beneath your fingers. Deftly using your palm and your fingers, you roll the cigar back and forth on the table until the cigar is a smooth and perfect cylinder. All that remains is to finish the head of the cigar and trim the tuck end—the end to be lit.

"Capping" Off the Cigar

Because you're making a belicoso with a delicately pointed head, you've already formed this pointed tip as you made the cigar. It's trickier to do this than to roll a cigar with the usual flat head, which is why only expert *tabaqueros* such as yourself are assigned to these cigars.

You trim the quarter-inch or so of filler tobaccos that protrude from the head, and then reach for the quarter-sized piece of leaf that you cut out of a scrap from the wrapper. A small jar on your table contains a white glue—an all-natural product called *gum of traga-canth*.

Dabbing the glue on your finger, you smooth the cap of tobacco over the head of the cigar, which is called the *perilla* in Spanish. You apply the cap so expertly that it's difficult to tell that it's a separate piece of tobacco.

To cleanly finish the cap, many cigar makers run a thin strip or two of tobacco around the cigar to cover the line of the cap's edges. On a flat-headed cigar, the cap covers the head and extends about ⅛ inch up the body of the cigar. These strips clean up any ragged edges of the cap and add an extra aesthetic touch to finish the cigar. Finally, you place the cigar in the small guillotine sitting on your table and lop off the tuck end to make a clean, perfect surface for lighting.

Finished cigars start to pile up on the roller's table.

As a formality, you check the cigar against a wooden block to make sure it's the right dimension, but your skilled fingers and experienced eyes tell you that it's perfect even before you measure it. You set the cigar carefully aside and move on to the next.

As it is, the cigar should be perfect and smokeable, but it has a journey remaining before it's boxed and shipped to some fortunate smoker. A small, proud smile might cross your face, but you have a quota to fill. You must move on, and your newly made cigar, now a star, must continue its adventure. This adventure includes marriage with other cigars, resting in a cedar cabinet, being placed in a vacuum chamber, and traveling thousands of miles. In Chapter 11, you'll see how the delicate cigar survives this tumultuous process!

A factory manager checks the finished cigars to make sure quality levels are high.

The Least You Need to Know

➤ The experience of the people, not the equipment, makes for a perfectly constructed, rolled, evenly burning cigar.

➤ Exact amounts of tobaccos are used to blend your cigar, which allow quality manufacturers to produce a consistent cigar.

➤ Book-rolled cigar filler, which is the Cuban style used throughout the Caribbean, smokes cooler and slower than concentric-rolled filler from Indonesia.

➤ A great cigar is finished off with a smooth, flawless, silky wrapper leaf.

➤ The head of the cigar should be perfectly covered with a cap of tobacco that's almost indistinguishable from the wrapper.

Few images are more alluring to a cigar connoisseur than the thought of sitting on a breezy veranda, watching a tropical sunset, and preparing to enjoy a fine Havana smoke.

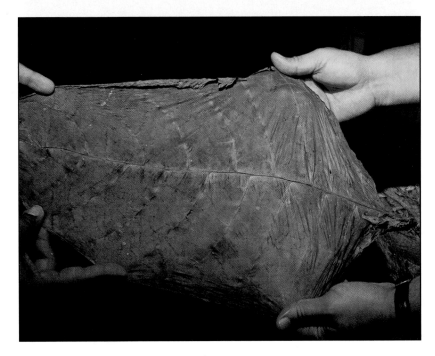

Tobacco leaves are large, and when you see a fully aged, supple leaf, it becomes obvious why only a half leaf is used to make cigars. The leaf displayed is relatively mature. The few subtle greenish spots still remaining will disappear when the leaf undergoes final aging in bales—a process that can take up to seven years.

Delicate tobacco seedlings get their start under a mesh canopy to filter out harsh sunlight, prevent drops of rain from marring the tender leaves, and to help keep out insects that find cigars at this early stage very tasty. (Photo courtesy of Tabacalera A. Fuente y Cia)

These humidors, designed and built by Eric Haskell of Sonoran Humidors, represent the best in beauty and functionality. Trays with dividers separate different brands so flavors don't mix; the humidifying element is sized for the box; and the large precision hygrometer (the round gauge on the lid of the open humidor) provides an accurate reading of the humidity level.

A tobacco field, ready for harvest, is inspected by members of the Fuente family. (Photo courtesy of Tabacalera A. Fuente y Cia)

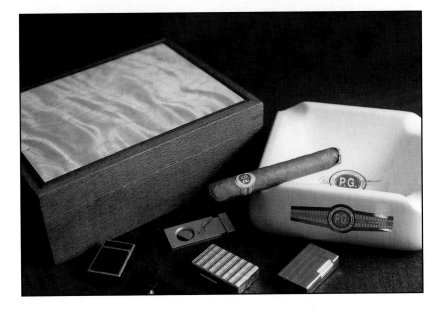

All you need to enjoy cigars in high style: A limited-edition PG ash tray; an assortment of gold and Chinese lacquer S.I. DuPont lighters; a quality guillotine cutter; and a handsome humidor lined with Spanish cedar. Artisan Rex Poggenpohl used African lacewood for the sides; the top is pillowed maple veneer trimmed out in bloodwood.

Cigars have long been a ritual after dinner. This early 19th-century humidor shaped like a beer stein was passed around the table. Diners lit their cigars from a flame on a wick in the gryphon's mouth. Inside are special Adipati Philipno cigars with a personalized gold band.

Ashtrays can be fun and inexpensive to collect. The absurd alligator ashtray and simple Italian terra cotta ashtray contrast with an elegant, elaborate (and expensive!) humidor from Elie Bleu.

Collectible cigar art is hot, and one of the favorites in my collection is Rosa de Santos. The cigar is long forgotten, but the beauty of the label artwork makes it popular among collectors.

PG belicoso-shaped cigars nestled in a boite nature (natural cedar) box. Note how the Dominican tax stamp must be broken to open the cigars, just as you have to break a tax seal to open a bottle of liquor.

Pictured are the most common cigar wrappers you'll encounter. The tan-colored *claro* is seen on (from left) the MacClellan Honduras Selection, the Punch Gran Cru, the Dunhill Vintage, and the Ashton. The Davidoff is wrapped in a reddish brown leaf called *colorado claro* or English Market Slection. The Partagas has a dark brown Cameroon leaf. The Punch Gran Cru has a light *maduro* wrapper, while the cigars at the far right have dark, rich *maduro* wrappers.

A celebration of beautifully made, premium stogies and their bold, splashy cigar bands.

A variety of short but flavorful premium hand-made smokes. At each end are small but delicious offerings: Macanudo's "Ascot" (left) and Ashton's "cordial." For size comparison, a Davidoff corona is in the middle, flanked by four different robustos (left to right): an A. Fuente Chateau Fuente; a Punch Gran Cru; an A. Fuente Hemingway series; and a Davidoff "R."

With a classic corona cigar in the middle for comparison, these are some of the larger cigar sizes you're likely to encounter. The MacClellan cigar (far left) is a presidente—larger than life. The rest would classify as either Churchill or double-corona sizes. Note that although they're called double coronas, they really aren't twice as long as the standard-sized corona pictured.

A selection of unusual, or figuarado, cigar shapes, including (left to right): an Avo petit belicoso, a PG belicoso, an A. Fuente Hemingway series double corona with a perfecto (pointed) tip, and a Fonseca pyramid.

At a quality smoke shope, you can expect to find a well-stocked, temperature-controlled humidor such as this one at Chicago's well-known Up Down Tobacco Shop. (Photo courtesy of Up Down Tobacco Shop)

Filler Up, Bind It, Wrap It Up!

In the last chapter, you learned how to roll a cigar like a true *tabaquero*, or roller. While you wait for your finished belicosos to move through the factory on their way to humidors around the world, this is a good time to take a closer look at all the different tobaccos lying before you in neat piles on the *tabaquero*'s rolling table. It's all tobacco, but the variation in the characteristics of different cigar leaf plants is astounding.

In cigar-making countries other than Cuba, cigar leaf may come from a wide variety of countries. Each country, and often several regions within those countries, have climatic variations that are particularly suited for certain kinds of tobacco. Certain nations and regions have become famous for particular tobaccos. In Chapter 13, we'll talk about why tobacco varies so greatly between countries and regions. For now, let's explore the basics.

Fillers: Bulking Up

You know how important filler is to a good cigar: It delivers most of the cigar's flavor and comprises 98 percent of the cigar's tobacco. Which countries produce the best filler tobacco, and why? Let's take a look.

Cuba: The One and Only

Cuba produces all the leaf for its cigars: wrapper, binder, and filler. Different regions are noted for particularly excellent production of one of these elements. The warm center region, the Remedios or Vuelta Arriba, and the far southern Oriente produce mostly filler tobacco.

The Vuelta Arriba, although not considered the premier growing location in Cuba, produces a great deal of the filler leaf used in the finest Havana smokes. The climate produces rich, lush crops and thick, aromatic leaves that are ideal for adding body and flavor to the cigar filler.

Growing regions of Cuba.

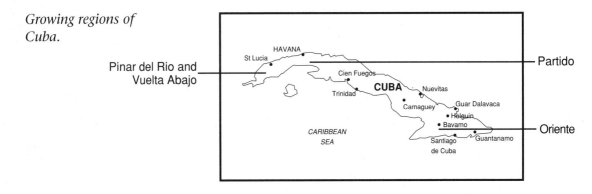

The tobaccos from Vuelta Arriba and Oriente are considered inferior to the leaf grown in the Pinar del Rio, located in the far western tip of Cuba. This location contains the famed *Vuelta Abajo*, considered the finest growing region in the world.

Most of Cuba's delicate and prized wrapper leaf is grown in the *Vuelta Abajo*, but acres are also given over to binder and filler tobaccos. During centuries of tobacco growing, the Cubans have had the chance to experiment and discover how the different soils and climates affect the tobacco.

The Cuban expatriates who took their skill and seed to nations such as the Dominican Republic and Honduras haven't had centuries to experiment, but in four decades

> **Cigar Speak**
> Cuba's **Vuelta Abajo** (roughly pronounced *voo-el-tah ah-bah-o*) is the world's most famous cigar leaf-growing real estate. This region in northern Cuba is divided into five subzones, all with slightly different growing climates and soils that affect the taste of tobaccos.

they've just about caught up with the Cubans—their success a case study in fortitude and determination.

Smooth Dominican

The Dominican Republic is now one of the world's leading producers of filler tobaccos. Twenty years ago, that nation yielded just a handful of tobacco, but manufacturers have taken advantage of the climate and soil and have cultivated some exceptional tobacco.

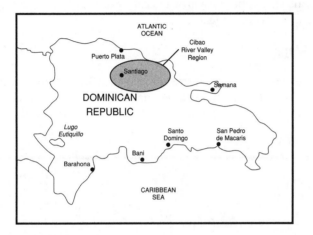

Growing regions of the Dominican Republic.

Located in the same basic chain of islands as Cuba and Puerto Rico, the Dominican Republic has regions with climate and soil composition similar to Cuba's. Nestled among mountainous terrain, the Cibao River Valley is the prime area for production, located well inland in the northern part of the country. Santiago, the area's main city, is home to numerous cigar factories.

It's quite a journey just getting into Santiago. Although you can fly to the city, a usual plane trip ends in the coastal resort town of Puerto Plata, and you then have to drive inland. On your approach by air, your plane spirals sharply downward, bouncing as it hits the warm thermals coming up from the land. You finally land, grab a four-wheel-drive vehicle, and make your way to Puerto Plata on a combination of two-lane highways and unpaved trails.

The mountainous countryside is green and lush, covered with royal palms. The contrast is amazing between this country and what you see flying in as you pass over Haiti. Although the two countries share the same island (once called *Hispañola*) Haiti is brown, barren, and denuded from years of tree felling. The border between the two nations can easily be traced from the air: one side is arid, the other lush and green.

The Cibao Valley is home to two primary types of filler tobaccos, both famous: Piloto Cubano and Olor. Having undergone extensive cultivation and hybridizing, these two varieties deliver the rich, peppery quality of fine Cuban leaf. The climatic and soil

113

differences yield a leaf that tastes slightly different from Havana leaf, but comes very close in quality and character. In Chapter 13, we'll take a closer look at how soil and climate affects tobacco.

Dominican leaf is known for being smooth and mild, but growers have proven that with the right mix of fertilizer, irrigation, soil, and climate—combined with different aging procedures—Dominican leaf can also be rich and spicy.

Around the world, filler tobacco is the most commonly grown type of tobacco, not only because it's the most heavily used, but because growers can more easily produce good filler and binder than outstanding wrapper leaf.

Honduras: Packing a Punch

Until the past few years, Honduras had severe restrictions against importing leaf from outside the country. The climate in Honduras is somewhat drier and hotter than the island nations of Cuba and the Dominican Republic, and so growers produced a stronger tobacco.

Growing regions of Honduras and Nicaragua.

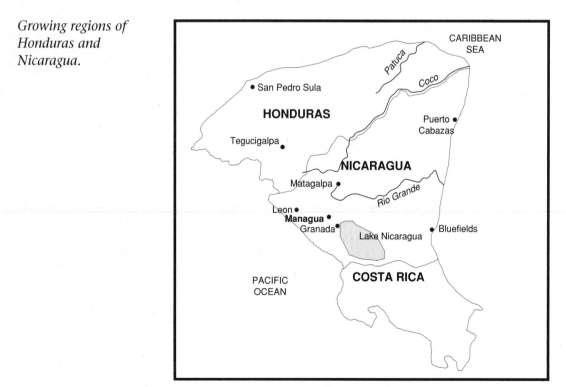

Those restrictions have been lifted, and today most Honduran-based manufacturers can import leaf from other nations. Cigar makers are now able to blend cigars combining

Cuban-style power with mellower filler tobacco. As a result, some of the finest full-bodied cigars made are coming out of Honduras.

Located in Central America, and jutting into the Caribbean Sea, Honduras has a tropical island climate that mimics that of Cuba. Although the country hasn't had much success producing world-renowned wrapper or binder leaf, it is home to great filler tobacco.

When cigar makers first left Cuba in 1959, many chose Honduras as the nation with conditions closest to their former homeland. Full-bodied cigars such as Punch found a home in Honduras, and the Cuban seed smuggled out of Havana took root and flourished.

Cigar Esoterica

While Punch might sound like a perfect name for one of the most full-bodied and powerful of all cigars, the name was actually taken from the cartoon character in the English humor magazine *Punch*. The famed Mr. Punch smoked a stogie and pummeled everyone with his club, including cartoon cohort Judy. The brand was created for the English market around 1840.

Honduran tobaccos have been plagued by the feared blue mold disease, which took its toll on Honduran crops in the 1980s. (We'll talk more about blue mold in Chapter 14.) Like *phyloxera vastatrix*, a bacterial disease that is a constant plague for wine makers in France and California, blue mold requires complete vigilance by tobacco growers whose crops are affected. Growers must carefully apply chemical sprays to arrest the mold's development, and also monitor the leaves to ensure they don't get overly moist. If there's an unexpected rainfall, growers may go so far as to walk through the fields, shaking each tobacco plant to remove excess water!

Blue mold can devastate a tobacco crop in the fields within 48 hours. Unlike *phyloxera*, fortunately, blue mold can be kept under control. Since 1980, Honduran manufacturers have been winning the battle against blue mold.

Doing the Samba in Brazil

The dense, hearty, and sometimes harsh filler tobaccos grown in Brazil can make you get up and dance—if they're grown carefully. The hot climate and relentless sun make Brazilian tobaccos spicy and dark, but they're also noted for their sweet flavor.

Many cigarillos—those short, sneaky smokes—are made using Brazilian tobacco. As a filler for fine handmade smokes, Brazilian tobaccos can add a hint of spice and sweetness.

Similar to a gourmet chef adding red-hot chile peppers, a master tobacco blender uses Brazilian tobacco in small quantities. You can't usually tell that Brazilian filler has been used in a cigar, but it adds a "kick," with the taste of the Rio de Janeiro Carnival.

Oh, Mexico, the Sun's So Hot...

The hot and relatively dry climate of Mexico's San Andrés Valley, nestled among the mountain range of the same name, yields a considerable amount of filler tobacco used in Mexico and around the world. Like most of the world's best cigar-growing regions, Mexico's region is a valley, has a more moderate climate than the surrounding countryside, and catches the runoff of rainfall from the mountains.

Mexican growing regions.

Although the blazing sun and crumbly soil of Mexico is not, by most aficionados' opinions, ideal for growing cigar leaf, it does nurture a spicy, earthy tobacco. Many of the cigars made outside Cuba use in their blends a hint of Mexican filler to add spice and character.

The first Europeans to take a stab at formal cigar cultivation in Mexico were the Dutch, who got tossed out of Indonesia when General Sukarno took over. Although the Dutch didn't stay long in Mexico, the cigar industry flourished.

Tobacco cultivation in Mexico began with the ancient Mayans, who cultivated native leaf. Cigar makers in Mexico have had their ups and downs since then, as we'll see later in this chapter, but spicy Mexican filler remains a staple ingredient of many blended non-Cuban cigars.

"Hey Mon, Come to Jamaica"

Jamaican tobacco has the undisputed reputation of being the world's mildest. Many veteran stogie smokers would say that Jamaican filler tobacco is not only mild, it's bland. Unlike the Dominican Republic, where several cigar makers have attempted, and succeeded, to create a rainbow of flavors and bodies, little effort has been made to change Jamaican tobacco from what it is: mild.

A few cigars are still assembled in Jamaica, most notably General Cigar's Macanudo, but Jamaican producers use tobacco from other nations to create their blends. Jamaican leaf never truly took off, and today it remains a nice element for smoothing out and bulking up the leaf used in a filler.

Nicaragua: Revolution and Cigars

Nicaragua is right next door to Honduras, so if you expect that its soil and growing conditions would be similar, you're correct. There is one huge difference between the two regions, however: Although Honduras has had more than its share of political unrest, it has never undermined the cigar industry. Not so with Nicaragua.

Nicaragua's cigar industry suffered disaster during the reign of the *Sandinista* guerrillas. Tobacco fields were neglected and tobacco growing suspended as any cigar makers in their right minds fled the country. During the 1980s, you couldn't even find the country's premier brand, Joya de Nicaragua (Jewel of Nicaragua).With the exit of the regime, cigar production has slowly resumed.

Unfortunately, the neglected tobacco fields of this country are still recovering. A few manufacturers are resurrecting the cigar industry, but in the rush to rejoin today's hot cigar market, Nicaraguan cigars are nowhere near the quality they were in the 1970s.

On a positive note, some of the quality in filler tobaccos from Nicaragua is coming back. Like Honduran leaf, Nicaraguan-grown leaf is spicy, hearty, and full-bodied.

More and more manufacturers located outside Nicaragua are using this leaf to spice up their blends. Cigars that rely primarily on Nicaraguan tobacco, however, show signs of very harsh, very young leaf because this industry hasn't had time to get back on its feet.

Costa Rica and Panama

Honduras is the leading Central American tobacco producer, but a few brands of cigars are assembled in Costa Rica and Panama. A small amount of cigar leaf—primarily filler—is grown in these nations.

Neither country is renowned for producing great leaf of any kind, although a few growers are trying. As our friends in the Dominican Republic can vouch, it takes a long, long time to cultivate a good tobacco crop! Costa Rica and Panama have a ways to go.

Dutch Treat from Indonesia, Java, and Sumatra

The Dutch were among the first Europeans to completely embrace tobacco, especially for the pipe. When that tiny nation was a colonial power, it established tobacco plantations throughout what was once called the Dutch East Indies.

A lot of cigars are still made in Indonesia using all Indonesian tobacco, but none have ascended the royal stairway to take their place among the world's fine handmade smokes. Growing conditions are good, but not ideal, and filler leaves tend to burn hot and dry. The Dutch did, however, cultivate some interesting varieties of tobacco throughout these small islands, and a lot of the seed has made its way around the world.

Binders: Keeping It All Together

You've learned (budding aficionado that you are), that binders play a critical role in keeping a cigar "together." Beneath every princely cigar lurks a frog. Yes, Virginia, under that silky, shiny wrapper that's a delight to the touch, the lips, and the eye, your cigar has warts.

The wrapper of your cigar is like the sheriff from an old-time Western: white hat, pearly teeth, shiny gun, and attractively groomed horse. But the binder that's beneath the shiny wrapper is like Clint Eastwood's "Man With No Name": tough, coarse, and full of character. Despite its coarse appearance, the binder is the real hero of your cigar.

In fact, your super-premium cigar without its wrapper looks a lot like those gnarly cheroots that Clint used to bite, spit, chew, and puff while he mowed down bad guys in the American (or was that Italian?) West.

Unless you're willing to dissect your $10 cigar with a razor blade (as I have), or take a very expensive trip to a warm Caribbean spot to watch cigar rollers do their thing, take my word for both the appearance and the importance of a binder.

Even though the binder is a single leaf (actually, a half-leaf) of tobacco, you know what an important job it has in holding your stogie together. What else does the binder do? It can be used to deliver flavor. Cigar makers use the tough, spicy, sun-grown binder leaf to add a peppery "POW" to your cigar.

Ecuador, Java, and Sumatra: Bound by Binder

Sumatran and Javan cigar tobacco seeds have made their way around the world. Ecuador, a small South American nation, is among the many places the seed has taken root.

Sumatra-seed Ecuadorian binder is prized for the same reason Mexican binder is prized. Its flavor is sweet and peppery, and its texture is tough enough to hold the filler in check. Binder leaf plants are grown in valleys nestled among the mountains of Ecuador. It's a small industry with relatively few acres planted, but some great Ecuadorian binder leaf makes its way around the world.

Java and Sumatra still produce binder, but cultivation—and certainly the all-important aging and fermenting processes—aren't particularly refined or controlled. Although the leaf itself is good, the finished product isn't up to snuff for a premium cigar.

Stay Outta My Tobacco Patch: Cuba

As we talked about in Chapter 7, Cuba imports no cigar leaf. The Cubans have many different growing regions, each with its own micro-climate. Some of these regions are best-suited for wrapper tobacco, some for filler, and some for binder leaf.

Remember I said that Cuban tobacco tends to be spicier and more robust than leaf grown in other parts of the world, yet it's also smooth? Non-Cuban makers turn to spicier, stronger-flavored binders to give their cigars this Havana "bite."

Because most Cuban tobacco has this peppery character, however, it's not as important for Cuban manufacturers to use a stronger-flavored binder. Cuban filler tobacco delivers most of the cigar's flavor; the binder is used mostly to hold the cigar together, and the wrapper makes it look pretty.

Honduras and Nicaragua Spice It Up

We've talked about the generally spicy, peppery qualities of Central American tobaccos, so it makes sense that these nations produce very fine binder tobaccos. The hot, sunny climates of Honduras and Nicaragua produce tough and tasty binders that are frequently used to accent milder fillers and wrappers.

Wrappers: Pretty as a Picture

If fillers and binders are the chassis and engine of your cigar's "car," the wrapper is the graceful exterior. A shiny, smooth, delicately veined wrapper gives your cigar "curb appeal."

This quest for perfect appearance makes wrapper leaf the most difficult and time-consuming to grow and process. It makes sense, then, that wrappers are also the most expensive and rarest of all leaves.

Blowing Smoke
A common misconception is that Cuban cigars are made only with a wrapper and filler—without a binder. It's virtually impossible to make a good cigar without a binder, and all Cuban handmade smokes use the same elements and construction as cigars all over the world.

Hot Tip
The leaves used for the dark maduro wrapper and the lighter natural wrapper are quite different. Leaf for maduro wrappers has to be tougher to withstand the additional growing time and processing needed to make this leaf. As a result, maduro wrapper is thicker, tougher, and has more prominent veins than other varieties. These characteristics are completely acceptable in maduro wrappers.

A good light-colored natural wrapper has to be free of large veins. It needs to be silky and delicate, yet elastic enough to be pulled smooth and taught as the *tabaquero* stretches it around the cigar. Variations in color are a no-no; wrappers are supposed to be one single, even color. Light-colored spots, a common wrapper flaw, are not acceptable to the picky cigar smoker.

Spots are about the size of a pin head, random, and generally lighter than the wrapper. Although there has been some debate about what causes the spots, general consensus is that these are just splashes of water that have marred the leaf.

Remember that wrapper leaf is very delicate, and can be bruised by something as seemingly harmless as a steady pelting of rain. The spots of water then act as lenses to focus sunlight on these points and slightly discolor the leaf.

Spots are common on sun-grown wrappers, and do nothing to detract from the flavor. For the sake of aesthetics, however, some wrapper leaf tobacco plants receive an even higher level of care than the usual tobacco plant.

Snuggled Under a Blanket

Visitors to tobacco fields have been puzzled by the sight of field after field, draped in white cloth suspended about eight feet over the fields by wooden frames. A warped landscape by an outlandish European artist? No!

To protect the aesthetic perfection of their delicate wrapper leaves, tobacco growers use wooden stakes to suspend cheesecloth over rows of plants. The cheesecloth provides a pleasant, cool shade for the pampered plants, yet it's porous enough to let in plenty of light, air, and water.

Cigar Esoterica

Near the turn of the century, a peculiar fad cropped up among stogie smokers. A few cigar dealers, probably trying to make the most of their low-grade, water-speckled Sumatran wrappers, effectively convinced smokers that spots were good. Some dealers even spotted their cigar wrappers with a mixture of ammonium carbonate and chlorinated lime. Moral: Beware of fads!

The leaves are never directly pelted by droplets of rain (or sprinklers), and the even, filtered light produces a perfect and blemish-free leaf. Another reason for the blanket of cheesecloth is to shelter the plants from direct sun, which makes tobacco grow faster, and produces a tougher, darker leaf.

Most of the wrapper leaf tobacco plants are carefully grown under cloth to prevent overexposure to the sun and avoid water spots. Not only is the growing process labor intensive and expensive, the curing and fermenting process is also time-consuming and costly. These processes add to the price of premium smokes with shade-grown wrappers, but the mild, silky wrappers are a delight to behold and taste.

Obviously, covering and tending these plants is a laborious process, which is why prime shade-grown leaf is among the rarest, most expensive in the world. For the sake of a perfect appearance, most cigar connoisseurs agree that the product justifies the price. Virtually every tobacco-growing nation produces some wrapper leaf, but certain places are famous for their wrappers.

The Wrapper King of Connecticut

Wait a minute! We've been talking about tobacco grown in one tropical country after another, and all of a sudden, we're talking Connecticut? Yep. This state produces some of the finest wrapper leaf in the world.

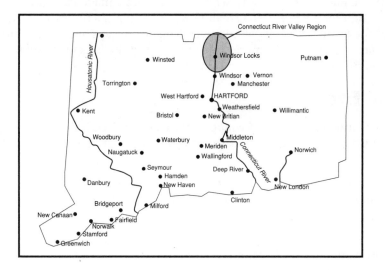

The Connecticut River Valley, where fine cigar leaf is grown.

The United States produces a lot of tobacco, but it isn't generally known for producing great cigar tobacco. At one time, as you'll see in Chapter 13, a great deal of mediocre cigar leaf was grown in the States. For some reason, however, the Connecticut River Valley— just south of the Massachusetts border—offers the perfect climate for wrapper leaf tobacco, even though it doesn't fit the tropical profile of most cigar-growing nations.

You'll usually see the wrapper advertised as "Connecticut shade-grown," which is self-explanatory. Most of the Connecticut wrappers come from a variety of tobacco called *broadleaf*. The leaf is wider than many types of tobacco leaves, which, when divided in half, makes it appropriate for covering even the largest, longest stogies.

Cameroon: The African Connection

The tiny West African nation of Cameroon would seem like an odd place to produce cigar wrappers, but the Cameroon wrapper is highly prized. Cameroon still produces wrapper leaf, but the seed for this type tobacco plant has been transplanted to other nations. Recently, a few countries—notably the Dominican Republic—have been successful in growing Cameroon leaf.

The sun-grown Cameroon leaf is darker than shade-grown leaves. It's also covered by little bumps, almost reminiscent of the goose pimples you get when you shiver. Overall, it's thicker, with more pronounced veins than shade-grown wrappers.

These characteristics, which would be considered flaws in perfect shade-grown wrappers, are readily accepted by connoisseurs because of the Cameroon wrapper's beautiful, oily texture and rich taste. It's one of the most aromatic and flavorful of all wrappers, and it lends more taste to a cigar than any wrapper but maduro. Can you tell the Cameroon wrapper is my favorite of all wrappers?

A few cigars, such as the A. Fuente Hemingway Series or Dominican-made Partagas, are made exclusively with Cameroon wrappers. A small number of manufacturers offer the Cameroon wrapper as one of their wrapper alternatives. This has always been a very rare leaf, with limited production, and is even more scarce today with the large demand for premium smokes. If you find it, buy it!

Wrappers from the East

Shade-grown Indonesian and Sumatran-seed wrappers have been prized for centuries. Their primary characteristics are elasticity, a pleasing appearance, minimal veining, and neutral flavor.

Sumatra-seed wrapper was particularly prized in the United States, where ultra-mild smokes were favored until the early 1980s. Today, American smokers have turned to fuller-bodied cigars and the complexity offered by a wrapper more flavorful than traditional Sumatran seed.

Some manufacturers use a Sumatra-seed or Indonesian wrapper, but its lack of flavor only means everything else has to work harder! One exception is the relatively recent development of a Cameroon-seed wrapper in Indonesia, which is beginning to appear on cigars that formerly used Cameroon wrappers, which as I mentioned is becoming quite difficult and expensive to obtain. This wrapper is a relatively new development, but it tastes great and packs a lot more flavor than the traditional Indonesian wrapper.

The Mojo of Mexico and Maduro

Mojo, a kind of magic, is exactly what Mexican maduro leaf provides. Maduro is the most flavorful of all wrappers, and the hearty, tough leaf grown under the Mexican sun is the perfect candidate for maduro treatment.

Maduro leaf gets its dark color from the sun (it is left on the plant longer before picking) and extra fermentation. What better place than Mexico to produce such a leaf? Some of the finest maduro wrappers come from Mexico.

Sweet, yet peppery, the maduro wrapper delivers the full-bodied flavor that suits the Spanish taste. Ironically, Cuba doesn't produce maduro wrappers, even though Spain is one of that country's major markets for export.

Maduro wrappers can be made from wrapper leaves grown in any country, and great maduro wrappers also come from Connecticut and Honduras. Any grower willing to take the extra time and expense to create a maduro wrapper can do it, but Mexican leaf is ideally suited for the rich, blackish maduro leaf.

The Least You Need to Know

➤ Great filler tobaccos are grown all over the world.

➤ Cuban cigars use only Cuban filler, but other cigars use filler from many different countries.

➤ Binder tobacco leaves are tough and ugly, but they hold your cigar together and often add a spicy flavor.

➤ A shade-grown wrapper leaf is difficult to grow and adds cost to your cigar, but it looks great.

➤ The darker the wrapper, the more flavor it contributes to the cigar.

Happily Ever After

In This Chapter

➤ Finished cigars need time to rest

➤ How cigars are matched for color and appearance

➤ Getting the bugs out of cigars

➤ Different ways to package cigars

Finished cigars come off rollers' tables in factories all over the Caribbean, and they're almost ready to enjoy. As a handmade product, created by many individual rollers using individual tobacco leaves, cigars are not consistent in appearance after they're produced. In addition, they need time to rest after their rather quick journey from leaf to a finished product.

Although they're a relatively small part of the entire cigar-making process, these final stages of aging, grading, and quality control are what separate the good cigars from the great ones. They help ensure that every cigar you select is ready to smoke and enjoy the minute you buy it. Let's follow our cigars to the "finish line."

Why New Cigars Get Married

A good marriage involves two compatible people. In cigar society, a good marriage involves 25 individual cigars, presented in a box. Ideally, when you open a box of cigars, the cigar wrappers should have a uniform color and no variation in consistency, draw, and flavor.

The master blender who grouped the leaves and sent them to the roller was responsible for creating the perfect combination of leaves. The result should be consistent flavor and style from cigar to cigar, and from box to box. Cigars made by the great manufacturers will have little variation even from year to year, which is why you can find a particular brand you like and enjoy it for the rest of your life!

To make a perfect marriage of appearance, however, takes a bit of work. Once the finished cigars are removed from the rollers' tables, they're taken to a room for yet another round of sorting and grading.

Same-sized cigars are laid on a long table and a master grader enters the scene. It's my idea of a cigar lover's dream job: You're in a room filled with cigars, and you have first pick of all the product!

Finished cigars are sorted and graded.

Every cigar is checked by hand for proper firmness. Cigars that feel too hard or too soft, or that have any spongy spots, are rejected on the spot.

The grader also examines all wrappers for blotches or tears that might have occurred while the cigars were being rolled. A manufacturer with the highest standards rejects cigars with these imperfections.

Take heart; rejected premium cigars aren't thrown away! They're separated from the perfect smokes and used as smokes by the rollers and workers, turned into unbranded seconds (discussed in Chapter 1), or sold to a less discriminating distributor who will band and sell them.

The grader also groups cigars by wrapper color, ideally creating bunches of 25 or 50 smokes with the same color wrapper. This consistency in appearance is an aesthetic treat that an experienced cigar smoker appreciates.

In Chapter 5, you read about the five main color categories. The Cubans have about 70 different wrapper color classifications—most of them subsets of the five main groups. The master cigar grader keeps all 70 grades in his eyes and his head!

Not all cigar makers are so discerning. Makers of many of the new brands are happy if the 25 cigars in a box are anywhere near the same color. Exact color matching is not a lost art, however; wrapper color consistency provides a big clue that you've found a quality maker. Stick with that maker.

The cigars are bundled by shape and tied with a ribbon or bound with simple paper. The next stage of the process varies from maker to maker. Almost every quality manufacturer will give these bunches of cigars at least a month of "marrying" time.

Blowing Smoke
You might think, by this point, that cigar-making involves a ridiculous number of quality-control stages. This gauntlet of checking is surprisingly effective at catching most badly made cigars. If these steps aren't followed and the maker doesn't weed out bad cigars, you will—after you've purchased your stogies! The better the cigar maker, the more quality control steps he employs.

Hot Tip
Cigars that are rejected by top manufacturers can be pleasant and smokeable. Seconds (when priced cheaply enough) are a deal worth checking into—provided you're willing to accept the occasional speckled wrapper or tight draw.

Graded cigars are bundled into groups of 25 or 50.

Tobacco readily absorbs and gives up flavors to anything around it. Put a cigar and a slice of onion anywhere near each other, and in a few days, you'll have an onion-flavored cigar. Bundle a group of 25 cigars together for a month and they'll swap flavors with each other.

Stacking bundled cigars in the cedar-lined marrying room.

This marrying process smoothes out differences in taste due to variations in the exact tobacco content of each stogie. It also gives the cigars time to rest and dries some of the excess moisture required during rolling.

The Three-Month Wedding Night

In Cuba, sorted and bundled cigars are transported to a special cabinet, called the *escaparate*, which holds approximately 18,000 cigars. Here they rest and marry, sharing their unique flavors with each other.

Many connoisseurs believe this marrying stage is extremely important, although it's a mere "blip" when compared to the time between planting the tobacco seed and completing the cigar in the factory. Many cigars, including Cubans, arrive in stores without having gone through any apparent marrying process.

Although you can age cigars yourself (which is covered in Chapter 17), the ideal time for cigars to go through the marrying and mellowing process is just after production, with other cigars, in special rooms.

Some manufacturers stretch this aging process even further, opting to give cigars a three-month honeymoon in cedar-lined aging rooms. This extra step enables the bundled cigars to marry flavors and pick up a subtle hint of cedar. Six months in an aging room would be even better, but that would be unrealistically long for the manufacturer to wait.

> **Hot Tip**
> Aromatic cedar wood plays an important role in aging and storing cigars. Cedar has a pungent aroma and blends well with cigars, so cigars are often exposed to cedar-lined rooms where they pick up a slight cedar scent. Cedar also absorbs humidity when conditions are too moist and provides humidity when the cigars' surroundings are too dry.

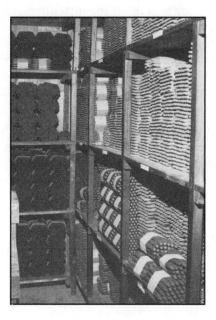

Thousands of perfect cigars stacked wall to wall in a cedar-lined aging room.

The cigars in the marrying room are packed closely together so that they have a chance to share flavors and mellow with hundreds of nearby stogies! Some manufacturers who use this process explain the process on the cigar box or on a slip of paper accompanying the box. If you buy individual cigars, ask the storekeeper whether he or she has any extra material from the manufacturer describing the cigar-making process.

During this aging period, a few cigars are selected and subjected to expert taste tests. When they're considered ready, they're removed. Believe it or not, the stogies still aren't ready for shipping.

Once again, the cigars are inspected and graded by an expert. Color and appearance might have changed slightly during the aging, so individual cigars in a group of 25 may be replaced with others. If, during the aging process, a cigar's wrapper splits, the cigar is discarded.

Gotta Crush That Bug Right Outta My 'Gar!

During the final stages of readying cigars for export, manufacturers have to deal with a nasty pest. In a warehouse or factory, hatched tobacco beetles can devastate storehouses. Fortunately, these destructors can be controlled.

Blowing Smoke

Tobacco beetles are persistent pests that lay sturdy eggs. These eggs can travel with a finished cigar and hatch in a smoke shop humidor. The worms (immature beetles) eat holes in cigars and can quickly infest an entire shop. A simple way to crush them is to put the cigars in a vacuum chamber before they're shipped, which crushes the eggs. Most manufacturers take this important precaution.

The tobacco beetle enjoys laying eggs on aged leaf, which gets turned into finished cigars ready to travel around the world. The eggs then have to be destroyed. Tobacco beetle eggs are hearty and can survive a nuclear bomb blast, but they can't take pressure!

To destroy the eggs, most manufacturers place finished cigars in large vacuum chambers. Some do this before the cigars are boxed, and others do it immediately after they're boxed or bundled. The chamber door is sealed, and the air is sucked out. This process doesn't damage the cigar, but it crushes the heck out of any beetle eggs that might be lurking, still viable, inside the stogies.

This vacuum step is necessary; just ask any retailer who's had a beetle infestation. If the beetle eggs survive and hatch, they start eating their way through cigar after cigar, and then they breed, and the adults lay more eggs, and, well, you get the idea.

The idea of smoking bug eggs is not particularly appealing, and neither are the holes and trails left by the larvae. Beyond the simple repulsion factor, holes in cigars destroy the draw because you're sucking air in through the holes rather than the lit tip. Bottom line: Tobacco beetles are bad news, and vacuum fumigation is a perfect way to eliminate them without using chemicals.

Farewell to the Tropics

Fumigated cigars are ready for the finishing touches. They've been sorted by color and size, graded, and are ready for banding and boxing.

Before being boxed or packed up, virtually all cigar brands are given a colorful, unique band. The bands are the only identifying mark a manufacturer can put on the cigar, and they help you keep track of individual cigars in your humidor.

Most bands are paper and are printed on flat sheets and cut out. In the cigar factory, a band is wrapped around the cigar, usually close to the head, and held with a dab of glue.

Manufacturers can use one of three ways to pack individual cigars into a box:

➤ Glass or metal tubes

➤ Clear cellophane

➤ Naturally, with no cellophane sleeve

Cuban makers almost never use cellophane, choosing either to tube cigars or pack them naturally. As you might expect, there is debate over which method is best.

Totally Tubular Cigars

Tubes protect a cigar in transport and make it easy to slip into your pocket, but they don't keep cigars moist. Some tight-sealing tubes, particularly those that come on Davidoff cigars, can help retain moisture for a day or two, but you can't count on them in dry conditions.

You're also at a disadvantage when you buy cigars in opaque metal tubes because you can't as easily inspect individual cigars. If you buy a box, you're completely trusting that every cigar in that box is fresh and has a nice wrapper. Tubes also add to the cost of a cigar. For many reasons, I just don't like 'em.

Blowing Smoke
Some makers claim that their glass-tubed cigars are sealed so tightly that the cigar will stay fresh until the tube is opened. A tightly sealed glass tube may help a little, but the cigar will still dry out unless it's properly humidified. Don't count on tubes to keep a cigar fresh and moist.

The Cellophane Debate

Cellophane, a type of clear plastic, has been used on cigars since at least the late 1930s. I like cellophaned cigars because they're easier to carry around individually without fear of damaging the wrapper.

Cellophane also helps protect cigars that are sold individually. If I'm caught without a leather cigar case and I need to cart my cigar around for awhile before I smoke it, I'll lean toward choosing a cellophaned cigar.

If you've kept a cellophaned cigar in your humidor for a few years, it's fun to haul out the cigar, pull the cellophane off, and see how the oil from the cigar has given the clear plastic a golden hue. Cellophane *does not* indicate a cheap cigar. Many super-premium brands are sleeved in cellophane.

A lot of smokers believe that a cigar will fail to age or breathe in a cellophane sleeve, that the sleeve should be removed immediately after purchase and before the cigar is placed in your humidor. Perhaps they're right, but over the years I've experimented with storing the same cigars: some cellophane sleeved and some unsleeved. I haven't noticed any difference between the two, even after several years of aging.

> **Cigar Speak**
> You'll hear cedar cigar boxes called **boite nature**, which is French for "natural box." These boxes take many shapes: Some are hinged with metal clasps, while others have a simple wood top that slides into grooves cut into the box. Either way, an all-cedar box is boite nature.

I like to remove cellophane sleeves from cigars I plan to smoke in a month or two, just to give them a little extra airing in the humidor. I've stored cellophaned cigars for up to 10 years, however, and they're just as good as when I bought them.

As I explained earlier in this chapter, if a cigar is aged properly by the manufacturer, it doesn't need to age any more. I'm content if I can buy a great cigar and smoke it right away—or smoke it 10 years later and get the same great taste! In Chapter 17 I talk more about aging cigars.

On rare occasions, makers will wrap their cigars in a thin, pliable sheet of cedar and then either tie the cedar or slip the whole affair into a cellophane sleeve. It looks elegant, and I've noticed cigars with individual cedar wrapping do pick up a little more of the pleasant woody flavor and aroma of the wood.

Boxed and Ready to Travel

Boxes are stacked in the factory, awaiting their precious cargo. Some manufacturers purchase raw materials such as cedar for *boite nature* boxes and basswood for boxes that will be covered with paper; they then make the boxes at the factory. Other makers buy their boxes already stamped or labeled.

For most manufacturers, it's most cost effective to have their boxes made in whatever country the cigars are assembled. It doesn't make much sense to ship bulky, empty cigar boxes from one country to another!

A factory worker carefully packs A. Fuete 8-5-8 cigars into finished wood boxes.

We've already talked about the different types of boxes in Chapter 4, and the aesthetic and possible flavor benefits of cedar (boite nature) over paper-lined boxes. Many manufacturers add their own special touches to boxes: Some use a velvet lining on the lid or apply colorful labels.

Some manufacturers insert a plastic tray on the bottom of the box with protruding *pincers* that gently hold and separate the cigars. Pincers are especially common with large cigars packed in flat boxes with one row only of 10 stogies.

Some makers wrap their bundles in tissue before boxing them. Although the options are seemingly limitless, the main criteria is that the box is properly sized, holding the cigars with just enough pressure to keep them from bouncing around during transport.

The boxed, banded, and fumigated smokes are ready to be quickly transported from their tropical home to distribution points around the world. Although cigars can be taken by container on ships, the stogies can be damaged during a slow trip atop a cargo ship in the blazing sun.

Cigars are relatively light and very costly if damaged, so many manufacturers pay the extra cost of a quick flight in the hold of a cargo plane. When the cigars arrive at their destination, they're rushed to temperature- and humidity-controlled warehouses. They then await shipment to retailers, where those prized cigars are waiting for you to appreciate them.

The Least You Need to Know

➤ The cigars in a box of quality handmade smokes will be perfectly matched by color.

➤ Cedar is an aromatic wood used to lend a subtle flavor to cigars.

➤ A nice touch is a cigar that has been aged in a cedar-lined room, wrapped in a sliver of cedar, or boxed in cedar.

➤ Individual metal tubes will not keep your cigars humidified, and glass tubes have only limited use for keeping cigars fresh.

➤ Finished premium cigars are sorted and graded numerous times to ensure quality, perfect construction, and consistent, flawless appearance.

Part 3
Portrait of the Cigar as a Young Leaf: Where Cigars Grow Up

So far in our journey through the world of cigars, you've selected cigars, learned about cigar shapes and sizes, figured out what's mild and what's wild, and sat at the tabaquero's table to make the hefty belicoso. What you haven't done yet is to take a trip back in time to explore how cigars and cigar tobacco evolved. Understanding the history of cigars helps you to understand just how amazing, and sophisticated, this process has become.

Tobacco has undergone many evolutions: from hand-rolled native stogies to the painstakingly cured and aged handmade smokes of today. Although it's native to hot, tropical climates, tobacco is grown all over the world. In this part, you'll see how this fascinating and adaptable plant has been cultivated almost everywhere.

We'll also talk about how the nearly microscopic tobacco seed is grown and nurtured, and about the time-consuming steps required to process the cigar leaf once it's picked from the plant. Finally, we'll take another look at the many cigar leaf growing regions around the world, and why each is unique.

BABY CIGAR   FULL GROWN

I Was Born in a Log Cabin...

Like so many things, Europeans claim to have "discovered" tobacco. But tobacco was certainly no secret to the native North and South American peoples, who smoked and cultivated tobacco for centuries before Columbus landed in the New World. Native Americans from the Incas in South America to the Inuits at the Arctic Circle knew of, and smoked, tobacco.

Among native American peoples, tobacco was assigned special properties. It was considered magical: The Central American Mayans believed that lightning and thunder meant that the Gods of the Four Winds were striking fire and lighting up! And because being seated by a fire with a good cigar on a stormy night is one of the great pleasures of life, who's to argue with the Mayans?

Cigar Esoterica

The real origin of the word *tobacco* is lost to us. Some say the first Europeans to visit the New World used the Spanish word *tabago*, which was close to the native Caribbean word for the pipe used to smoke tobacco weed. When the Spaniards asked about the smoking substance, they were told *tobago*. So the substance was named for the pipe.

Tobacco also played a vital role in the native American community: We've all heard of the peace pipe. Smoking a pipe or some form of tobacco provided an opportunity to sit down, take a load off, and commune with friends—and sometimes foes. It's hard to be angry or argumentative while relaxing with a good smoke.

An Aztec drawing taken from an ancient stone carving depicts early cigar smoking.

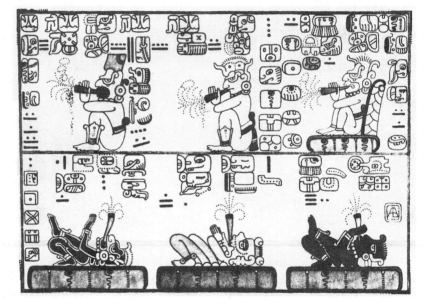

All tobacco comes from one simple variety, *Nicotina Tabacum*, named after Jean Nicot, a Frenchman who presented the leaf as a medicinal herb to Italy's Catherine de Medici in the mid 1500s. Over the centuries, this plant has been hybridized in hundreds of thousands of ways, leading to the many sub-varieties grown worldwide for cigar filler, binder, and wrapper, not to mention cigarette and pipe tobacco. The Spanish explorers, however, were probably the first to discover and popularize this incredible leaf.

Native Smokes: Close, but No Cigar

The word *cigar* was probably coined by the Europeans who landed on the island of Hispañola in 1492. (If that date sounds familiar, the familiarity is with good cause: "Columbus sailed the ocean blue, in 14 hundred and 92...")

The European landing is the first documented exposure of the western world to tobacco. And what a bizarre set of circumstances surrounded the event. Christopher Columbus figured that if you could get to India and the Orient by sailing west from Europe, you could probably get there by sailing east, as well. (Hey, give the guy credit for believing the world was round!)

As a historical aside, and not to take anything away from old Chris Columbus, he did not sail because he was an explorer trying to discover the world. He was an Italian mercenary sailor and navigator who'd been given the boot by his home country.

Columbus went to Spain, and under direct orders from Isabella and Ferdinand, the Spanish queen and king, he searched for a western route to the Orient with the directive to find booty for the mighty Spanish empire. This treasure included gold, silk, and spices. (Spices were valued because they were used to preserve meat and other perishables in those pre-refrigeration days.)

> **Cigar Speak**
> Cojoba, or Cohiba, was the term for the tobacco natives used on the island Christopher Columbus called **La Española** or **Hispañola**. This term was also adopted by Cubatabaco when it created its famed cigar for Fidel Castro.

After sailing for India, China, Japan, or one of those places famed for gold, silk, and spices, Columbus sighted land in October 1492. With three ships full of seasick, nearly mutinous sailors, old Chris was thrilled to see any kind of dirt. Unfortunately—or fortunately—he had made a slight miscalculation about the size of Planet Earth; he only got halfway around the world, and the first land he saw was the Bahamas, not Japan or India. When he landed upon this island nation, he was sure he'd found Japan, and wandered around hoping the Lord would show him "where gold is born."

If Mr. Columbus had sailed about 200 miles south, he would have found the land of gold: Central America. As history tells, the Spanish *conquistadors* who followed Chris had a nose for Mayan and Inca gold, and did a good job of filling Spain's royal coffers with the pillage. Today, cigar smokers can thank Chris for his mistake.

> **Tobacco Leaves**
> "Hispañola is one of the wonders of nature. The mountain ranges, the hills, the valleys, and the fields are strikingly beautiful. The soil is so fertile...No man who has seen it will ever wish to leave."
>
> —Christopher Columbus

As it was, Columbus stumbled upon something today's cigar smokers might say was better than gold! In a total twist of irony, he arrived on the island in October, which is the optimal time for planting cigar tobacco throughout the Caribbean.

While Chris checked out the Bahamian white-sand beaches in the Bahamas, Martin Alonso Pinzon, Columbus' second-in-command, took one of the ships (the Pinta) in search of gold, jeopardizing the entire expedition. After exploring Cuba in the other ships (the Santa Maria and Niña), Columbus sailed east along Cuba's coastline.

Soon afterward, the Santa Maria ran aground on the northern coast of Hispañola and was wrecked. Unable to transfer all personnel and goods to the Niña, Columbus established a colony. Hispañola today is the island split between the former French colony of Haiti and the former Spanish colony of the Dominican Republic. Guess who figured out how to make cigars?

At his new land, Columbus saw dark-skinned people puffing a flaming weed and blowing smoke. Imagine what a fascinating and terrifying sight that must have been. Still convinced he had landed in India, Columbus called them "Indians." Some of these native peoples smoked pipes, while others smoked long cylinders of rolled tobacco.

In a report to Columbus, advance-men Luis de Torres and Rodrigo de Jerez described their experience:

> On their way, these two Christians came across many people walking through the towns, women and men; all the men had firebrands in their hands and certain herbs to breathe in the smoke, dried herbs enclosed in a certain leaf, also dried, a sort of musket made of paper, like those children make on the feast of the Holy Spirit, lit on one end, while on the other they were drawing or sucking, breathing in that smoke; with which they numb their flesh and which is almost intoxicating, and in this way they say they never feel fatigue. These muskets, we shall call them, they call tabaccos.
>
> —Recorded by Barolomé de las Casas, *Historia de Las Indias*

Hmm, sounds like a modern cigar bar! This magical herb really perplexed the European explorers. They just couldn't figure how this blowing of smoke made the natives so laid back.

I don't believe that anyone has yet figured out the exact combination of psychological and physical ingredients that make smoking a cigar so relaxing, but the native peoples of the Caribbean seem to have come close to solving the mystery—and didn't ask a lot of questions. By the way, de Jerez did more than just observe smoking. He took up the pastime himself, becoming the first European (but hardly the last) to smoke a cigar.

Eventually, Columbus met up with the Pinta, struck an uneasy truce with Pinzon, and set sail for Spain in January 1493. In September, the intrigued Spaniards sent another fleet to the Caribbean, with Columbus at the helm. He didn't find gold in the Caribbean, but he found enough that was interesting to convince the king and queen to finance another venture.

"This Is Better Than Gold!"

Upon arriving at Hispañola on his second voyage, Columbus discovered that all the colonists left behind had been slaughtered. The killing was probably not done by the peaceful Arawak natives, but by the warlike cannibal Carib people from modern-day Venezuela, who frequently descended on the peaceful islands for a raiding and a taste of human flesh. You have to wonder why the area was named for the warlike Carib tribe instead of the peaceful, cigar-smoking natives—until you think about how "Arawakabbean Sea" sounds.

The colony on Hispañola was re-established for a short time, but upon hearing rumors of gold in the southern part of the island, the greedy European mercenaries soon abandoned the settlement to establish Santa Domingo on the island's southern coast. This bustling city is today the capital city of the Dominican Republic.

Columbus praised the natives of this lovely, mountainous island for their beauty. He wrote: "They go about as naked as when they were born, they are all young, strongly built, shapely and handsome."

Ironically, the native races that Columbus found so appealing failed to survive their meeting with Europeans. The diseases and germs carried by the Europeans, to which the Caribbean natives had no immunity, decimated the population within a century.

Cigar Esoterica

How did the cigar get its name? The most common tale is that the word comes from the Spanish word *cigarrel*, meaning "orchard," because the newly discovered tobacco plant was transplanted to the gardens of wealthy Spaniards. Speaking with pride of their crop, these Spaniards would say to guests who received the rolled tobacco, *"Es de mi cigarrel"*: "It is from my orchard."

So what were the native smokes like? In a word, awful. The tobacco was not hybridized for smoothness, and the only processing involved picking the leaves and drying them in the sun. Even today, if you smoke the finest cigar leaf that has undergone only the first stage of processing—air curing—the tobacco is so filled with nicotine and ammonium nitrate that it makes even the toughest smoker sick.

Perhaps this harshness accounts for early European explorers reporting native smokers as "falling down as if dead" after indulging. The magical and curative powers of tobacco were somewhat exaggerated, as described by one English explorer in North America:

In the West Indies it hath divers names according to the several places and countries where it groweth and is used. The Spaniards call it tobacco. The leaves…purgeth superfluous and other gross humors; openeth all the pores and passages of the body, by which means the use thereof not only preserveth the body from obstructions, but also if any be so that they have not been too long continuance, in short time breaketh them; whereby their bodies are notably preserved in health and know no many grievous diseases wherewith we in England are oftentimes affected."

—Thomas Harriot, *Briefe and True Account of the New Found Land of Virginia,* 1588

Wow! So much for the tobacco smoked by native Americans! The relative poverty of all Caribbean nations attests to the fact that Columbus never found the gold that he sought. He came back to the Caribbean, where he eventually died, still looking for gold and never realizing he'd discovered another kind of treasure. He had no idea that he had stumbled upon a natural resource that would some day give pleasure to millions and, at times, would be used as money and have a greater value per ounce than gold.

The Indians have a certain herb, of which they lay up a store every summer, having first dried it in the sun. They always carry some of it in a small bag hanging around their necks. In this bag they also keep a hollow tube of wood or stone. Before using the herb they pound it into powder, which they cram into one end of the tube and plug it with red-hot charcoal. They then suck themselves so full of smoke that it oozes from their mouths like the smoke from the flue of a chimney. When we tried to use the smoke we found it bit our tongues like pepper.

—Henri Cartier, describing his encounter with tobacco-smoking natives in Canada

Aging: It Worked for Wine

What is it about tobacco that worms its way into the hearts and souls of those captivated by it? I'm not sure any cigar lover has ever figured out its seductive powers, and I, for one, don't try! But I do know that, armed with an outstanding cigar, we don't ask too many questions. Thank goodness the early Spaniards did!

Someone, somewhere, decided that this native leaf grown throughout North and South America was worth a second look. To European palates, it was unacceptably rough and harsh. No one knows exactly who had the brilliant idea to apply the same techniques to tobacco cultivation as had been applied for centuries to grapes. (By the time Columbus discovered the New World, wine, beer, and spirits had long been a staple in Europe.)

Cigar Esoterica

Tobacco has always had its ups and downs. In the early 1600s, Russia's Tsar Michael condemned tobacco users to death, but in 1634 revised the punishment to merely slitting the smoker's nose with a knife. By 1696, his grandson, the legendary Peter the Great—an avid smoker—was turning Russia into one of the world's leading tobacco-exporting nations.

Apparently someone reasoned that if grape juice can be fermented and turned into something totally different, why can't tobacco? Who was the brilliant soul? We don't know, but we owe him (or her) a round of applause! If you understand how wine is made (or how fine scotches or brandies are made), you'll understand how much the creation of the modern cigar resembles wine-making techniques.

What Tobacco Learned from Wine

Grapes are just grapes, and even the best wine grapes are simply plump, juicy orbs that taste nice with cheese. To make wine, the grapes have to be harvested at their peak, crushed, allowed to ferment in vats with yeast (which converts the sugar to alcohol), and then placed in wood barrels and allowed to age. It's a long process that's best saved for another book: *The Complete Idiot's Guide to Wine*! In Chapter 15, I talk about how this process was applied to tobacco.

The Europeans who discovered tobacco, notably the Spaniards (who are no wine-making slouches), realized that tobacco might benefit from the same kind of aging and fermenting that wine undergoes. How somebody made this connection is a complete mystery to me and everyone else, but what an idea!

Soon after the Spaniards discovered tobacco in the Caribbean, the English discovered the same thing in North America. The English concentrated on tobaccos grown for pipe smoking, while the Spaniards focused on the rolled tobacco leaves they called *cigarre*.

All these discoveries happened at approximately the same time: the 1500s, the age of Sir Walter Raleigh, who first colonized the east coast of what would later be the United States. It seems everyone had a similar idea: Make this incredible weed more palatable to refined tastes. But how?

It probably started with taking the native tradition of air-curing the picked leaves a step further. Tobacco is a natural plant material, and if you pile it, it heats as do weeds and grass clippings in a backyard compost heap. At some point, someone must have tried stacking leaves and found that with a bit of heat, something happened to the tobacco leaves: They mellowed.

When introduced to sugar-eating yeast, what starts out as grape juice turns into an alcoholic beverage. The same is true for hop-laden, sugary malted water when yeast is introduced: It becomes beer. Similarly, lightly sprouted barley seeds, when toasted, allowed to ferment in water, and then heated and distilled, become malt whiskey.

No foreign ingredients such as yeast need to be introduced to help raw tobacco leaves turn into something different from how it began. The natural enzymes and chemicals in tobacco, combined with the heat of composting, handles the transformation. Although we know nothing about who began the process of mellowing tobacco leaves, we know that perfecting the procedure required centuries. We'll look at this complicated process in Chapter 15.

Tobacco Farming: Getting Your Hands Dirty

Similar to growing of wine grapes, growing tobacco is a superb labor of love. Great cigar leaf is founded on experimentation, and today's cigar manufacturers continue to experiment to create the best possible leaf.

Many top manufacturers own acres upon acres of prime tobacco-growing land. Others "lock up" the best leaf in their homeland by striking deals with tobacco farmers. Usually, the well-capitalized manufacturers provide the "front" money to relatively poor growers to obtain prime seed, the best fertilizer, and the cultivation equipment needed to grow a good tobacco crop.

Blowing Smoke

Remember: Your best bet for a consistent, high-quality smoke is to buy established brands. Large manufacturers have the best access to leaf and have first rights to thousands of acres of tobacco because they've helped finance the growing. Some established specialty brands, such as Avo, Butera, or PG, also have access to top leaf because of good connections with larger players.

In return for their financial contribution, these manufacturers have first rights to the tobacco grown. If they think the crop shows promise, they buy it and keep it. If they find the crop to be inferior, they'll still buy it, but they'll sell it to other manufacturers.

Tobacco growing has progressed from a simple native practice to a true art. We'll look at every detail of this art in Chapter 14. At every stage of the growing process, a great deal of expertise comes into play. Growing good cigar leaf involves an established procedure, and the grower and manufacturer work together to plant and nurture just the right kind of hybrid seed.

Many centuries of experimentation and hybridizing have brought the uncultivated Indian seed of *Nicotina rustica* to the sophisticated Cuban-seed cultivars that comprise today's great cigars. A few cigar guides tell you what kind of leaf is used in various brands, but knowing where the leaf came from isn't nearly as important as how the cigar tastes to you.

Manufacturers never, ever, give away the exact combination of leaf used in their cigars. By checking descriptions of newly rated cigars in magazines such as *Smoke* or *The Cigar Aficinado*, you can get some broad knowledge of the wrapper, binder, and filler leaves used in particular cigars. That knowledge is interesting, but how they're blended makes all the difference.

The Least You Need to Know

➤ Tobacco is native to the Americas, but has been transplanted all over the world.

➤ Native American peoples from South America to the Arctic Circle smoked, sniffed, and chewed tobacco for centuries before Europeans "discovered" it.

➤ Tobacco in its original native form was rough and harsh to smoke.

➤ The Europeans, notably the Spaniards, successfully applied the processing techniques to tobacco that were used to make wine, brandy, and beer.

From Green Bay to Bombay

In This Chapter

➤ The origins of tobacco

➤ How tobacco traveled around the world

➤ The challenge of growing tobacco

➤ Nicotine and tobacco

➤ Why cigar leaf is different than all other tobacco

Have you gotten the feeling that growing great cigar leaf usually involves tropical weather and valleys? You're right, but tobacco—one of the world's most adaptable plants—can be found almost anywhere in the world, growing happily in small patches and on large plantations.

Tobacco's journey around the world began with Christopher Columbus, but as we saw in Chapter 12, this indigenous American plant had been widely cultivated and used for at least a thousand years, and probably much longer, by native Americans.

How tobacco has been used, the purposes it has served in culture, religion, and society, and how it has been literally and figuratively transplanted is so interesting that it deserves a few words. Light up a premium smoke, settle back, and take a break from the "how to" of cigars to enjoy a bit of the "where, what, when, and why!"

You'd Be Amazed Where This Stuff Grows

> **Cigar Speak**
> Nicotine in its pure state is colorless, burning to the taste, and highly poisonous. Tobacco contains a small percent of nicotine, and cigar leaf contains the smallest amount of nicotine of all tobacco—only about 2 percent of the leaf's content. Much of this disappears as your cigar burns, so you take only a tiny amount into your mouth when you puff. Nicotine is addictive, so the less that gets into your system, the better.

If you took a globe and put red dots everywhere tobacco is grown, the only two empty continents would be Greenland and Antarctica. But if you think this warm-weather crop hasn't found its way into the coldest regions of the earth, you'd be wrong. Even Inuits, or Eskimos, smoked tobacco in pipes made of whale tusk, stone, and wood. But I'm getting ahead of myself; let's begin at the beginning.

Tobacco was used in the Americas for a variety of ceremonial purposes—and for plain enjoyment. In its wild state, *Nicotiana Tabacum* grows two to three feet high and sprouts delicate pink flowers. Tobacco is a distinctive-looking plant. Today several hundred distinct species of N. Tabacum are scattered around the world.

A popular garden flower, *nicotiana* has been hybridized over the centuries to produce a spray of sweet-smelling pink or white flowers and small leaves. Cultivation of tobacco for smoking, chewing, and sniffing took a different course. Plants were bred for broad, luscious leaves, and the flowers weren't important.

Tobacco is a perennial plant, meaning that in its wild state, it sprouts anew from its roots each year. A first-year plant sprouted from seed produces far superior tobacco, however, so cigar-leaf tobacco plants are always grown from seed each year.

The original tobacco smoked by natives resembled today's cigar leaf about as much as the bland, small-eared Indian corn, or maize, resembles today's juicy sweet corn. Centuries of hybridizing and cultivation has led to hundreds of species and thousands of sub-species of tobacco.

Tobacco probably found its way around the Americas quite easily. Evidence shows that tobacco was chewed or smoked by the Incas and Aztecs, the tropical Carib and Arawak islanders, the native North American tribes, and the Inuits. No one knows who carried what plants where, but it's likely tobacco traveled northward through the Americas from its original home in the lush, tropical climates of South and Central America.

> **Cigar Esoterica**
> Tobacco had many different names among native American peoples. In Aztec Mexico, it was *picietl*; on the east coast of North America, *uppowoc*; in Canada, it was *quiecta*; and in Peru, it was called *sayri*. In Brazil, the natives called it *petum*; in Columbia, it was *yuri*; and in Trinidad, it was *vreit*. The origins of these words has for centuries provided fodder for etymologists!

Tobacco in Europe's Backyard

The first European tobacco "crops" were probably planted in the gardens of wealthy Portuguese and Spanish merchants and noblemen. The plant took a liking to the hot climate of the Iberian peninsula and flourished. I've talked before about the Spanish preference for stronger, more full-bodied smokes; this preference could partially be a result of early exposure to powerful (what most of us would find unacceptably harsh and bitter) tobacco.

Cigar Esoterica

The first tobacco users tried the leaf in a myriad of different ways. Whole leaves were chewed; dried tobacco powder was sniffed through hollow reeds; dried shredded leaves were smoked in pipes; and sun-dried leaves were rolled into something resembling a modern cigar. The explanation for why native Americans cultivated and used this plant is about as logical as our modern reason for smoking cigars: It tastes good, and we like it.

Growing great cigar leaf is an art, and it requires the perfect combination of cultivation and climate. Tobacco itself, however, is exceptionally hardy and can grow in nearly any climate. Granted, tobacco grown in some climates won't taste very good, but it does grow, and it *is* smokeable!

Over the centuries, tobacco has made its way to the islands of the Pacific, Asia, the Middle East, Africa, Europe, and throughout North America. It became a huge cash crop in the American colonies—particularly the warm states of Virginia, Maryland, Kentucky, and North Carolina. These states are renowned for growing some of the best pipe and cigarette tobaccos in the world, but except for Connecticut, they're not ideal for cigar leaf.

Cigar Esoterica

By the early 1500s, the Spaniards had established permanent colonies on Hispañola (today's Dominican Republic) and had begun to explore Cuba. Despite Cuba's cigar-growing reputation, formal cultivation began in the Dominican Republic. The first tobacco plantations in the Caribbean, run by Spaniards and staffed by natives, were up and running by the mid-1500s. At this time, growers began experimenting with ways to improve tobacco crops.

149

In the English-held American colonies, homegrown tobacco was chewed and smoked in pipes, but never made into cigars. It was so valuable in colonial times that the leaves were pressed into cylinders and used as money. Someone wanting to use tobacco to buy something would cut off a chunk from the cylinder and hand it over!

The English were extremely fond of pipe tobacco and snuff. The Dutch were, also, and so they began planting tobacco in their colonies in the Pacific. During the same time—from approximately 1600 to 1800—Spanish colonists moved most of their tobacco-growing efforts to Cuba and began staking out plantations in multiple locations. Although much of Europe took to the pipe, the Spanish preference was the cigar.

Cigars did find some favor in Europe and in America. By 1850, cigars had become popular in the U.S., and tobacco farmers—already experienced in growing pipe tobacco—tried their luck at growing cigar leaf that could match Cuban leaf. Tons of cigar leaf for the proverbial "nickel seegar" was grown in Florida, Ohio, Pennsylvania, Georgia, Texas (filler), Connecticut (wrapper) and, yes, even Wisconsin (binders)!

How good was the cigar leaf grown in the United States? Despite all efforts, tobacco didn't take to the North American climate—not even Florida. Nothing grown in the U.S. could rival Cuban leaf, so American cigar tobacco was used in cheap cigars and Havana leaf was reserved for the finest smokes. Only Connecticut broadleaf gained stature as a good cigar tobacco.

The World's Most Sensitive Crops

Although the adaptable tobacco plant could grow happily all over the world, it couldn't produce great cigar leaf anywhere besides a tropical climate. While connoisseurs can argue about the merits of cigar leaf from various nations that border the Caribbean, few dispute that from Green Bay to Bombay, the native home of tobacco—the Caribbean—still produces the best cigar leaf.

Cigar Esoterica

Ever find yourself at a loss for conversation while enjoying a cigar with friends? How about jump-starting the banter by discussing the chemical composition of tobacco? Chemicals and minerals found in tobacco include nicotine, potash, lime, ammonia, iron oxide, malic and citric acids, polyunsaturated fats, resins and oils, and cellulose.

I'm no horticulturist, but I find the similarity between cigars, coffee, and wine fascinating. These crops all thrive in challenging climates: They all prefer hilly or mountainous areas and dry, crumbly soils. If they're slightly deprived of moisture, the flavor of the crops concentrates and improves. And, as final products, wine and coffee both go great with a cigar!

There's no documented proof that the early growers of these three sensitive crops learned from each other. All three are very labor-intensive crops, however, and they require exacting cultivation and hand-picking at the absolute peak of ripeness.

When harvested, all three crops undergo treatments that create chemical transformations. Coffee beans are dried and roasted to bring out the oils and "cook" the bean; otherwise, they're unpalatable. Wine grapes are fermented using yeast to create alcohol. Tobacco is also fermented using heat (we'll talk about tobacco fermentation in Chapter 15).

Why Cigar Leaf Is Different

When you smoke a cigar, you're enjoying one of the most delicate and hard-to-grow of all tobacco crops. Let's talk about the special soil and climate that cigar leaf requires.

Most tobacco grows best in sandy, loamy soil with a heavy mineral content. In other words, it likes loose, somewhat lousy soil instead of the rich, black dirt that pleases crops such as corn and wheat. Let's look at Cuba's soil, which arguably may be the best for growing cigar.

Cuba's *Vuelta Abajo* region is considered the world's greatest plot for growing cigar tobacco. The soil is reddish-brown because of a high content of ferrous minerals, better known as iron. The soil is loose and granular and sits atop mountain ranges that were pushed out of the ocean millions of years ago when continental tectonic plates collided.

Vuelta Abajo soil contains lots of minerals but is almost pulverized rock: It contains little organic material. The soil is crumbly, filled with iron, quartz, sand, and a bit of clay. This kind of soil, which is common throughout the Caribbean, is inhospitable to many plants, but tobacco loves the fight to survive in this terrain.

Tobacco needs a lot of care and attention while it grows, and a dry or exceptionally hot growing season will stunt the tobacco plants' growth. With a little help—including water and fertilizer—from the farmer, tobacco enjoys its fight for life, producing rich, broad leaves in an effort to soak up moisture and shield the all-important stalk from the sun.

Change the Conditions, Change the Taste

So what makes cigar leaf tobacco different when it's grown in different countries, or even regions of the same country? First, as anyone who has smoked pipe tobacco or cigarettes can attest, cigar tobacco has a unique flavor. Regardless of where it's grown—from Cuba to Africa to Sumatra—this leaf has a striking and easily identified taste that says "cigar."

Nicotine content, the growing conditions, and the particular species of tobacco all play a part in creating this distinctive flavor.

Regional soil differences have a pronounced effect on the quality and flavor of cigar leaf. Although cigar tobacco seed will produce a plant with cigar-tasting leaves, smoothness and taste vary greatly based on the soil. Cuban tobacco, for example, has a natural peppery quality that is owed greatly to the mineral content of Cuban soil.

Cigar Esoterica

Francisco Fernandes, a physician sent by Philip II of Spain in 1558 to investigate the products of Mexico, was the first to bring tobacco to the European continent. However, it was Jean Nicot, a French ambassador, who staged the public-relations coup (and had his name memorialized in Latin) by bringing it back from Iberia and introducing it to the queen of France in 1560.

The Dominican Republic has slightly different soil, and only in the past decade have growers mastered soil management to be able to replicate the soil of Cuba's famed Vuelta Abajo. With this replication, the Dominican growers have been able to create a taste in the Cuban seed tobaccos that's close to Cuban.

Tropical climate also plays a major role in differences in cigar leaf. Rainfall varies from country to country, and within regions of each country. To you or me, the climates of Honduras, Cuba, and the Dominican Republic would seem almost identical. Not so with tobacco.

To the sensitive cigar tobacco plant, slight differences in rainfall or the presence of underground streams have a profound effect. If the season is dry, farmers irrigate their fields to compensate. Farmers don't have to miss the mark by much either way—by under- or over-watering—to destroy both yield and quality.

Of course, farmers can't control the sun unless they're growing the expensive and pampered shade-grown wrapper leaf. Fortunately, tobacco loves sun, and as long as it gets enough water and nutrients, it usually does fine.

Because the cigar tobacco fields are so sandy and arid, farmers have to apply fertilizer to give them enough nutrients to grow green and lush. Tobacco is hearty, and it would grow happily in the soil without fertilizer, but the resulting leaf would taste more like that bitter native *Nicotiana Tabacum* than a modern 'gar.

When you look at the delicate balance needed to grow luscious cigar leaf tobacco, a good cigar seems like a miracle. The best of Mother Nature and human ingenuity (along with lots of trial and error) have combined to give us the cigar.

Although this chapter might seem like a geography lesson, it's really to help you understand why good cigar leaf is so valued—and so expensive. If you looked at all the land around the world that's dedicated to agriculture, the acreage used for growing cigar leaf tobacco is small enough to be statistically insignificant.

Only a few regions in a few countries worldwide have proven suitable for growing fine cigar leaf tobacco. Even seed planted in a classic cigar tobacco region costs money and requires a lot of hard work and skill to ensure a good crop. Unless all the variables we've talked about happen in perfect combination, an entire tobacco crop can be ruined or rendered inferior.

All of these factors point to one thing: It's tough to grow a great leaf, and when you find a cigar filled with great leaves, you can appreciate what a treasure it is! Ultimately, this challenge adds to the price of your premium smoke, but high quality can help justify high price.

The Least You Need to Know

➤ Tobacco is native to the Americas, and has been transported around the world.

➤ The right combination of soil and climate makes cigar-leaf tobacco grown in the Caribbean region of the Americas the world's best.

➤ The chemical nicotine provides that unique "tobacco" flavor and smell.

➤ Cigar leaf contains the least amount of nicotine of nearly any type of tobacco.

➤ The price of a cigar reflects the challenge of growing good cigar leaf tobacco.

"Growing" a Good Cigar

Here we are, standing at the beginning of your cigar's long journey. It's early September in the Caribbean, and the weather is becoming milder after the hot summer. There's a hint of rain in the sky, and tropical squalls blow up, dump rain for a few minutes, and disappear.

Millions of tiny tobacco seeds—*Piloto Cubano, Olor,* and other varieties—lie dormant in bags and envelopes. It's time for the annual cigar tobacco season to begin, and we're about to witness how in a few weeks, a nearly microscopic seed grows into a lush green plant taller than an adult.

The Care and Feeding of Baby Tobacco

Tobacco growers (called *vegueros* in Spanish) begin the process in early September, sowing tiny seeds into special beds close to the farm's main buildings so that they can be carefully and frequently tended. These beds are prepared with a bit of fertilizer and are usually turned with a cultivator so that the soil contains no large lumps. The farmers drive tractors through the nursery beds, mounding up the soil in long, straight rows and creating a path down the beds for the tractors. The tractor wheels straddle these mounds, which are about three feet wide.

Infants in the Nursery

> **Blowing Smoke**
> Many independent tobacco farmers don't have enough money to buy the seed, fertilizer, and pesticides needed to nurture a good crop. Larger manufacturers finance these farmers, then buy the tobacco at a set price so they get first pick. The manufacturers use exceptional tobacco for their products and sell the rest to other makers. Consequently, large manufacturers typically obtain the best leaf and produce the best-quality cigars.

The planters scatter tobacco seed on the mounds, just dense enough to ensure many plants germinate, but not so dense that the seedlings will struggle with each other for life. If the seeds are placed too closely together, the young plants put all their energy into growing roots to reach water and nutrients, which stunts their top growth.

After they plant the seeds, the growers gently cover them with straw or porous cloth. This covering protects the seeds from the late-summer sun but lets in water from sprinklers. Without protection, the seeds could burn or dry out faster than they could be watered. The seedbeds get regular watering, and in about a week, they sprout.

After about 10 days, growers remove the covering every day in the early morning and late afternoon to give the seedlings some direct sun. They replace the covering during the middle of the day to protect the delicate seedlings. About this time, they also begin applying insecticides and fungicides to kill off the many pests and diseases that can afflict tobacco. The tractors move up and down the rows, efficiently spraying a mist of pesticide.

Taking It to the Field

In about a month—generally around mid-October—the seedlings are a few inches tall and ready to be transplanted from the seedbeds to the growing fields. While the farmers were pampering their tiny tobacco plants, they were also preparing the growing fields to receive seedlings. The farmers apply calcium carbonate to help the soil achieve the slightly acidic pH balance that tobacco enjoys.

The sandy, granular soil in the growing fields always gets an application of fertilizer. A traditional Cuban fertilizer was *guano* (bat and bird dung) gathered from nearby mountain caves. Guano is very rich, but it will burn seedlings if applied too heavily, so a little went a long way. Today, the usual fertilizer used in tobacco fields around the world involves a combination of organic (manure) and chemical fertilizers. The growers till the soil a bit to break it up, and it's ready for the transplanted seedlings.

The growers go up and down the seedbed rows, selecting by hand only the healthiest, hardiest seedlings. (They need to be hardy to withstand the shock of being dug up and moved to the growing field.) The tobacco farmers quickly transport the seedlings and plant them in furrows dug about three inches deep into the soil. These furrows help retain precious water.

The seedlings are planted a few inches apart and are left to grow in the warm October sun. The blazing heat of summer is over, and the conditions are perfect for growing tobacco. Wrapper leaf tobacco plants may be treated differently from filler and binder leaf. Some wrapper leaf is grown in direct sun, which results in a darker and more flavorful leaf.

Blowing Smoke
Pesticides are applied heavily when tobacco is initially growing because the delicate plant is vulnerable to insects and various molds and fungi—all prevalent in warm tropical climates. You might worry about heavy pesticide application on something you light and smoke, but the early application means that most residue dissipates by the time the leaves are picked. Without pesticides, little of the delicate crop would survive.

If the leaf is destined to be the finest shade-grown variety (discussed in Chapter 10), the transplants are set in fields covered by cheesecloth hung on wooden frames. The cloth keeps direct sun and pelting rain off the leaves.

The tobacco seedlings get another application of fertilizer about two weeks after they're transplanted, and if rainfall is light, they receive regular irrigation. At this point, field hands go through the rows and thin out the growing plants. They pull plants to allow about two feet between the seedlings—the amount of room they'll eventually need to spread their leaves.

The rows of tobacco receive regular weeding and cultivation to loosen the soil and keep out any plant that would compete for nutrients with the tobacco plants. If the growing conditions are right, the tobacco plants grow rapidly, sprouting long green leaves from an ever-thickening central stalk.

Pinch Me, I'm Budding

Like all plants, tobacco wants to reproduce, and that means growing a mass of lovely and sweetly fragrant pink flowers at the top of the plant and producing seeds. A plant expends much of its energy in making flowers and seeds, which saps energy from big, luscious leaves.

Debudding is nipping off the flower buds sprouting from the top of a tobacco plant. This procedure forces the plant to expend all its energy to grow bigger, better leaves. Growers pinch these buds by hand; they also pinch off some of the small top leaves that will never grow large enough for cigar production. In Spanish, debudding is called *desbotonar* (literally, "de-botanizing" or "preventing growth").

Tobacco Leaves

"Guided by the results of long experience handed down by his ancestors, the farmer knows, without being able to explain it scientifically, the way to increase or decrease the strength or mildness of tobacco. His right hand, as though guided by instinct, knows which buds to remove to limit the development or growth of the plant or what may be necessary to do to leave only the best quality leaves."

—Samuel Hazard, writing about Cuban tobacco farmers, from *Cuba a Pluma y Lápiz, v. VII,* 1928

Tobacco growers know from experience exactly where to break off the buds. By the time debudding begins, the tobacco plants have nearly reached their optimal height of about four feet. The *vegueros* pinch the buds and smaller top leaves, taking the top off each plant. This snapping motion has to be quick and clean to avoid tearing the tobacco stalk; a torn stalk can invite disease.

If the tobacco was left to grow without this trimming, it would put its energy into growing taller, sprouting small top leaves, and developing flowers and seed pods. Taking off the top gives the plant no choice but to direct all its sap and nutrients into making the remaining leaves bigger.

The tobacco plants keep trying to sprout new flowers and small leaves, called *suckers,* so this process has to be repeated time and again until the tobacco leaves are ready to harvest. In Spanish, this ongoing debudding is called *repasar* ("removing suckers"). Not all tobacco plants are treated this way; specially cultivated tobacco plants are allowed to produce flowers and seed pods to furnish future crops.

If the growers only had to worry about pruning and watering the plants, they'd be tickled as pink as a tobacco flower. From the time the tobacco seeds are set in the ground to the time they're picked and taken to the curing barns, however, *vegueros* must worry day and night about an army of pests just waiting to consume their crop.

Mold and Pestilence at Play in the Fields of Tobacco

Native tobacco is extremely hardy, but hybrid varieties, such as those used for cigar leaf, are vulnerable to many kinds of pests. Growers have to keep a 24-hour vigil on their crops. The warm tropics are a comfortable and happy home for bugs, and fungus can attack and destroy a field within hours.

The Beetles: Live on Stage

The most tenacious pests are various beetles that lay their eggs on the underside of tobacco leaves. Actually, it's the hatched larvae that causes the problem. Several varieties of beetle plague tobacco in the fields, and the various larvae have been given names such as *cutworm, grub, wireworm, hornworm, tobacco budworm,* and *green worm*. Each variety essentially does the same thing: hatch and grow fat on tobacco leaves.

In previous chapters, I talked about how the tobacco beetle can be the bane of cigar makers and smoke shop owners. The tobacco beetle is a different variety than these field beetles; it prefers to feast indoors on dried tobacco leaves. Tobacco beetles can become a problem in the factories and warehouses, but they're not a major threat in the fields.

Bugs are a huge problem for cigar-leaf tobacco growers because of the tropical climates. Cold weather helps keep tobacco beetles under control in northern climates, so tobacco growers in the U.S. don't have the same level of problem. But various types of tobacco beetle grubs are a problem, even in the U.S. In tropical climates, however, nothing but fumigation and pesticides stop these pests. They keep eating and breeding and eating and breeding! They must be actively controlled.

Without getting too deep into the varieties and types of bugs, let's just say that if these grubs appear on tobacco plants, they have to be killed immediately. Growers routinely apply pesticide to seedlings, which is easy because the seedlings are small.

It's a lot tougher to kill the worms when you have a field full of large tobacco plants, and the little buggers are hiding under the leaves. Farmers can apply pesticide from above, but the grubs would still eat a lot of leaf before they died. The best way to get these guys is to spritz them directly, which means spraying the undersides of the leaves by hand.

Tobacco Leaves

"(The grower's) principal task, to which he devotes most of the hours of his life, is the extermination of the voracious insects that attack the plant. One of these insects, called the cutworm, chooses its home on the underside of the leaves; the green June beetle larvae attacks the ends of the leaves; the grub eats away the heart of the plant and all cause some degree of damage. The tobacco grower spends entire nights with lights, freeing the sprouting seedling of the destructive pests."

—Samuel Hazard, from *Cuba a Pluma y Lápiz, v. VII,* 1928

Growers also don't like to apply pesticides to the leaves so late in the growing process for the obvious reason: This product is not only going to be consumed by humans, but burned, which ignites chemicals and makes them even more detrimental. Sometimes, late spraying can't be helped, but often applying pesticides in the early growing stages provides a good shield of protection from the worms.

Mold: Good in Blue Cheese, Bad on Tobacco

Creatures with legs aren't the only things that threaten tobacco crops. Tobacco is a natural product, and like many crops, it's susceptible to fungus, mold, and rot. Even more devastating than insects is blue mold, which has nearly destroyed the tobacco crop of entire nations, and is very difficult to eradicate once it gets a foothold in the fields.

The spores of this fungus are everywhere, just waiting for a little extra dampness so that they can spring into action. Even an especially damp evening can trigger blue mold fungus, which attacks tobacco leaves and rots them very quickly.

The warm, dry breezes of the Caribbean growing season help keep tobacco leaves dry. After a rainfall, growers hope for a stiff breeze to follow, which quickly dries out the leaves. When they have to supplement rainfall, growers prefer to irrigate the plants using hoses laid on the ground, rather than sprinklers, so that the plants' roots can be soaked without wetting the leaves.

As I mentioned in Chapter 10, in recent years blue mold has plagued Honduran tobacco crops and wiped out significant portions of the crops during the 1980s. It has been less of a problem in Cuba and the Dominican Republic. Farmers can keep blue mold under control by avoiding sprinklers and shaking plants after a rain to get rid of extra moisture on the leaves.

Pick a Winning Leaf

After the laborious growing process, growers are finally ready to begin harvesting. In the Caribbean, leaf harvesting usually begins in January, but the exact date depends on the growing season. Warmer temperatures or more rainfall will accelerate plant growth, while dry conditions or less sunlight will prolong it.

In Connecticut, where planting seeds for shade-grown wrapper leaf begins in late May, the leaves are ready to harvest toward the end of August. In Indonesia, the planting time happens from April through June, and the leaves are ready to harvest from July through October.

Yet again, the skill of the tobacco grower comes into play in deciding the perfect time to begin the harvest. When you're ready to harvest, you don't just mow down tobacco plants as you would corn or wheat. In fact, field workers may comb the rows of tobacco every day for two weeks, each time picking particular leaves as they reach perfection. No one can predict which leaves will mature first, but the skilled *veguero* can tell when the leaves have matured and are ready for harvesting.

When correctly grown and debudded, tobacco plants look exactly like the shape of a tobacco leaf. They're small at the top, where the short, young leaves grow. They're wide in the center, where the large, fine leaves reside. And they're narrow at the bottom, where the sun-deprived bottom leaves grow.

Tobacco plants have three basic sections: the *corona (top leaves)*, the *volado (lower leaves)*, and the prized *seco (middle leaves)*. The sophisticated grower knows that the leaves from each section have different characteristics. This is where things get a little confusing, so hang with me.

Some tobacco growers, particularly Cuban growers, reserve leaves picked from places on a single tobacco plant for different purposes. A Cuban *veguero* may use top leaves from the corona for filler, for example, because these leaves are stronger in flavor. He might use the rich bottom leaves for binder because they burn well. And he might set aside the large, lush central leaves to be used as wrappers.

Other tobacco growers produce plants that they intend to harvest for a specific purpose, such as binders. This specialty planting especially holds true for shade-grown wrapper-leaf tobacco, which is grown exclusively to be used as a wrapper on some fine cigar.

I can't make these two different approaches to selecting leaves any less confusing! However, let me explain how the Cubans generally describe the leaves on a tobacco plant, and how they tend to use them.

> **Cigar Speak**
> The tobacco plant is divided into three basic sections. The top leaves, which comprise the **corona**, are small and somewhat harsher because of their exposure to the sun. The lower leaves are called **volado**, and they burn well and have higher nicotine content. The prized middle leaves are the largest, and are called **seco**. (These terms apply only to sungrown tobacco!)

Tobacco plants have three main sections (*corona*, *seco*, and *volado*), and these are divided into sub-sections. The top leaves of the plant comprise the *corona* (crown) and *semi-corona*. The middle consists of the *centro gordo* (thick center), *centro fino* (finest center), and below those leaves, the *centro ligero* (lesser center). At the bottom, you have the *uno y medio* (one-and-a-half, due to the smaller size) and *libra de pie* (at the base) leaves.

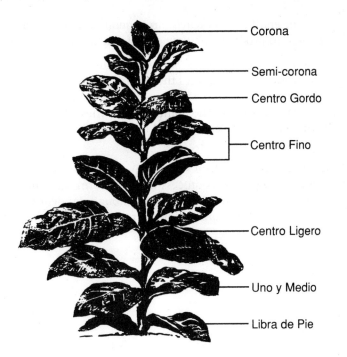

Corona
Semi-corona
Centro Gordo
Centro Fino
Centro Ligero
Uno y Medio
Libra de Pie

The parts of the tobacco plant.

Leaves at the corona are smaller and stronger in flavor because of their exposure to the sun. They make decent filler tobacco—as a peppery accent. The lowest, sun-deprived leaves are tough and make good binders. The middle leaves are like the filet mignon of the tobacco plant, and are reserved for fillers in the finest cigars, and sometimes used as wrappers because of their smooth texture, large size, and mild flavor.

Are you confused yet? Me too. I know what happens, but this is one part of tobacco growing that's a lot easier to do than to explain!

Just remember that the leaves differ in flavor, size, and quality, depending on where on the plant they grow. How various leaves are selected and classified (as filler, binder, or wrapper) is the joint decision of the grower and any manufacturer with whom he might be partnering.

Cigar Esoterica

In Cuba, wrapper tobacco grown under cloth has a whole different set of names because the sun doesn't affect the leaves as dramatically. You want to know these names? The most prized leaves are called *ligero* (light), *seco* (dry), *viso* (glossy), and *amarillo* (yellow). Flawed leaves are called *medio tiempo* (half texture) and *quebrado* (broken). Aren't you glad you don't have to remember all this?

A tobacco plant contains different sizes of leaves. In general, one particular field will grow plants specifically cultivated to produce one type of leaf, such as wrapper, binder, or filler.

Some of the picked leaves have obvious flaws. Sometimes, they have big holes chewed by worms that survived the pesticides. Sometimes they aren't perfectly shaped. Unless the leaf is a total loss, it's separated from the perfect leaves and bundled separately with similarly damaged leaves. Depending on the manufacturer, these leaves might still be used as filler. In Cuba, these imperfect leaves might be fermented and shredded for use in short-filler, machine-made cigars.

Now that the leaves have matured and been selected, it's time for them to start the amazing process of curing and aging. This process will transform them from something less useful than dandelions dug up in the front yard (although dandelion leaves *do* make a nice salad) into something you'll puff and enjoy after a long day at work or a wonderful meal!

The Least You Need to Know

➤ Many growers team up with large manufacturers, who provide the financing to buy tobacco seed, fertilizer, and pesticides, and to pay the many laborers required to manage a tobacco crop.

➤ Pesticides are applied liberally to young plants to ward off pests and fungus, but they dissipate by the time the leaves are picked.

➤ Tending to growing tobacco plants is a 24-hour-a-day labor of love during the entire three-month growing season.

➤ The best-tasting and largest leaves come from the middle of the tobacco plant.

.Snııııf..

Fermentation: Sweating the Small Stuff

The name of this chapter refers to one of the important stages, *fermenting* or *sweating*, required to turn tobacco into something you can smoke and enjoy. Many steps are critical in making a good cigar, but if I had to pick the single most important one, I'd choose the long and laborious process that takes a tobacco leaf from a green, living plant to an aged product ready to smoke. This important stage hasn't been thoroughly explained in any cigar book I've read, but I believe that it's important and interesting information. I'm going to do my best to help you understand how this magic happens.

During the process that involves air curing, fermenting, and aging, the tobacco leaf makes a physical transformation as its structure and chemical makeup changes. You might ask, "If this stage is so important, why did you wait until *now* to tell me about it?" I have my reasons!

Now that we've talked about how cigars are made, how to judge a good one, and how they're "grown," I think you'll better be able to appreciate this remarkable process. You'll know what I'm referring to when I talk about wrapper, binder, and filler leaves and all those other tobacco terms; it's important to have those basic terms down because we're going to cover some new and wild terminology in this chapter.

Finally, because you've been smoking and enjoying cigars, you won't get discouraged when I tell you about the foul-smelling heaps of tobacco that fill the fermenting barns; you'll know that everything works out okay in the end!

Airing It Out

Lush, green tobacco leaves—all carefully hand-picked at their peak ripeness—are carried to large barns dotted throughout the tobacco plantation. These barns, or *casas de tabaco* in Spanish, don't look like the barns of the American countryside. They are large, glorified, open-air sheds with roofs made from dried palm leaves. In fact, they are designed to let in as much air as possible while keeping the rain out.

These ratty-looking structures dot the landscape in tobacco-growing country, and they look haphazardly scattered around the fields. In fact, they are very carefully situated to always face west so that they catch the breezes (which almost always travel east to west) and so that only the morning and afternoon sun shines into them. Growers don't want direct sunlight on the tobacco, which they'd get with a south-facing barn.

> **Cigar Speak**
> **Curing** the newly harvested tobacco leaves is the first stage in creating cigar leaf. The time-honored method is to hang bundled green leaves in open-air curing barns, where the warm tropical breezes dry the leaves over several months. In the curing process, the flavors concentrate as moisture evaporates.

In a job mostly handled by women, the leaves are gathered into bunches by their long, thick stems. The women tie the stems of each bunch, braiding rope-like strips made from palm leaves. The women then hang the bunches of tobacco from floor to ceiling on long wooden poles in each barn.

The Cubans even have a preferred wood for making these poles—the mangrove tree—and the poles, called *cujes*, are cut by *cujeros*. Can you believe the wood is even soaked in salt water for two months to remove all flavor of the wood? Then, all the knots are removed—because they might ooze sappy resin or damage the fragile leaves. As you can see, tobacco keeps a lot of people busy!

In the Caribbean, the late winter weather is warm, dry, and breezy—perfect for beginning what's called the *curing process.* Bundled green leaves are hung in open-air curing barns, where the warm tropical breezes dry the leaves during the course of several months. The flavors in the leaves concentrate as moisture evaporates.

Cigar leaf benefits from *air curing,* which promotes the natural evaporation of moisture. As you might remember from our discussion of wrappers (in Chapter 5), a once-popular type of wrapper was the *candela*, or green, wrapper. The green color indicated a high level of chlorophyll, and the color was achieved by curing tobacco leaves in heated barns to accelerate the drying process.

Heat curing stops the loss of chlorophyll, but the speed of drying also prevents flavors in the leaf from concentrating, which gives the leaf a bland taste. The curing process—which requires from 45 to 60 days, depending on the weather and the winds—can't be rushed.

Many other kinds of tobacco, especially cigarette tobacco and some pipe tobaccos, are *flue cured*—another term for heat curing. Certain types of tobacco leaves benefit from this accelerated process, but cigar tobacco doesn't!

As the bunches of cigar tobacco leaves hang in the sheds, they gradually lose almost all their green color. The chlorophyll disappears along with the moisture, and the leaves turn from deep green to light green to varying shades of yellow and gold; they then finally turn to tan.

The expert tobacco growers and factory representatives monitor the leaves every day to determine exactly when they've gotten the full benefit from air curing. Timing is everything: If left too long in the barns, the leaves will wither too much and begin to give up their concentrated oils and flavors to the tropical winds, which would ruin the tobacco.

Growers watch for the first rains of spring in early March, which help raise the humidity and moisturize the dry leaves, making them less brittle and easier to handle. Then it's time to take the tobacco off the poles and move on! Heck, they even take care to remove the tobacco from the poles in the morning, when humidity is highest and the leaves are less likely to shatter.

Can a Leaf Make the Grade?

Now that the tobacco has gained as much as possible from air curing, the process of sorting, re-sorting, grading, and sorting again begins. The bunches of leaves need to be transported from the fields to warehouses near the fields. These warehouses are huge, long, and virtually empty buildings. They're completely enclosed but well ventilated. In a minute, you'll understand why they're made this way.

At this point, the manufacturer is likely to show up and, with the grower, take a sample leaf, and use a lit cigar to burn a hole in the middle of the leaf. They then smell the smoke coming from the burning leaf, using their experienced noses to judge its quality. This step is their first chance to sense how good the crop is likely to turn out.

In or near these warehouses, the first sorting of the leaves takes place. The bunches of leaves, stems still intact, are untied and carefully spread out on tables. Many of the sorters are women, who have developed great skill in knowing exactly what to look for.

Skilled sorters organize air-cured cigar leaf into a variety of groups and grades.

These sorters laugh and talk, but their eyes are so skilled that grading and sorting is almost automatic. Their fingers work quickly, and their eyes dart from leaf to leaf, sorting them into orderly piles.

At this point, the sorters group the leaves by how they look. Even though the leaves are slightly withered and wrinkled, they've stayed pretty supple in the moist tropical climate and they're easy to handle—not at all like the dry tree leaves that you find on the ground in mid-winter. The leaves are sorted and graded using several factors.

Sorting Leaves by Size

The leaves are grouped from large to small, and also by width. Even at this early stage, the largest, widest leaves are the most prized because they have the potential to be used in large, long cigars. By looking at the size, the skilled sorter also knows what part of the plant they came from: whether they're small, mild leaves from the top of the plant, tougher leaves from the bottom, or the "prime cut" leaves from the center.

Sorting Leaves by Texture

You can feel a leaf at this stage and determine whether it's a smooth, silky leaf or a rough, heavily veined leaf. Of course, if you're growing binder leaves or leaves for tough maduro wrappers, you expect the tobacco leaves to be a little tougher. If you're growing a wrapper leaf crop, those leaves had better feel smooth!

Sorting Leaves by Appearance

The color of each leaf should be even, although individual leaves may vary from light tan to medium brown. The leaves shouldn't have any green splotches. Bunches of tobacco hanging in the shed are checked for overall maturity, but you can't tell about every leaf until you unwrap the bunches. Uneven color and green splotches means that the leaf didn't cure properly or had a flaw, and the ultimate taste of the leaf will be inconsistent. You toss it out. You also look for ragged edges or torn leaves, which aren't worth processing any further. You toss them out.

Bring on the Heat

This next stage of processing tobacco is one of the most fascinating ever devised to alter a natural vegetable product!

When you make wine or beer, you add yeast to grape juice or water with malt (a type of sugar) and hops. The yeast, an amazing little organism, eats the sugar and converts it to carbon dioxide and alcohol.

While the yeast is consuming the sugar, the liquid looks like it's boiling as it foams with carbon dioxide; you can see that something important is happening.

What yeast does for beer and wine, heat does for tobacco. Adding yeast to grape juice or "beer juice" (called the *wort)* transforms these liquids into something very different. This process is called *fermentation,* which is the same term used for heating up tobacco.

Cigar Speak
The process of placing air-cured tobacco leaves in large piles to heat up is called **fermenting**, **bulking**, or **sweating** the tobacco. If you garden or mow and leave piles of weeds or grass, you might notice they heat up inside very quickly. Called **composting**, the chemical composition of the plant changes and the plant begins to break down, producing heat. Tobacco fermentation is basically composting.

Air-cured tobacco leaves are placed on the floor of the fermenting sheds and built into piles called sweats.

The sorted leaves are taken into the fermentation warehouse and are meticulously stacked into neat piles, or *bulks*, sometimes called *sweats*. Another term used is *bulking the tobacco.* Yet another in a long line of skilled experts, the *zafador* handles this task.

The zafador oversees a growing bulk of tobacco.

Here's where things get ugly. The tobacco leaves are carefully stacked in the warehouse in piles from three to six feet high. The invention of polyvinyl chloride tubing (the same plastic tubing used for plumbing) enables tobacco makers to insert lengths of tubes every couple of feet as they pile up the tobacco, which enables them to insert thermometers into the sweats. To accelerate the heating process, the bulks are often covered with burlap or mats woven from palm fronds.

Sweats of tobacco, covered by burlap or palm frond pats, fill the floor of a fermenting warehouse.

The bulked tobacco begins a chemical process. Call it whatever you like: fermenting or composting or—the most accurate description—rotting! The piled leaves begin to heat up. The rising temperature begins to turn the starch in the leaves to sugar. The heat breaks down the leaves' structure. Oils and fats in the leaf concentrate.

These piles of tobacco are called *sweats*, by the way, because the tobacco actually seems to sweat! Oils come out of the leaves, and then are re-absorbed back into the leaves, intensifying the flavor.

Okay, bottom line, these fermenting warehouses really stink! Many plants contain a great deal of ammonium nitrate, and tobacco is one of them. You've probably smelled ammonia, and that's the smell of tobacco fermenting in a warehouse. Now you can understand why these warehouses are well ventilated!

But hold on; this stench of ammonia is a good thing. If it doesn't come out during fermenting, it will when you smoke the cigar. One of the most important transformations that happens during fermentation is the heat forcing ammonia out of the leaf. Good riddance.

You don't just walk away and leave this composting mess to take care of itself. If left to compost, the tobacco would eventually turn into wonderful fertilizer, but it sure wouldn't make a good cigar. Experts check out these bulks regularly, and when the temperature inside the bulk reaches somewhere between 115 to 140° Fahrenheit, the pile is rotated. The skill of the manufacturer dictates how hot specific bulks need to be; they determine prime temperature based on the kind of tobacco inside the bulks.

The outer leaves are piled up on the inside of a new bulk, and the steamy leaves inside are placed outside. This process ensures that all the leaves get an even fermentation. A pile might be rotated several times before the manufacturer decides the tobacco has been perfectly fermented.

Blowing Smoke
A major reason that a cheap cigar stinks is because the tobacco in it hasn't been properly fermented. If the tobacco isn't properly sweated, it won't give up all the ammonium nitrate that naturally occurs in the leaf. When you smoke a cigar like this, you're actually burning ammonia, which is a very unpleasant smell for anyone near you.

Hot Tip
Insufficiently fermented tobacco is the main reason you'll feel nauseous when smoking a cigar. Even full-bodied tobacco won't make you feel sick, although you may not like the style. If the cigar is harsh or you feel nauseous, don't buy that brand again. If it's incorrectly fermented once, it'll probably be so again.

A newly uncovered bulk of steaming tobacco is ready to be reorganized so the outer leaves get transferred to the center.

> **Hot Tip**
> All types of cigar leaf—wrapper, filler, and binder—are put through some kind of fermentation process. The exact process depends on the type of leaf, and understanding the different techniques is one of the great skills of a great tobacco manufacturer.

Each time a new sweat is created, the internal temperature is lower and lower, which tells the experts that the tobacco is nearing the end of fermentation. During the process, the tan leaves turn a rich brown color. Any uneven coloring or slightly green spots disappear.

A careful cigar maker may create up to 10 sweats, until the tobacco is completely fermented. This process takes weeks. When the tobacco is finished fermenting, it can be turned into cigars. Most quality-minded makers, however, give the cigar leaf even more aging. First, however, the leaf has to be *stripped*, removing the thick stem that attached the tobacco leaf to the stalk.

A Tobacco-Leaf Striptease

> **Cigar Speak**
> **Stripping** tobacco means removing the thick stem attaching the tobacco leaf to the stalk. Until this happens, the stem provides sap and nutrients to the leaf. In essence, the leaf is alive and changing. After the stem is stripped, the leaf truly dies, and the transformation process essentially stops.

Fermented leaves, which are very soft and pliable after their sweaty adventure, are taken to the factory to be stripped. A worker places each leaf on a machine that draws in the leaf and cuts out the thick stem. The machine leaves the whole leaf intact, but the stem, which is like a tail, is gone.

Tobacco experts say this process is the *coup de gras* for the tobacco leaf. While attached to the stem, nutrients and sap moved throughout the leaf, propelled by the stem. Once the stem is gone, the leaf loses its "heart." After the dramatic changes brought about by fermentation, future changes to the leaf will be subtle.

The manufacturer then returns this weary leaf to yet another bulking process, this time very slow and subtle.

Temperatures in the bulk probably won't exceed 85 degrees as the final starches in the leaf turn to sugar and the last of the ammonium nitrate disappears.

The maker carefully rotates the sweats and packs them just high enough to exert enough pressure to flatten the leaves. This pressure continues to force out moisture, which then sinks back into the leaves to concentrate the flavor.

When the relatively dramatic and violent process of fermentation is over, the maker checks progress by sniffing the leaves and by burning a few of them. Like a wine maker who can discern a potentially great wine long before it's finished, the cigar maker can judge how the leaf is faring. He might even roll some of the leaves into a makeshift cigar and try them.

At this point, he has to decide whether this crop has the potential to be good, excellent, or great. His judgment will determine how many years the tobacco is allowed to rest—and that can be a very long time.

Cigar Speak
After tobacco leaves have finished fermenting, they need to be packed up in a **bale**, called a **tercio** in Spanish. These sturdy bales, made from the tough sheath of the palm tree and encased in burlap, provide a home for the leaves while they age, and also serve to transport them safely.

Baling Out: Putting Tobacco to Rest

After the central stem is stripped, the tobacco is once again sorted, classified, and baled.

In Cuba, and nowhere else in the world, the stripped and fully fermented leaves get placed in cedar wood barrels to rest and pick up a bit of cedar flavor. Frequently, the tobacco ages in these barrels for a couple of months and then is taken to the factory to be turned into cigars. In most of the cigar-making world, however, the fermented tobacco will end up in bales: rectangular packages made from the sheath of the palm tree.

Not only do the bales protect the delicate leaves while they're allowed to age, they also provide an excellent vehicle for transporting the leaf. With blended cigars, makers import cigar leaf from all over the world, and the bales protect the leaf.

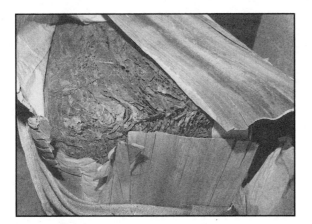

A bale of tobacco covered by burlap.

173

Bales of tobacco (*tercios* in Spanish), as they're traditionally made in the Caribbean, are an art form in themselves! The tobacco can be baled only in burlap, but the classic method is to first wrap these bales in the woody sheath to protect new leaves that sprout from the royal palm tree.

Royal palms are tall, majestic trees that grow everywhere in the Caribbean. Each palm produces only ten or so new leaves each year, and so each tree has only 10 of these woody sheaths to harvest.

The royal palm of the Caribbean. To the left of the trunk hangs a woody front sheath, or yagua.

This woody base, called a *yagua* in Spanish, is not the green, lush leaf you see swaying in the tropical breezes. It's the "anchor" out of which the long-stemmed leaves grow, and it feels like a cross between bark and leaf. It's very tough and fibrous, can be moistened and molded to create part of a square bale, and provides a surprisingly good case to protect the delicate tobacco leaves.

Cigar Esoterica

Manufacturers like to bale tobacco in palm leaves because the leaf acts as a humidity control. When weather is moist, the bark absorbs moisture, protecting against mold. When conditions are dry, the bark gives some of its retained moisture to the tobacco. The palm sheath serves the same purpose as the cedar lining in a humidor: It helps regulate the climate around the cigar leaves.

The yaguas are stripped from the trees, flattened out like large sheets, and allowed to dry. It takes many sheets of yagua to create one of these large bales. Even though the royal palm is plentiful, collecting the leaves is time consuming. Some manufacturers don't bother with this classic Cuban method of packing tobacco; burlap alone is used in tobacco-growing countries that don't have palm trees.

When the neatly packed tobacco has been wrapped in *yagua* and burlap, each bale is tightly tied with rope. The old-style rope is made from the fibrous interior of the *majuga* or corkwood tree, but most modern manufacturers use plain old hemp rope. Cuban makers omit the burlap if the tobacco is destined for a Havana cigar factory: It doesn't have to travel far.

The Long Sleep

The *tercios* are transferred to storage warehouses, where the tobacco inside begins its long sleep. Most cigar leaf is given the chance to rest for at least a few months. During this time, the leaves have the chance to "settle" after enduring their long, hot voyage in the bulks. In these huge sheds, you'll see hundreds of bales stacked up. The bales get stamped with the harvest date, the species of tobacco (such as Olor or Piloto Cubano), country of origin, and information on how the tobacco will be used: wrapper, filler, or binder.

If the maker has decided the leaf in particular tercios is superior, he might let them age for up to seven years. After it's fermented and stripped, the leaf won't change much chemically. It will, however, age and mellow with time. Tercios containing the same tobaccos are grouped together in the warehouse and left to sleep.

With the huge demand for cigars, manufacturers feel a lot of pressure to get as much finished leaf as possible into production. Top-quality cigar makers, with large amounts of stored, aging leaf, continue to set aside leaf for several years to fully age the tobacco.

After leaves finish fermenting, they're about 90 percent of the way to being fully matured and ready to become cigars. Taking the time to achieve that extra 10 percent separates the great cigar makers from the good ones. This difference is similar to the difference between 8-year-old single-malt scotch and 16-year-old single-malt scotch. The 8-year-old scotch is very good, but the older bottle is smoother, richer, and more flavorful.

Blowing Smoke
Cuban cigar makers seldom age the finished, fermented tobacco for more than a few months—at most, up to a year. Consequently, some Cuban cigars that smoke harsh when you buy them may improve greatly if you age them for a year or two. They need time to mellow.

Allowing tobacco to age is costly. It requires a lot of storage space, the tobacco (which is very smokeable at this point) can't be placed into production and then sold, and the storehouses are in constant risk of fire. Over the years, several of my cigar-making friends have lost entire warehouses to fire—thousands of pounds of aged leaf literally going up in smoke. It's a blow to manufacturing and represents a tremendous financial loss, as well. Tobacco warehouse fires are the best-smelling infernos, but the loss is a tragedy to anyone who knows how many great cigars could have been made from those leaves.

During their long sleep, the cigar leaves aren't disturbed or even checked. Once the maker, who keeps very accurate records, thinks it's about time to turn these leaves into cigars, he'll open one of the tercios. He'll light a leaf or two, and, once again, his nose will tell him whether the tobacco has reached its peak of maturity. If so, the tercios are removed and taken to the factory to begin their life as cigars.

Members of the Fuente cigar-making family light tobacco leaves to see whether they are ready.

If you have any question of how much commitment it takes to be a tobacco manufacturer, just remember that throughout this long process, the maker doesn't see a penny of income. In fact, he bears all the costs of buying seed, fertilizer, and pesticides; paying farmers to grow the leaf and workers to process it; and many other costs. Then the leaf sits in warehouses, quietly aging—susceptible to mold, pests, and fire. Only when the leaf is sold to another maker, or the cigars are made and sold, does the manufacturer realize a profit for all this hard work and capital outlay.

The Least You Need to Know

➤ Drying just-picked tobacco leaves in open-air sheds is an important step in getting cigar leaf ready to use.

➤ Avoid cigars with green wrappers; they've been cured by using heat instead of by drying naturally.

➤ Tobacco leaves have to be fermented using heat before they can be turned into cigars, and you'll know the tobacco wasn't fully fermented if it tastes harsh or makes you nauseous.

➤ Leading manufacturers take the time to age their finest cigar leaf for several years—just as fine scotch or brandy is aged.

Tobacco Doesn't Like to Relocate: Making a Home for Your Cigars

In This Chapter

➤ How free trade revolutionized cigar making

➤ The advantages of blending tobaccos

➤ What happens to cigars when they leave the tropics

➤ Caring for your personal supply of cigars

You've seen how cigars are made, grown, and blended. Now, it's easier to imagine how those tobaccos make their way around the Caribbean—and around the world. For cigar leaf, whether in bulk form or as a finished cigar, a tropical location is everything.

In this chapter I talk briefly about how cigar leaf travels, and how leaves grown in one country end up in a cigar made in another country. (This cross-cultural cigar making is a fairly recent phenomena.) Finally, I touch on the important subject of what's required of you when you buy this delicate product that doesn't like to leave the balmy weather.

Gettin' Around the Tropics

As you learned earlier, blended cigars, often using tobaccos from many countries, have become a staple outside of Cuba. Many cigar factories in Caribbean nations are located within highly regulated *free zones* that have been set up by the governments to monitor the flow of goods and raw materials in and out of the country. In the Dominican Republic, for instance, most businesses using foreign raw materials—from garment manufacturers to cigar makers—have factories located in free zones.

Cigar Speak

A **free zone** is specifically set aside to receive shipments of foreign products—the only place where free movement of non-domestic materials is allowed. All shipments in and out of these zones, which encompass thousands of acres, are checked and monitored by guards. Because of free zones, Caribbean-based cigar makers can legally import tobaccos and other materials for use in creating their smokes.

Tobacco Leaves

"Although the demand for cigars… has spread throughout the world, the islands of Cuba and Jamaica, where the crudely rolled leaves were first seen by Europeans, have remained the home of the best cigars to this day. This is largely due to the fact that the cigars are made in the same conditions of humidity in which the leaf is grown."

—Alfred H. Dunhill, from the Dunhill of London family, in his classic *The Gentle Art of Smoking*

Decades ago, most Caribbean nations imposed stiff rules against importing raw materials. Only products created in a specific country could be used in products manufactured in that country. What kind of problems did this cause for cigar makers? Let's look at Honduras.

Until the 1980s, cigars made in Honduras could use only Honduran-grown tobacco. While Honduras grows fine cigar leaf, it's not known for great wrappers or mild tobaccos. So if you ran a factory in Honduras and wanted to make anything other than a very spicy, full-bodied cigar with a tough maduro wrapper, you were out of luck.

The advent of free zones enabled Honduran makers to import leaf from other nations, and suddenly some of the best cigars in the world were coming from Honduras! True, most still had the characteristic robust quality of Honduran smokes, but they were balanced with some milder tobaccos and wrapped in a nice Ecuadorian or Connecticut shade-grown leaf.

Arguably, free zones have been an economic boon for several Caribbean nations, notably the Dominican Republic.

Some cigar makers in the Caribbean even take advantage of free-zone status to import raw materials such as cedar for making cigar boxes. All in all, free zones have enabled tobacco to travel freely from nation to nation, and have provided a major boost for cigar manufacturing outside of Cuba. In fact, without this development, you probably wouldn't be able to enjoy most of the great cigars available today.

Blending in and Around the Caribbean

Most of the world's cigar leaf used for blended cigars moves in a relatively restricted area bordered by Mexico on the west, Honduras and Nicaragua on the south, the Dominican Republic on the east, and Miami on the north.

Other tobaccos travel into this "golden quadrangle" of cigar-making from places such as Connecticut, Ecuador, Cameroon and Central Africa, and Indonesia.

Even when the voyage is a long one, such as from Asia to the Caribbean, it takes place in tropical latitudes. For the most part, then, manufacturers don't need to worry about the tobacco leaves contained in *tercios* (bales). Temperatures and, most importantly, humidity levels are just about the same in these equatorial climates.

Location Is Everything

In real estate, they say that location is everything. Like a lovely home next to a noisy highway, a perfect premium cigar in a dry environment isn't worth much.

In order for you to enjoy it, that stogie must leave its tropical home and head to a place that's probably less hospitable for cigar leaf. As you'll remember from Chapter 11, cigars are rushed from the tropics to humidified warehouses around the world. They're then shipped out to smoke shops, liquor retailers, cigar clubs, and restaurants. So far, so good.

You'll also recall (from Chapter 2) how important it is for the cigar seller to maintain proper humidity for the cigars, and you know what happens if the cigar seller doesn't: tinder-dry, crumbly cigars that burn hot and fast. A reputable retailer who's interested in having long-term success will have invested in proper equipment and storage. But do you have any hope of replicating the tropics in your own home?

Until now, I've talked mostly about buying individual cigars and smoking them relatively quickly. But there will probably come a time (if it hasn't happened already), that you'll find a special cigar that you really enjoy. You may find some price breaks on full boxes, or you just want to lock up a tasty supply for future enjoyment.

After you start buying more cigars than you can smoke in a week or so, you become a "cigar steward." You are now personally responsible for taking care of your premium smokes and ensuring that when you get around to smoking them, they're as fresh and moist as the day you bought them.

> **Hot Tip**
> Remember to use your best detective skills when checking out whether a retailer has done a good job of maintaining that tropical climate for the smokes. Before you spend $100 or more on a box of premium smokes, you should see the conditions under which the retailer stores stogies. (See Chapter 2 for more details.)

> **Cigar Speak**
> As mentioned in Chapter 1, a **humidor** is an enclosed device that keeps cigars in a tropical climate. A humidor can be a huge walk-in room, a box made of wood or Plexiglas that sits on your table, or something as simple as a sealed plastic bag—anything that maintains the relatively high level of airborne moisture, or humidity, cigars require to keep from drying out.

If you buy more than a few cigars at a time (and in Chapter 17 I explain the reasons why stocking up is a good idea), you'll need something in which to keep your cigars—something that provides an enclosed tropical "micro-climate." Keeping cigars in good condition at home is even more important and difficult than keeping fine wines. You will need a *humidor*.

You can spend a fortune on fancy devices in which to store your cigars. You can also do a pretty decent job of storing them with relatively little expense. Before we get into all the different ways of storing your cigars, let's take a look at what happens to cigars under different conditions.

Making a Home for Your Cigars

Without question, the most important thing for cigars is proper humidity: the amount of moisture in the air surrounding them. A distant second is proper temperature. Cigars are tropical creatures; they were made in the tropics, and they don't like leaving home. You need to "fool" them into thinking they're still in a tropical climate or they will not be pleased. What happens to a cigar in different temperatures and humidity levels?

Too Dry

If the humidity around your cigars drops below 60 percent, moisture and the volatile oils that pack a lot of the flavor begin to evaporate from the cigar. The lower the relative humidity, the faster this process occurs. The stogie gets dry, brittle, and hard. If you smoke it in this condition, the wrapper will probably unravel and the dry tobacco will burn hot and fast.

Almost any state in which you need heat during the winter is much too dry for cigars. Heat dries the air, which is already dry because the cold weather has robbed the air of ambient moisture.

Cold isn't the only enemy of your stogies. A desert climate is also too dry for unhumidified cigars. Even if you live in Florida or the Caribbean, don't get too smug. Air conditioning removes moisture from the air, so if it's 75-percent humidity outside, the climate inside might be too dry for cigars. You need to humidify them. Remember, a humidity level that's comfortable for you is not comfortable for your cigars.

Too Moist

On the other hand, if the humidity exceeds 80 percent, mold can start to develop. In the early stages, you can wipe off the mold. If it lingers unattended, however, it'll take over your cigars, and moldy cigars taste like a musty basement smells. The excess moisture will also be absorbed at a faster rate by the springy filler tobacco than by the binder or wrapper, so the filler will swell and split your cigar wide open.

Too Hot

If your cigars are exposed to a heat source such as a radiator or heating duct, it'll be tough to keep them humidified because the moisture will evaporate very quickly. If you live in a hot, dry climate, the cigars will tend to dry out unless they live in a regulated environment.

Cigars cannot stand long periods of intense heat, so don't lock them inside an automobile on a hot summer day.

Cigars also hate sunlight, so never put them near windows or in a car. At best, they'll discolor and very quickly give up the essential oils that contain most of their flavor. At worst, they'll dry out and split open. Unlike your friends and co-workers, your cigars will thank you for being kept in the dark.

Too Cold

You probably couldn't stand indoor temperatures lower than 60 degrees Fahrenheit for very long, but as long as your cigars are humidified, they can tolerate this temperature. Even if you leave your home for extended periods and turn the heat down to 50 or 55 degrees Fahrenheit, the cigars should be fine if humidified.

On the flip side, however, cigars can get too cold. A myth prevails among smokers that refrigeration or freezing preserves cigars. In fact, this treatment ruins them because freezers and refrigerators, like air conditioners, remove moisture. Never, *ever* chill your cigars. For the same reason, don't leave them in a car during winter.

Just Right: The 70/70 Rule

An indoor climate that's pretty comfortable for you—say 75 degrees Fahrenheit with 40 percent relative humidity—is not good for your cigars. If you're going to keep cigars around the house, they need a "home" with its own special climate.

I mentioned the 70/70 Rule in Chapter 2 as it relates to judging how well cigar dealers preserve their stock. Now, box of cigars in hand, you're the one responsible for enforcing proper humidity.

The basic rule is to keep your cigars in an environment with 70 percent humidity, at a constant 70 degrees Fahrenheit. This mimics the tropical climate in which your cigars were made. Maintaining these conditions isn't always easy, especially if you live in a dry desert climate or in cold northern areas where indoor relative humidity can plunge to five percent.

> **Cigar Speak**
> A **hygrometer** is used to read and measure humidity levels. There are a few digital versions, but most look like a meat thermometer, with a needle and markings from 0 to 100 percent humidity. They're helpful, but you can also tell whether your cigars are properly humidified just by feeling them (remember the pinch test from Chapter 2); based on how they feel, you can then add or remove moisture from the humidor.

Some exacting connoisseurs feel that at 70 percent humidity, cigars will eventually dry out. They claim that 73 percent is ideal, because the tropics are closer to 76 percent relative humidity. Because you virtually can't measure these subtle differences without a serious and expensive *hygrometer* (a device used to read and measure humidity levels), the best advice is to check for proper humidity by giving your stored cigars the "pinch test" at least every two weeks.

Of course, the horrible pictures I've painted of what will happen to your cigars if they're not given the proper climate are leading to one thing: You gotta get a humidor for your cigars! You have thousands of choices for humidifying your cigars, and in Chapter 17, we're going to explore some of the basic options.

The Least You Need to Know

➤ Open trade in the Caribbean has revolutionized cigar making.

➤ Because many cigars are now made from tobaccos from different countries, country of manufacture doesn't mean what it used to mean.

➤ Cigars are tropical creatures, and they need humidity.

➤ It's your job to keep stored cigars in a humidor, at a constant 70 degrees Fahrenheit and 70 percent humidity.

Part 4
"Turbo Smoke": Adding to Your Enjoyment

As you continue your cigar adventure, you may find that your enjoyment of good smokes is expanding beyond just an occasional stogie at a cigar bar or on the golf course. If so, this is a great time to "turbo-charge" your smoking experience.

An excellent way to fuel your growing passion for cigars is to begin buying modest quantities of your favorite smokes and storing them. In this part, we'll talk about buying boxes of cigars, the important basics of how to store them, and even how to age them. We'll talk about boosting your enjoyment of cigars with small cigars, which you can enjoy in places where you may not be able to smoke a larger stogie. We'll also talk about cigar and smoking collectibles—a great way to complement your enjoyment of fine smokes.

Finally, we'll really fire up the engines by giving you all the tools you need to analyze and rate your smokes. You'll get an inside look at the elements that go into describing and scoring a cigar, and you'll be able to compare your ratings with the experts using your own cigar "encounter log."

Stashing Your Stogies: Keeping Them Fresh

In This Chapter

➤ The advantages of buying a box of cigars

➤ Options for storing and humidifying cigars

➤ Aging cigars as you would wine

➤ Traveling with cigars

A lot of the fun of cigars is finding a smoke you like and nabbing a box or two. You never know when you'll find that brand, or even one cigar from a particular batch, that tastes so wonderful, so you just have to stock up. And when you bring that box home, you have to take special care to preserve that freshness and flavor that caught your attention.

You now understand the long, tropical journey your cigar has traveled. You also, then, completely understand why your stored stogie needs a safe resting place. Remember that a lot of people went to a lot of trouble to create a moist, fresh cigar for you. Take the time to give it the proper treatment. Let's take a look at how simple and easy it can be to store your cigars.

Top Reasons for Stashing Stogies

You can sometimes get a small discount—usually no more than 10 percent—if you buy a box of cigars; volume purchasing isn't a top reason for buying a box. Although saving a little money is a valid consideration in buying a box of cigars, there are better reasons:

➤ Because premium cigars are handmade and involve varying crops of leaf, even the best cigar differs slightly from batch to batch. If you find a cigar you like and the retailer has a full (or almost full) box, odds are that each one in the box will taste more or less the same. You can assure that you'll have at least 25 of these prizes by locking up a box now, rather than waiting for the next batch to arrive.

➤ The overall market for bulk filler, binder, and wrapper leaf is very unpredictable and demand far outstrips supply—and the situation probably won't improve in the next several years. Many smaller and newer brands don't have a guarantee of year-in, year-out access to great leaf, as do the major players. A brand you like today may taste very different—probably worse—in six months if the maker can't obtain the same quality leaf in the next order. Buying a box or two now assures you that you can keep smoking your favorite stogies without experiencing a decline in quality.

➤ You have the chance to hedge against price increases, which are now occurring regularly.

➤ Stocking up gives you the chance to age cigars as you would fine wine, and while most cigars won't change as dramatically as wine, some do benefit from several months to several years of aging and mellowing.

> **Cigar Speak**
> **Aging** under humidified conditions improves some cigars, but a properly made cigar should be delicious the day you buy it. Very little change occurs once a cigar is made, and aging won't make a bad cigar tasty. Certain cigars undergo a slight change with aging, and you can experiment to determine which cigars benefit from a little time in the humidor.

Everyone has a different idea of what "stocking up" means. To some, it might be keeping 25 cigars around so you always have one when you want one. For others, a stockpile of cigars might run into the hundreds or thousands. As long as you have the patience to care for your cigars, and the equipment and conditions you need to keep them humidified, you can store as many as you like.

Keep in mind that *storing* or *aging* cigars still involves keeping them humidified. In other words, you cannot store cigars in a brown paper bag in a dust-dry attic and then trot downstairs with a handful, put them in your humidor, and expect a premium smoke.

From the day you buy your smokes at the store to the day you light up, humidifying a cigar is a "lifetime" commitment—at least for the life of the cigar! Now, let's talk humidors.

Humidors: From Palaces to Plastic Bags

When they hear the word *humidor*, many people think of a lovely wooden container designed to hold cigars. When I think of a humidor, I think of a device that holds in moisture and creates a self-contained environment for cigars. No matter how lovely a humidor is, if it can't maintain a tropical climate, it's just a box. The job of a humidor is to maintain a constant balance of moisture around the cigars—with assistance from you, the chief rainmaker.

You have to make some level of commitment to caring for your cigars. Unless you have an expensive self-regulating walk-in humidor or cigar vault, you'll need to monitor your stored smokes regularly for proper humidity. You'll have to add water to whatever humidifying element you use: sometimes every few days in the middle of winter when the heat's on, or in dry desert climates.

Before we start discussing humidors, let's go over a few cardinal rules to remember when deciding where to store your cigars or locate a humidor:

> **Blowing Smoke**
> Whatever type of humidor you use, you should separate different brands of cigars. They can be in the same container, but they should not touch. Remember from Chapter 11 how readily cigars like to "marry"? Two different stogies placed together will share flavors, which will destroy their distinctive characteristics.

➤ Cigars should never be kept anywhere that's prone to growing mold or fungus. Primarily that means no damp basements! No matter what you use to store your cigars, those mold and fungus spores will conduct a search-and-destroy mission for the tobacco because it is a natural vegetable product. (If your basement is cool and dry, then it's a fine place to store cigars.)

➤ Never store cigars in any room that has dramatic swings in temperature. No matter how well you try to humidify cigars, they won't survive the combination of the blasting heat of summer and the chill of winter.

➤ It's best to store your cigars inside the house, even if you don't smoke them inside. Avoid storing cigars in garages or outbuildings; not only is the climate variation too dramatic (unless you live in the tropics), but cigars kept outside the house invite bugs and mold. If you have an attached, heated garage, you can probably store your cigars there with no harm.

Remembering from Chapter 16 that the goal is to keep your cigars at 70/70, let's take a walk through some of the available homes. These sections start at the bottom of the price ladder and work up. Don't be discouraged; with humidors, the most expensive solution isn't the only solution!

Cigar Shop and Cigar Club Lockers

If you don't want to fuss with storing cigars yourself, and you live in or near a large city, try locating one of the growing number of cigar clubs and retailers offering humidified lockers. For an annual fee, you rent a locker and you can come pick up any cigars you need during store hours.

Hot Tip
Annual dues for lockers at cigar clubs or smoke shops can run up to a few hundred dollars, depending on the demand for the lockers. In addition, you'll still need to invest in a humidor for home to hold your short-term smokes.

Although cigar lockers are relatively maintenance free, they do have a few drawbacks. Your access is restricted by store hours, and if that Ashton Churchill you crave at 8 p.m. is in that locker, you're stuck. Second, most retailers who offer these lockers start to act a little funny if you trot into their stores with loads of cigars you bought somewhere else. Most prefer you buy your cigars at the store. (If you buy most of your smokes at that store anyway, this second consideration isn't a drawback.)

Finally, I don't know whether I completely trust retailers to maintain cigars properly. A few years ago, for example, several boxes of pre-Castro Dunhill Havanas were sold at auction for astronomical prices.

People were not allowed to view the cigars—only the boxes—but were assured of quality because the stogies had been stored in a prestigious retailer's locker since the day they were purchased in 1958. I happened to hear from friends who later saw the opened boxes. The cigars were dust-dry and unsmokable. Personally, I'd rather trust myself to keep my cigars moist.

Zip-Seal Bags

You'd think that plastic zip-seal bags would be stretching the definition of a humidor. Would you believe that this is one of my favorite ways to store my smokes? I regularly dip into my zip-seal stock and pull out smokes that have been stored six to ten years, and they're still fresh and perfect.

Blowing Smoke
If you use a bag as a humidor, test it for air-tightness before you put in your cigars. Zip it up, place it on a table and press on it. It'll have a certain amount of air inside, and this air shouldn't go anywhere. Sometimes the bags are torn during the manufacturing process. If the air hisses out of the bag and you've checked the seal to make sure it's completely zipped, toss the bag or use it for Monday's leftover meatloaf—not your cigars!

You have to work a bit to maintain humidity in plastic bags. Although the bag manufacturers claim that their products are air-tight, my "humidifying elements," which are pieces of florist foam (yes, the stuff used in flower arranging) dry out in time, so the bags can't be perfectly sealed.

If you have several bags set aside and don't open them regularly, you should open them for an hour at least once a month. This allows some air to circulate around your cigars, and is a perfect excuse for you to check them for proper humidification. If you only keep a few cigars at a time, you'll probably be opening and closing the bag regularly as you retrieve your smokes, so plenty of air will get in without this special airing.

Later in this chapter, I'll explain how to keep your cigars moist. For right now, trust me when I tell you plastic bags work just fine—and they're inexpensive to boot. Buy the best zip-closure bags you can find, and stick with the freezer bags, which use heavier plastic that's more resistant to tearing or puncturing. Look for the quart-sized bags, which hold 25 cigars and still leave room for your humidification element.

I guess I should include those heat-sealing food storage bag contraptions in this category. I've never used them because I'm leery of using something I can't open to check my cigars and adjust the humidity. Likewise, I have no experience with the do-it-yourself vacuum storage bags used for sealing food.

I don't know what the outcome would be if you enclosed perfectly humidified cigars in an airless, moistureless environment. I would think that after several months, there would still be some air and moisture transfer through the plastic and your cigars would eventually dry out. Some day I'll have to try it.

Plastic Boxes

Remember I said that the real purpose of a humidor is to hold in humidity? Well, they aren't pretty, but sealing plastic containers—the kinds you can buy at most large grocery stores—are very effective for holding in moisture! Rubbermaid and Tupperware are two leading brands to look for.

These boxes are cheap, costing only a few dollars. In addition, you'll have to purchase a humidifying element—which I'll get to in a few moments.

The downside is that these plastic containers, like zip-seal bags, don't allow your cigars to "breathe," and a modest amount of air flow helps inhibit mold and keep your cigars fresh. If you use plastic containers, open them at least once a month to check your cigars for correct moisture. While you're at it, let the cigars breath some fresh air for an hour or so.

If you're going to use a plastic container, please buy a new one! If you use one that has held food, you increase your chance of attracting mold and imparting food flavors to your stogies. You may, if you like, wash the new container thoroughly in warm soapy water and dry it carefully before you use it. You want to make sure there's no residue from manufacturing and remove the plastic smell.

> **Hot Tip**
> You can easily create your own cognac-flavored cigar. Take a few mild smokes and toss them in a tight-sealing plastic container large enough to hold the cigars and a shot glass filled with brandy, cognac, or Calvados. Snap on the lid and leave in a dark place for a few weeks or until the brandy evaporates. Your smokes will acquire a subtle, "spirited" flavor!

Tabletop Humidors

Not since the heyday of cigars in the early 1900s has such a beautiful array of tabletop humidors been available. There are lacquered boxes of exotic, hand-worked woods;

mind-boggling creations that resemble castles and famous buildings (and cost as much); and brightly stained woods with outrageous inlays.

Most of these humidors are also functional—as opposed to older models. I collect antique humidors, and while they are lovely, I'd never store a cigar in one. I can't imagine that they are able to maintain a 70 percent humidity level; they're just not crafted to seal tightly.

A *tabletop humidor* holds anywhere from 10 to 250 individual cigars. The ideal humidor is lined with Spanish cedar to absorb and release moisture and buffer the outer wood against the moisture changes that could cause the outer liner to swell, shrink, and crack. The outside wood can be almost anything, but it should be thick and tightly joined at the corners to resist cracking as the cedar liner inside expands and contracts.

Remember that while your cigars bask inside at 70 percent humidity, less than an inch away the indoor relative humidity might be 10 percent. Thin wood or wood without a cedar liner is likely to crack with that kind of moisture variation.

My test of a good wooden humidor is to raise the lid about three inches and let it drop. If the box is crafted well enough to create a tight seal, a "whoosh" of air will escape and prevent the lid from slamming loudly. If you try this in a cigar store and the lid crashes shut, you'll attract some attention but you won't waste your money. For this reason, be cautious about mail-order humidors. You absolutely must test the seal before you buy!

Some humidor makers trim out the inside of the box with a rubber gasket to enhance the seal. No matter what's used, the "whoosh" will tell you it's a well-crafted piece.

A large, professional-quality hygrometer isn't practical for tabletop humidors. Don't bother paying attention to the little circular gauges included with tabletop humidors. They run on a cheap spring coil and simply won't give you an accurate reading. Check your cigars for proper humidity by applying the pinch test (see Chapter 2).

In today's market, a box with top-notch craftsmanship will cost at least $500. Expect to pay more than $1,000 for a well-crafted humidor with exotic wood or fancy inlay.

That's a lot of money, but many humidors double as exquisite tabletop decorations, and they'll last forever—possibly something you hand down to future generations.

You can also find tabletop humidors made from clear and smoked Plexiglas. They give you the chance to admire your stogies—kind of a high-tech approach to storing cigars. A humidor doesn't have to be wood to hold in moisture, but you have to be very careful when buying a Plexiglas humidor because it's tough to create an airtight seal with this material.

Today, a number of high-quality Plexiglas humidors are being made, with excellent seals. You need to treat these models as you would the plastic container mentioned earlier in the chapter. If you're using the humidor for storage and not regularly opening and closing the box to retrieve cigars for smoking, you should open the lid occasionally to let the cigars breathe.

Your best bet would be to find a Plexiglas humidor with some kind of sealing gasket, such as rubber or nylon, and a lock that holds down the lid. The weight of a wood lid is enough to create a seal, but because Plexiglas is lighter than wood, the same isn't true of Plexiglas. Expect to pay $200 to $400 for a high-quality Plexiglas humidor.

> **Hot Tip**
> Examine the humidor's hinges before you buy a tabletop humidor. They should be solid brass, attached with at least two screws each to the top and base, and should work smoothly and easily. There should be no "wobble" if you jiggle the lid back and forth. Cheap hinges will break and repairs can be difficult. A top maker will use expensive hardware.

Free-Standing "Vaults"

I've seen a lot of free-standing cigar vaults and furniture being offered these days. The vaults are often made by the same companies that make temperature- and humidity-controlled vaults for wine. You can get a lot of stogies in one of these things. They're electric and some hook into a water source, like a refrigerator with an ice maker, so they pretty much take care of themselves.

A cigar vault could be a wise investment if your love of cigars has you spending a few thousand dollars over several years. Remember, the life of your cigars depends solely on how you control the climate. I've even see a few handy individuals make a "poor-man's" cigar vault out of an old refrigerator and a passive humidity source such as water-soaked clay bricks.

Cigar "furniture" is also being made today—kind of a hybrid between a humidor and an end table. The ones I've seen have either solid wood exteriors to hide your boxes of cigars, or glass panels to show them off! They seem to work fine, but they are very pricey and don't hold all that many boxes.

Built-In Humidors

A built-in humidor would go very nicely with the wine cellar in your multi-million dollar dream home! All kidding aside, having a built-in, cedar-lined, humidity- and temperature-controlled humidor in your home involves a lot of expense—unless you're very handy with a hammer and nails, at which point it involves a lot of work.

If cigars become one of your major passions, and you choose to start accumulating a significant number of boxes, turning a closet or basement spot or recreation room into a walk-in humidor might be a good idea. A nicely built walk-in will probably cost you at least $7,000 in materials and labor.

The mechanics of a walk-in humidor are pretty simple. You only need shelves that don't rust and walls that won't crumble or mold under the relentless humidity. I've seen people tile closets or panel them with cedar and, bingo! They have a humidor.

Ideally, a walk-in has cedar walls laid against backer board drywall (the same type drywall used as a base for tiled showers). The drywall will help balance moisture fluctuations by absorbing or giving off humidity. Cedar lining is a nice touch, but isn't essential. The door has to seal tightly and should be made of a material that doesn't easily warp.

If you can regularly monitor the room, you only need a drum-type humidifier that you can switch to high, low, or off to control moisture. You can also buy automatic humidity controls. If the room isn't against an outside wall, you probably don't need a heating or cooling source. The general acceptable temperature range—68 to 74 degrees Fahrenheit— is fine for cigars as long as they have the proper humidity.

When you reach this level of cigar appreciation, look for ideas by going to retail cigar shops with humidors. You can modify some of the ideas yourself. If you see a design you really like, ask the shopkeeper for the name of the carpenter.

How Do I Keep These Things Moist?

Now that we've looked at all the different ways to store your cigars, you're probably asking, "So how do I keep them moist?" Well, you obviously need something that will hold moisture and gradually give it off. The word "sponge" comes to mind!

Cigar Esoterica

In the old days, the most common humidifying element was an absorbent clay brick for large humidors and display cases, and small clay discs for small humidors. You can still find these, and some retailers still use them. But this special absorbant clay is hard to locate, and dries out faster than some of the newer materials.

If you build a walk-in humidor, you may use a drum-type humidifier—the same kind you'd use to keep a home humidified during the dry winter months. You may also use an electronically controlled humidifier that spritzes mist into the air when the humidity level falls below 70 percent.

If you're starting off humidifying an area smaller than a walk-in humidor, you'll simply need to use a small piece of porous material. Most tabletop humidors come equipped with some type of humidification element that attaches to the lid.

The cheap humidifiers use a piece of foamy sponge. Most of the expensive ones use simple, cheap florist foam, even though they may tell you it's some magical material. Florist foam is that stiff, absorbent stuff placed in the bottom of flower vases. For flowers, it holds the stems and retains moisture very well. While you probably won't use it to create a floral arrangement for your smokes, it works equally well at holding and gradually releasing moisture.

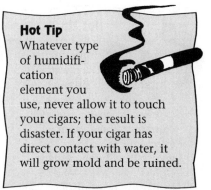

Hot Tip
Whatever type of humidification element you use, never allow it to touch your cigars; the result is disaster. If your cigar has direct contact with water, it will grow mold and be ruined.

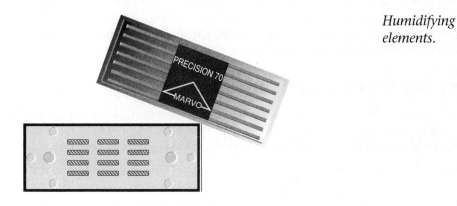

Humidifying elements.

Built-in humidifying elements are usually attached by a magnet to the lid of your humidor (or in a drawer below, for some larger tabletop models), away from the cigars. These elements are removable so that you can periodically moisten them. Generally, the foam is enclosed in a vented plastic box.

You can moisten the humidifying elements by dunking them in a half-filled sink, but it's best to use a small squeeze bottle filled with distilled water. Just drip water into the element. Manufacturer's instructions usually tell you how much to use, but you'll get a feel for the amount of water based on how your cigars are faring. If they're a bit too dry, add more moisture than you did the last time!

When you get to be an expert at storing cigars, it's sufficient to check them once a month because you'll know your humidification practices are sound. When you're starting out, however, it doesn't hurt to check your cigars every few days to correct overly dry or moist conditions. You should monitor cigars, regardless of the type of humidor you use.

Hot Tip
The best fluid for humidifying is distilled water or soft water, although I've used regular tap water with success. Tap water, however, contains minerals that will eventually build up and clog your humidifying element. Unless you have a lot of cigars, a quart bottle of distilled water will last a long time.

Keeping cigars moist is an inexact science, and if you use a tight-sealing tabletop humidor, you may sometimes have to open the top to out let moisture. If the cigars feel a bit spongy or contain a light white dusting of mold (which can be wiped off and shouldn't harm the cigar), you'll need to add less moisture to your humidifying element in the future.

If you're creating your own humidification element, nylon sponge works pretty well, but it can get moldy. Florist foam seems to resist mold. You can buy this foam at craft shops and cut it to size with a kitchen knife. Just drop the moistened sponge or florist foam into a small plastic bag, leaving the top of the bag open.

Place the smaller humidifying bag into the large zip-seal bag or plastic container holding your stogies. (Once again, I strongly advise that if you're using zip-seal bags, use the thick, high-quality freezer variety to prevent moisture from leaking directly onto your cigars.) You may even use a low-tech element like this to supplement the humidity in a regular humidor if you discover that the humidor's element is too small to store your smokes properly.

Help! My Cigar Dried Out

Despite your best efforts, you could still wind up with some dried-out cigars. Maybe you forgot to check the humidification element. Perhaps a friend gave you a really fine smoke that is showing signs of being dry and brittle. Do you have any recourse?

Smoking a dried-out cigar is no pleasure because it burns hot and fast, and it is more likely to unravel as you smoke. Although you could use such a cigar for a casual outdoor smoke, a better bet is to try to resurrect the cigar by rehydrating it. Sometimes, you get lucky and you can bring a cigar back to life, but it's a tricky process and doesn't always work. Here's how:

➤ Do your best to judge how badly the cigar is damaged. If it's simply hard and dry, you have a better chance of resurrecting it than if the wrapper has cracked or the binder has split open.

➤ Place the dry cigar or cigars in a humidor (and here's the perfect place to use that cheap snap-lid plastic container) and place in the box a lightly damp sponge in an open plastic bag. You have to bring a dry cigar back to life very, very slowly. Filler tobaccos absorb moisture faster than wrappers, and if you expose the dry cigars to humidity too quickly, the filler will expand, splitting the binder and wrapper.

➤ Every few days, check on your cigars and gently turn them a quarter inch. Add a few drops of moisture to your sponge if it's beginning to dry out. A sponge drying is a good sign: It means that the cigars are re-absorbing moisture.

➤ Continue this process for about a month and see what happens. You may salvage the cigars, although once they dry out, they'll probably never be as tasty as they were because some of the essential oils will have disappeared.

➤ If the wrapper cracks during the process but the binder is intact, peel off the wrapper (yes, this is a sad occasion, but most necessary). A cracked wrapper will start to unravel during smoking and get really messy. You may not want to smoke this ugly, wrapperless cigar in public, but it should still taste fine. Remember that the wrapper contributes only a small percentage of flavor to your smoke.

Rehumidifying a cigar is a desperate measure, but considering that your chances of salvaging it are reasonably good if you follow my instructions, it's worth the trouble.

Better with Age: Aging Your Cigars

As you'll recall from Chapter 9, when the central vein is stripped from the tobacco leaf, most of the major changes that occur during the initial air curing and fermentation cease. Unlike wine that has been bottled, in which yeast and bacteria continue to change the product, there isn't much inside a completed cigar that will change.

Some cigars, however, do seem to benefit from being set aside. Overall, the biggest beneficiaries of aging are Cuban cigars, which I think get shortchanged on aging and marrying. I've had Havana smokes that transformed from rough and raw to smooth and delicious with about six months of aging.

If you get into aging certain cigars, or simply storing them for long periods until you get around to smoking them, you may find that some improve with age while others taste about the same as the day you bought them. A well-made premium cigar should be ready to smoke when you buy it, but if you store it properly, you can maintain that flavor peak for years.

Some aficionados say that after you buy a cigar, it can go nowhere but downhill. Time does tend to rob a cigar of essential oils, but with proper storage, this won't happen for many years. Experts can't agree on which brands age best, so your best bet is to experiment with your stash as you build your stockpile of stogies.

Hot Tip
A good rule of thumb in aging cigars is that cigars with darker wrappers will benefit more from aging than those with lighter wrappers, and full-bodied cigars are more likely to mellow and intensify in flavor than mild cigars. This has to do with the higher amounts of oil in the darker and more full-bodied cigars.

I suggest that if you buy several cigars of the same brand and you find the first one to be somewhat harsh, you have nothing to lose by stashing the others for at least six months. Then try one and see if it's any better. You might find the flavor greatly enhanced—in which case you'll be thankful you didn't dispose of them.

You Can Take It with You

If you travel or want to take a smoke with you to a cigar-friendly bar, club, or restaurant, you'll need something with which to transport your booty. If you carry smokes frequently, you may want to invest in a cigar case or even a small traveling humidor.

Cigar Cases

A cigar case is a container for holding anywhere from one to five smokes. You probably won't believe you need a cigar case until that first time you lean over a rail for a few moments before realizing you've squashed the $8 stogie in your coat pocket.

Although designed to fit into the pocket of a sport coat or jacket, cigar cases are still pretty bulky. If you're a man, it's best to stash the case in a side pocket. If you're a woman, use your purse.

Cigar cases are generally made of leather and provide individual pockets for cigars. The best cases use thick, stiff leather. Less expensive cases will wrap a layer of leather around a plastic or cardboard frame to stiffen the case; these cases can work nicely.

A fancy leather case can cost several hundred dollars, but you can find a decent model for $50 or so. These cases don't humidify your cigars, so I don't recommend using them for longer than a few hours.

The most important consideration when shopping for a cigar case is to find one big enough to hold the longest, fattest cigar you prefer. You don't want to bring home a cigar case, only to discover that it's too short to hold your favorite Lonsdales or too thin to accommodate a robusto. You also don't want to buy a case that's too big for your smokes, or the stogies will rattle around inside and could get damaged.

Travel Humidors

If you travel and want to bring some smokes with you, consider investing in a travel humidor. You don't want to lug a wooden 25-cigar humidor in your suitcase, but you do need something to keep your cigars humidified. A number of small humidors are made especially for traveling; they usually hold anywhere from one to ten cigars.

Most travel humidors are boxes, with locking lids to keep moisture inside and various types of padding to hold the cigars in place. Most use small sponges, separated from the cigars. You can rehumidify the sponges at various destinations, so theoretically you could travel with the cigars for weeks without a problem. Travel humidors start at about $30 for a single-cigar tube and may cost up to $250, depending on size, use of rare exterior woods, and ornamentation.

Davidoff makes a nifty travel humidor that looks like a cigar case made of wood. They have small humidifying elements inside that you can moisten and re-moisten as you travel. These cases come in different lengths and sizes that can hold up to four cigars.

They're too bulky to place in a pocket, but they slip nicely into a suitcase, briefcase, or overnight bag, and they do a good job of keeping your cigars humidified and ready.

Because I love thrifty solutions, I'll let you in on a cheap version of the travel humidor. You can put a few well-humidified cigars in a zip-seal plastic bag and close the bag. By now, I can hear you saying, "Oh boy, there he goes again with those plastic bags."

While it's true that I love plastic bags, the pitfall of using them for traveling is that they provide no protection for your cigars. You have to pack your smokes very carefully in your bag or they'll get crushed. If you plan to carry them in your suitcase, I'd suggest putting the bag inside a cigar box for protection.

This trick only works if you'll be gone just a few days; much longer, and the cigars will start to dry out. In addition, if you're traveling to a very hot, very cold, or very dry destination, the bag won't protect your cigars for more than a day. You can't enclose a sponge in the bag because it could easily flop around and touch the cigars, ruining them.

The Least You Need to Know

➤ Buying a box lets you "lock up" a supply of great smokes for future enjoyment.

➤ You don't have to spend a lot of money to store your cigars and keep them humidified.

➤ Inspect your stored cigars at least once a month to check for proper conditions.

➤ You can "age" cigars, but they probably won't change much in flavor.

➤ You can transport cigars without humidity for a day; if you're going to travel with them, however, you have to keep them humidified.

Cigarillos: The "Other" Cigar

You're at a restaurant with some friends and you'd love to enjoy a cigar. You know cigarettes are allowed, and you're in the smoking section, but there's a big label at the bottom of your menu that says "Patrons are respectfully requested to refrain from smoking pipes and cigars." You're not stuck; you pull out a tin and remove a small, brown cigar the size of a cigarette.

It looks like a miniature cigar, and it packs a lot of taste. The waiter eyeballs you momentarily but keeps his distance while you finish. You've just had a cigar at a no-cigar restaurant, which is why I call the *cigarillo* "a sneaky smoke that satisfies."

The Sneaky Smoke That Satisfies

I'd been smoking cigars for quite a few years before I ever tried a cigarillo. These miniature cigars are descendants of the *cheroot*, a small cigar that was extremely popular in the

Cigar Speak
A **cigarillo**, or "small cigar," is generally not much bigger than a cigarette. It's made from cigar-leaf tobacco, but due to its small size, it generally contains short filler to promote proper, even burning.

Victorian era. With the challenge of finding the place and time to smoke a big cigar, cigarillos are once again popular.

There's sometimes a fine line dividing a small cigar from a cigarillo. I consider a small cigar to be handmade, to have at least a 30-ring gauge, and to give me a good 25-minute smoke. A true cigarillo, on the other hand, is machine made and has a 20 to 27 ring gauge: a similar or slightly thicker circumference than a cigarette. I also distinguish cigarillos from regular cigars because not only are they small, they require no humidification. I'll talk more about that in a minute.

Still life with cigarillo.

Small cigars can be great smokes, but with their generally larger size and fuller aroma, they're not necessarily "sneaky" like cigarillos. If you're enjoying a small cigar at an establishment that prohibits cigars, the fuller aroma and larger size might give you away.

Cigars, Cigarillos, and Small Cigars

It's difficult to say exactly where to draw the line between small cigars and cigarillos. To over-generalize, I'd say a cigarillo is closer to a cigarette in size. In length and ring gauge, small cigars look much closer to regular cigars than to cigarettes. These small cigars—some handmade and some machine-made—don't necessarily require humidification, but they don't have the same shelf life as *other* cigars.

You can leave them unhumidified for several weeks, but eventually they will dry out and their wrappers may begin to unravel.

Many Cuban brands, notably Partagas and Punch, make small cigars that come in small tins or paper containers. These cigars use Cuban leaf, so they provide an inexpensive opportunity to try Cuban tobacco. I haven't tried many, but I've found the construction a little sloppy and the tobacco green and inferior. You may want to try a few if you run across them, but I think many non-Cuban brands are far superior. Make no mistake: The best cigarillo or small cigar can't compare to a larger stogie. They're not thick enough to offer the same satisfying smoke volume, nor do they deliver anywhere near the complex and full taste. They *do*, however, have their value:

➤ Most cigarillos come in tins or stiff cardboard boxes, so you can slip them into a pocket and not worry about breaking them, as you could with a cigar.

➤ Although cigarillos give off a typical cigar-like aroma, the smoke volume is very small because of their size. Because you aren't exhaling big plumes of aromatic smoke, you can usually enjoy a cigarillo in places that allow cigarettes but prohibit cigars.

➤ Cigarillos not only give off less smoke, but because cigarillos are blended to be mild, their aroma is generally gentler and less noticeable than a full-blown cigar.

➤ Cigarillos are a quick smoke, lasting no more than 15 minutes. They burn slowly and evenly because they're perfectly made by machine. (This is the only time I will recommend that you buy a machine-made cigar.)

➤ Finally, cigarillos require no humidification, which makes them really convenient for transporting just about anywhere.

Cigarillos certainly don't offer the variety of taste and character you'll find in premium handmade cigars, but they deliver a great cigar taste at times and places where a full-sized cigar would be inconvenient or inappropriate. In addition, they offer their own distinctive taste that makes them a great alternative. Some of that difference is in the way the tobacco is processed, as we'll see.

What's Dry-Curing?

Although dryness is the sworn enemy of premium, handmade smokes, it's no bother at all for a *dry-cured* cigarillo. *Dry-curing* means that the tobacco is allowed to dry during the manufacturing process. Because of this process, cigarillos have to be made differently from regular cigars.

Most cigarillos don't use a rough binder or silky wrapper. Instead, the wrapper and binder are one and the same, holding inside a filler of shredded tobacco rather than long-leaf tobacco. (Cigarillos use short filler because bunching enough long filler leaves inside the cigarillo for an even burn would be nearly impossible.) For this reason, the wrapper leaf needs to be tougher than wrappers used on large cigars.

> **Cigar Speak**
> **Dry-curing** means that the tobacco is exposed to heat to dry it during the manufacturing process. Because of this moisture-removing process, most cigarillos don't require humidification, as do premium cigars.

The dry-cure process originated in Holland. Even today, you'll find that many brands of Dutch cigars (even full-sized) are dry-cured. Dry-cure tobacco has almost a "toasty" quality, and dry-cured cigars have a different taste than the long-filler stogies I've referred to in this book.

Many cigarillos are machine made, and as I discussed in Chapter 4, a machine is much better than a person at making short-filler cigars—especially cigars as tiny as cigarillos. The machines are able to pack the short filler with just the right pressure, which creates a very even smoke.

You'll also find a large number of cigarillos that feature Sumatran and Brazilian tobaccos. The very sweet and Brazilian tobacco is mild, but a bit harsh, as well.

What You See Is What You Get

In most cases, cigarillos contain shredded tobacco in a tough, bumpy wrapper that almost looks as if had been shrink-wrapped around the tobacco. Some wrappers are smoother than others, but all are very dry. Don't expect to see any oily sheen.

Remember that the cigarillo wrapper has to serve double-duty as both binder and filler. Most European-made cigarillos use a tough natural tobacco leaf to wrap the cigar, as do the few brands of cigarillos made in the Caribbean region.

These wrappers aren't the smooth, pretty, oily wrappers you'd look for on a fine cigar. They look like what they are: a cross between a binder and a wrapper.

Cigar Speak
Homogenized tobacco product is pulverized and reconstituted tobacco blended with natural binders; it's used as the wrapper for a number of cigarillos.

Wrapper colors range from a light claro to relatively deep brown, although no manufacturer I know creates a true maduro wrapper for cigarillos. (See Chapter 5 for a review of wrappers.) You can't apply the same color classifications to cigarillo wrappers as you can to full-sized smokes.

Brazilian leaf wrappers tend to be darker and richer in flavor than the lighter wrappers, and in most cases, the box will tell you what tobacco is used for the wrapper. Some manufacturers offer several cigarillos with similar fillers but different wrappers.

In some cases, mostly in American-made cigarillos, the wrappers are made from *homogenized tobacco product*: pulverized and reconstituted tobacco blended with natural binders. Don't discount less expensive cigarillos made with the homogenized tobacco wrappers. A couple of these brands are pretty tasty, most notably La Corona Whiffs, which are made by Consolidated Cigar Company.

Paying the Price

In my opinion, most cigarillos are pricey for the amount of tobacco they contain. I'm not sure why cigarillos are so expensive: Most average 70 cents to $1.00 per stick. The prices have gone up during the past few years, and the various taxes charged for cigarillos add considerably to the price of your smokes.

Be extra careful when buying cigarillos. Because they're a dry cigar, they have a long shelf life, which means they might sit around a smoke shop for many months. Although this doesn't hurt them thanks to the dry-curing process, the longer they sit, they more likely they could pick up tobacco beetles. Shops will generally gladly replace your product if it has beetle holes, but if you see tobacco beetles in your cigarillos, be wary of the shop!

Inspect every box of cigarillos you purchase. Many of the boxes come wrapped in plastic, but there's no reason not to open them if you are standing at the counter with every intention of buying them.

Opportunity Knocks: When to Smoke 'Em

I'm sure you can think of places where a cigar isn't appropriate but a cigarillo would be great—for example, restaurants that have a smoking section but don't allow cigars. I've never been asked to put out a cigarillo, and I doubt you will, either. I was asked once by a waitress if I was smoking a cigar, and I looked her straight in the eye and told her it was one of those little brown European cigarettes. It worked.

You can enjoy these little smokes during intermissions at plays, taking a work break in a non-smoking office (where you wouldn't have time to enjoy a cigar), when outdoors during a windy day in which you couldn't properly savor a handmade cigar, or in places that allow cigarettes but not cigars. After experimenting a bit, you may find that the flavor of certain cigarillos are more appealing to you than those of some cigars—or that they have a flavor you enjoy in particular situations.

A Selection of Sneaky Smokes

A few makers of handmade premium smokes also manufacture small cigars and cigarillos, notably Macanudo, Davidoff, H. Upmann, Punch, and Don Diego. These manufacturers make the smaller product by strategically using some of the scraps from larger cigars, so the tobaccos are identical to the quality leaf you'll find in their full line of smokes.

Cigarillos have long been popular in Europe, and even today, the majority of cigarillo makers are major Dutch, German, and Swiss tobacco companies. You'll encounter a whole new group of brand names when you go shopping for these tiny treasures.

The best way to learn what you like in cigarillos is to try various brands. Some shops sell them individually, but you'll usually have to purchase a box of 10 or 20. So let's run down some of the available smokes. You probably won't find all of them in one shop, but they're widely distributed and generally available, and you may be able to special-order a favorite brand.

Small Cigars from Handmade Brand Makers

I include small cigars in my listing because although most aren't made with the dry-cure process, they—like cigarillos—don't require humidification. (Of course, small cigars will eventually get dry and stale if left to sit around for more than six months.) Some of these are larger than cigarettes and look enough like a cigar to get you in trouble in a place that doesn't allow cigar smoking. You'll have a difficult time passing them off as "European cigarettes," and they generally have a fuller cigar aroma that may attract attention.

Still, they're short smokes, and you may enjoy them during occasions when you want a cigar but don't have time to savor a large stogie. Some are handmade with either long or short filler, and some are machine-made with short filler. I haven't listed all the brands, or any Cuban brands, but I've picked out some of my favorites that are readily available at many smoke shops.

➤ **Belinda**   These have a medium body and full aroma. They can be a challenge to find, as can Belinda cigars, but if you track them down, you'll find they have nice taste and a flavorful colorado wrapper.

➤ **Davidoff Special Selection**   These $3^1/2$-inch, premium-priced small cigars are available in packs of 10 and 20, and they convey a medium-bodied long-filler cigar taste. You'll find them at almost any smoke shop that's an authorized Davidoff dealer. They come in stiff cardboard boxes that do a good job of protecting them, and the presentation—complete with a white paper cover—is elegant.

➤ **Don Diego**   Don Diego makes a very mild, delicious small cigar, called "Preludes," that comes in a handy and attractive 10-pack tin. It features the mild and smooth tobaccos used in Don Diego cigars.

➤ **Macanudo**   These small cigars are among my favorite small smokes. They're very well-constructed, have a mild aroma, and burn evenly and slowly. They come in 10-pack tins that are easy to slip into a coat pocket, and are individually wrapped in cellophane to help protect the wrappers. They're called "Ascots."

➤ **Montecruz**   A dark, rich, sun-grown wrapper gives these smokes a little "kick." Like many of the other small cigars, they come in sturdy and attractive tins of 10, and are named "Chicas."

➤ **Oscar**   These have the characteristically medium-full flavor of the Oscar cigar, and are generally well-constructed.

➤ **Partagas**   These "Puritos" have the same nice, dark Cameroon leaf wrapper that makes the entire Partagas line tasty. They come in nice-looking tins of 10, and I've found them to be consistently well-made and even-burning.

➤ **Primo del Rey**   The "Cortos" are nearly four inches long and come in tins of 10. They have a dark, attractive EMS wrapper and a big-cigar taste. They have a fuller-bodied flavor than many cigarillos, and are what I'd call a small cigar, rather than a true cigarillo.

➤ **Punch**   These are slightly wider and longer than a classic cigarillo, and because they look like cigars, I wouldn't advise sneaking one into a cigar-prohibiting establishment. Called "Slim Panatelas," they have a distinctive peppery Punch taste and come in a striking black tin holding 10 cigars.

➤ **H. Upmann**   These small cigars incorporate the same tobaccos as the larger H. Upmann cigars. The cigars are of generally high quality and good consistency. Called "Aperitif," the Upmanns are also larger than the usual cigarillo.

A Selection of Cigarillos

Most of the following are what I'd call "true" European-style cigarillos, and most are dry-cured.

➤ **Agio**   A Dutch dry-cure cigar maker producing cigarillos of very high quality. See *Meharis* and *Biddies*. Agio cigarillos use two different tobaccos: Brazilian and Sumatran.

➤ **Backgammon**   A product of Germany, this tough-to-find cigarillo brand comes with a Sumatran leaf wrapper as well as a darker, more robust Brazilian wrapper.

A selection of popular and readily available cigarillo brands.

➤ **Biddies**   Several choices of Biddies are available, including ones with Sumatra-leaf wrappers and Brazilian-leaf wrappers. The Brazilian-leaf option is a little more robust and sweet than the Sumatra selection.

➤ **Braniff**   The Cortos No. 1 is more cigar-like in appearance than some cigarillos, but can pass for a cigarette if you're smoking on the sly. It has a nice, medium-bodied cigar flavor.

➤ **Captain Black**   These look just like cigarettes and have a filter. They're filled with pipe tobacco, not cigar leaf, but they're not bad and they provide a quick and easy smoke. They're artificially sweetened, like Captain Black pipe tobacco, but they're an interesting change of pace. You can find them everywhere.

➤ **Christian of Denmark**   This thin, elegant cigarillo is 3$\frac{1}{2}$ inches long with a very mild flavor and an inoffensive aroma. The cigar is manufactured by Nobel, Denmark's largest cigar producer.

➤ **Dannemann**   There are several different Dannemann selections, ranging in length from a little less than 3 inches to a little more than 4 inches. They come with either Brazilian or Sumatran tobaccos. If you like the taste of these cigarillos, you might want to try their two larger cigars: the Lights (Sumatra leaf) and Espada (Brazilian leaf).

➤ **Dutch Masters**   The line of "Dutch Treats" looks just like a brown cigarette. They're wrapped in a papery smooth homogenized tobacco product wrapper with a white filter. They're very mild and burn a bit more quickly than some cigarillos, but they have a decent flavor. Some are sweetened, but I'd stick with the natural flavor. The Dutch Masters cigar line is machine-made, but as a quick smoke, these are relatively tasty and also inexpensive. You can find them in many drug stores.

➤ **Garcia Vega Whiffs**   Another machine-made product, these cigarillos come with a natural wrapper. They're a bit large to pass as a cigarette, and the tobaccos aren't particularly good, but they're tolerable for a short smoke and are readily available in drug stores and many convenience stores.

➤ **Hamlet**   Made by the famed Gallaher in England, this has been the biggest-selling little cigar in the United Kingdom for years. It comes in a slim, regular, and special panatela, and even uses a Connecticut wrapper. It's hard to find, but very good.

➤ **Indiana Slims**   I'm not a fan of flavored cigars, but these rum-soaked smokes taste good. The gnarly wrapper is dark and flavorful.

➤ **La Corona Whiffs**   Available in convenient tins of 10 and 25, you can find these cigarillos in most drug and convenience stores. Although they are machine made and use a homogenized tobacco product wrapper, they're one of my favorite cigarillos. They're relatively inexpensive—priced at less than half the cost of many cigarillos.

➤ **Mehari's**   Another Agio product, this line includes several sizes, and includes versions that feature Sumatran, Javan, and Cameroon tobaccos.

➤ **Nobel**   The Nobel company is more than 150 years old and is the largest cigar producer in Denmark. It manufactures several cigarillos under the Nobel name, as well as under the Christian of Denmark name. The Nobel Petite Sumatra is nearly 3$\frac{1}{2}$ inches long, 20 ring, and packs a lot of flavor. Any Nobel product is a very good choice.

➤ **Panter**   A picture of the panther on the box tells you the cigar is named after an animal—not named after being out of breath! The Mignon is 3$\frac{7}{8}$ inches long, has a natural wrapper, and is packaged in a box of 10. At 3 inches, the Panter "Small" is a really short smoke, and the Panter "Sprint" is even shorter. The Vitesse, Limbo, and Silhouette are also available. Panter delivers a mild yet full flavor.

➤ **Schimmelpenninck**   This is probably the world's top manufacturer of dry-cure cigars. A Dutch company, Schimmelpenninck makes a wide variety of cigarillos using tobaccos from Brazil, Cameroon, and Indonesia. Most larger cigar retailers carry this brand. If you like the flavor of the dry-cure process, Schimmelpenninck also makes some larger sizes, although they're stick-thin.

➤ **Villiger**   This is an outstanding Swiss brand with a wide variety of cigarillos and larger cigars. The company, founded in 1888, is still family run. (By the way, the "g" is pronounced like the "g" in "goat.") Although Villiger cigars are machine made, it is a high-quality brand, using aged leaf from around the world.

➤ **Willem**   These Dutch cigarillos come in a variety of lengths, from the 2³/₄-inch Wee Willem to the 4-inch Brasilaantes. They incorporate primarily Brazilian and Sumatran leaf.

➤ **Henri Winterman**   With names like Cafe Noir (black coffee) and Cafe Creme, coffee is the obvious theme with these cigarillos. They're made with the Dutch dry-cure process and are generally mild and slightly sweet. They're widely distributed throughout the U.S.

Keep your eyes peeled for these interesting brands, and do some experimenting to see which, if any, you enjoy. Don't compare them with premium handmade smokes. Instead, appreciate them for what they are: sneaky, satisfying smokes.

The Least You Need to Know

➤ You can usually sneak a cigarette-sized cigarillo in places that allow cigarettes but prohibit cigars.

➤ Many cigarillos require no humidification, so they're ideal for traveling.

➤ Cigarillos made by companies that also manufacture large cigars often contain the same high-quality tobaccos as the larger product.

➤ Because of their small size, cigarillos are usually machine made and use short filler for even burning.

Baubles, Bangles, and Bands: Cigar Stuff

I'll admit it: I'm hooked on collecting! I collect antiques of all kinds—whatever catches my eye that I can afford—but I have a special fondness for cigar, pipe, and *tobacciana*-related merchandise.

If you enjoy collecting, you may find that your interest in cigars slowly starts to draw you into collecting both old and new items. In this chapter I offer a glimpse of the many types of collectibles you can pursue; with that knowledge in hand, you can let loose in flea markets, antique shops, auctions, and smoke shops!

Bands, Boxes, and Labels

The largest and most accessible area of cigar-related tobacciana includes cigar boxes, the art used to decorate those boxes (labels), and the bands that adorned the cigars. I also include humidors in this group. Let's talk about what's out there.

Cigar Speak
Tobacciana is a general term that refers to smoking-related collectibles and memorabilia. From advertisements to books to six-foot cigar-store Indians, tobacciana includes an almost unlimited variety of items. Often, even people who aren't smokers are fascinated by tobacco-related collectibles.

Collecting cigar boxes and labels is a popular pastime for cigar smokers as well as collectors who have no interest in smoking but find the items to be an interesting part of history. I'm not talking about new cigar boxes, but rather the older boxes used for thousands of brands of cigars once produced for American and European consumers. Virtually all of these brands have long disappeared, and many of the fine labels and boxes are prized by collectors for their beauty, historical interest, and rarity.

You can collect complete boxes—which held the cigars of yesteryear—or you can collect only the box labels. Cigar labels were printed by the millions, and while most found their way onto boxes, many were never applied and were left in their original form—as flat, printed sheets.

Other, related items are also collectible, including *printer's proofs* (the pre-printing test-run labels), *progressives* (the various one-color printer's sheets that combined to make a four-color label), and original artwork from which the labels were reproduced. In addition, you can buy *reproduction labels* that were printed from the original plates.

Cigar Speak
As you may remember from Chapter 1, a **cigar band** is the decorative strip of paper used to mark a cigar with the brand. The band sometimes includes information about the country of origin, as well as whether or not the cigar is handmade. Bands are a popular collectible, from small old bands that were once wrapped around long-extinct cigars, to huge bands used to bind entire bundles of cigars.

It takes a little detective work to tap into the world of smoking collectibles. You won't find shops devoted to this esoteric pastime, but there are many individual collectors. You can find cigar boxes at antique shops, flea markets, and garage sales, but they're not likely to be either rare or valuable. The more unique, pristine items can be found through auctions, and sometimes smoke shops. Your local retailer may also be able to give you names of customers who are collectors, and you can tap into the world of collecting through them. Many shops also carry information about pipe, cigar, and tobacciana shows and swaps being held locally. This is a great way to tap into this area of collecting, and meet others with the same interests.

If you intend to become a serious collector of boxes or label art, read up on what's available and become familiar with the prices, which are often dictated by rarity, condition, and historical significance. Some informative, comprehensive, and colorful books on antique cigar boxes and labels are available.

I'm no expert in this area, so I collect what catches my eye (and what I can afford). My home is decorated with framed cigar labels that are beautiful artwork. Not only are labels eye-catching, but they often portray historical events or sites. Others are simply fanciful and attractive.

You can also collect cigar bands. If you use my rating sheets (see Chapter 20), you'll already be collecting modern-day cigar bands by removing the band from your cigars and pasting them on a sheet.

The Cigar Box as an Advertisement

The heyday of cigar boxes, labels, and bands was from 1870 to about 1940. Before 1865, most cigars were sold in simple bunches of 25. In 1865, the U.S. government passed a law requiring cigars to be sold in boxes. Because the U.S. market for cigars was large and growing, most manufacturers routinely started putting cigars in boxes.

Somewhere down the line, someone had the bright idea that the cigar box could do more than just hold cigars: It could serve as a sales tool that would entice people to buy an entire box rather than one or two stogies! Thousands of brands appeared, and the artwork used to adorn these boxes ranged from ridiculous to sublime.

Whatever subject might attract attention (and sell cigars) ended up on boxes and labels: pretty women, U.S. presidents, catchy names inferring big bucks, literary greats, foreign lands, sports, aviation, Indians, actors, animals, nudes, current events…you name it. There were thousands of cigar brands, and most had distinctive and attractive labels.

The diverse subject matter of cigar-box labels also makes cigar labels a "crossover" collectible. For instance, a sports memorabilia collector will have no interest in tobacciana, but may collect cigar box labels featuring sports heroes or themes. Certain crossover subjects, such as sports or African-American memorabilia, are in large demand, making these labels particularly hard to find and pricey.

The names of cigars that the labels advertised are also fascinating. There was *Paid In Full*, *Uncle Jake's Nickel Seegar* ("Five Cents Worth O'Dern Good Smokin'"), *Honest Yankee*, *Irish Beauty*, *Madame Butterfly*, *Uwanta Cigar*, *Banker's Bouquet*, *Walt Whitman*, *Bible Class*, and thousands upon thousands more. You get the idea! By today's standard, most of the names are incredibly corny, but they all represent an important piece of history. It's fun to imagine a well-to-do Victorian gentleman settling back in his smoking den with a rare brandy and a cigar named *Uncle Jake*.

Most of these boxes housed inexpensive cigars. Many were made in the United States, although quite a few were made partially or completely with Cuban leaf.

Occasionally, cigar makers produced boxes or cigar jars in beautiful woods or crystal. These special gift packages were the equal of the finest humidors you could buy, and must have made a very attractive present.

It's not surprising that many of these elegant products came from the leading Cuban producers of premium handmade cigars: H. Upmann, Punch, Partagas, Por Larrañaga, and others. Unless the cigars came in one of these elegant containers, most of the really fine smokes bought by the real cigar connoisseurs came in simple wood cigar boxes. The box didn't matter much, because the smoker transferred his Cuban stogies to a fine humidor.

Humidors: The Fancy Stuff

Humidors are my favorite cigar collectibles. As my collection grows, the interior of my home seems to shrink, but I just can't help myself! Old humidors combine exquisite woods, glass, porcelain, or silver with amazing craftsmanship that rivals the finest collectible jars and vases available.

By collecting humidors, I have the chance to indulge my passion for fine craftsmanship and beauty while staying within a "discipline" that helps me focus my collecting interest and limit my spending. For instance, I like Wedgwood, a fine English decorative porcelain that features relief work such as leaves or Greek characters. I can indulge my interest in Wedgwood by purchasing Wedgwood smoking sets and ashtrays.

Assorted cigar-
related collectibles.

Anyway, back to humidors! As I mentioned earlier, old humidors are worthless for preserving your cigars; most don't seal properly. Even if you were to add a humidifying element, you'd probably warp the wood and severely damage the box. For collecting exquisite tobacciana, however, you can't beat vintage humidors.

I collect new and old humidors: new ones because they're beautiful and functional, and old ones simply because they're beautiful. I have old wooden boxes with incredible marquetry, inlaid woods, and metalwork. I collect sterling silver and also porcelain cigar boxes and jars with highly detailed figuring. You'll find a photo of some samples from my collection in the color section of this book.

Even though my personal cigar adventure began with a simple Cuban stogie at a conference in Toronto, I eventually got "hooked" on the entire cigar culture and all its accessories. Maybe the same thing will happen to you. Even if you only smoke cigars occasionally, you'll become a collector of sorts because you'll begin amassing cutting tools, lighters, and possibly a humidor or two. Believe me, it's only a small step from buying basic accessories to scouring antique shops and flea markets, searching for cigar paraphernalia.

Collectible Cigar Curiosities

Nothing is more satisfying than finding an old and rare cigar cutter or humidor for $10 at a junk shop. But I've also paid top dollar for cigar-related collectibles that caught my eye. Why do people collect these things? It may be for aesthetic reasons, or because of a passion for holding a piece of cigar history, or both.

In addition to collecting cigar humidors and jars, I collect ashtrays. I have ashtrays that range from a simple and silly tray guarded by a huge, toothless alligator to an assortment of elegant *Majolica* (a rare and expensive type of hand-glazed pottery) ashtrays. If you get "hooked" on cigar and smoking collectibles, you'll probably find your own favorite areas.

If you have lots of room to display collectibles, you might consider an authentic cigar-store Indian for about $10,000. For this, you need a lot of room and a wad of cash! You can buy reproduction cigar-store Indians that are well produced, but they have only aesthetic—not historical—value.

Cigar Esoterica

With Native Americans having introduced tobacco to the first European settlers in North America, the Indian became a natural symbol for all tobacco, which is how the cigar-store Indian evolved. Just as the striped barber pole said, "Here's a barber," so the statue of an Indian holding a handful of cigars said, "Cigar shop."

If you have a little less room, you might want to collect esoteric cigar cutters or table lighters. You can find modern-day lighters that work great with cigars, or older lighters that are mostly show pieces.

An assortment of antique lighters.

By the way, organizations have been founded for people who collect lighters, which just goes to show that if you search the world over, you can find a group of people who collect almost anything! I collect the French-made S. DuPont lighters, which are heavy and beautifully crafted with gold, silver, and lacquer finishes. Others collect lighters made by Dunhill, manufacturer of elegant smoking products since the early 1900s.

What strikes your fancy is entirely up to you, which is the fun thing about collecting. Some tobacciana collectors I know have a fascination with cigar cutters, which range from working guillotines to the cutters that have been used by cigar rollers for decades to lop off the foot end of thousands of freshly made cigars.

An assortment of antique cutters.

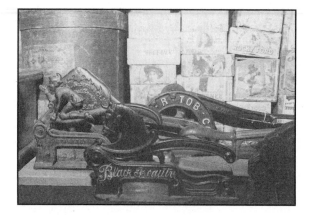

You can also collect *cheroot holders*, which you can find in almost any large antique shop. (Remember, cheroots were little cigars popular in Victorian times.) Most of these holders were made from *meerschaum* (a white mineral), have amber stems, and were delicately carved in Austria during the 1800s. They generally feature animals, hunting scenes, or pretty women: everything that appealed to Victorian men!

Cigar holders aren't very popular today, but they were considered an elegant way to smoke a cigar up until several decades ago. Rather than hold the cigar or cheroot in your mouth, the preferred method was to put this small cigar into an elaborate holder and puff away.

> **Cigar Speak**
> **Meerschaum**, German for "sea foam," is a white, calcium-based mineral mined primarily in Turkey. Soaked in water, it becomes soft and can be carved in detail. When dried and baked with a coat of beeswax, it becomes hard and looks like carved marble. It was commonly used for holding **cheroots**, or little cigars, which were very popular in the late 1800s and early 1900s.

A cigar holder, which has somewhat gone out of vogue in the past several decades.

No company manufacturers cheroot holders anymore, but the old European-carved holders pop up everywhere, which attests to how common and popular they were. The best guide you can use, without becoming a student of antique cheroot holders, is your own taste: Buy holders you think are attractive and nicely carved.

You can also find cigar holders, which are nothing more than a short mouthpiece that you attach to the head of the cigar. The holder keeps your lips from touching the cigar. Nobody uses these things anymore because, after all, the taste and feel of the wrapper in your mouth is a very enjoyable part of smoking cigars. The idea behind the cigar holder is that you don't get the tip all slobbery, but you wouldn't do that anyway, would you?

Cigar holders from the Victorian era can be interesting and attractive collectibles. Many were made from amber, a form of fossilized tree resin that's a clear or slightly cloudy orange-yellow color. It was as hard as glass and nearly as brittle, so many amber cigar holders that you'll find in antique stores will be damaged.

Other cigar holders are made from beautifully carved woods, ivory, meerschaum, or porcelain. You can sometimes find these holders in antique shops or flea markets. Many of them came in protective leather cases with velvet lining. Most were made to hold much smaller ring gauge cigars than we smoke these days, so you wouldn't want to use them. They are visually appealing, though, and a fun "find" if you enjoy collecting this type of cigar paraphernalia.

Modern Smoking Collectibles

You don't have to be an antique hound to enjoy collecting cigar-related merchandise. Capitalizing on today's cigar craze, many manufacturers are creating merchandise with cigar themes, from diamond-encrusted cufflinks in the shape of a cigar to cigar-print ties. I recently stumbled across a set of handmade martini glasses with a cigar and ashtray pictured on the base.

A lot of fun items are available that you can keep for your own private use—or wear to tell the world you enjoy a good smoke. With a little hunting, you can also find clothing designed for use while smoking. The most common item is the smoking jacket, which served the real purpose in the Victorian era of replacing the suit coat so the smell of cigars wouldn't linger on clothing.

Cigar Esoterica

Smoking jackets and caps (the classic fez) originated for a practical purpose. They were used in Victorian times because many women were highly agitated by the smell of smoke on their husbands' clothing and in their pomaded hair. When the men retired to the den for a smoke, they removed their dinner jackets, left them outside the room, and donned their smoking jackets and caps.

You can find antique smoking jackets, which are a little longer than a sports coat, full-length smoking robes, and even the occasional smoking cap, or fez. A few high-end clothiers sell elegant new smoking jackets made from velvet or silk, but be prepared to pay at least several hundred dollars for them.

You will probably not realize that you're on your way to becoming a collector until you've reached the point of no return! Take a look at what you have purchased by this point in the book. You may have a lighter, a cutter, and an ashtray. And have you forgotten the humidor you've had your eye on down at the local smoke shop?

Tobacciana provides the chance to meld a passion for collecting with a passion for cigars, which has to be the perfect combination.

The Least You Need to Know

➤ Cigar boxes, labels, bands, lighters, cutters, holders, and related items are popular collectibles.

➤ Until you learn prices for cigar collectibles, buy what you like and spend what you can justify.

➤ The best rule with collecting is not to buy because you think it's a good investment.

➤ Buy collectible cigar cutters and humidors for decoration only.

Chapter 20

Rating Your Smokes

> **In This Chapter**
>
> ➤ How cigar scoring works
>
> ➤ What to look for when describing a cigar
>
> ➤ The truth about cigar ratings
>
> ➤ How to conduct a cigar tasting like an expert

When it comes to wine, hotels, movies, restaurants, spirits, cigars, and more, we like ratings. If you're traveling, it's helpful to know whether the place you plan to stay is world-class or a haven for wayward bed bugs. A review might help you decide whether to check out a movie or restaurant or save your money.

A few years ago, nobody rated cigars. Today, everybody has an opinion! In this chapter I give you the tools you need to organize your thoughts, analyze a cigar, and keep a record. You can compare and contrast with the "authorities," as well as with your friends. Remember, though, that your own opinion is the most important decision maker.

Going by the Numbers

I use ratings all the time, for many different products and services, and I pay attention to them, too. Sometimes a rating will steer me away from something, but only if it includes pertinent details. I need to know why the reviewer did or didn't like something: what was good and what was bad. Like you, I've sometimes agreed with reviews and sometimes had a completely opposite reaction from the reviewer.

The same holds true for rating cigars. A meaningful rating has to go beyond a number and a one-sentence description, but most cigar ratings in books and magazines stop with this type of incomplete grading. While the reviewers may have detailed reasons for assigning a certain rating to a certain cigar, you're left in the dark when they don't share. Later in this chapter, I'll give you a rating sheet that will help you evaluate cigars like a pro.

Scoring Your Cigars

> **Blowing Smoke**
> A cigar is more expensive than a movie, but less than dinner at a fancy restaurant. Regardless of how the cigar is rated, don't hesitate to try at least one of any brand that strikes your fancy (and rate it). Experimenting with cigars is an affordable luxury, and even the bad ones help you learn what you like.

For years, wines have been rated on a 100-point scale. Specific attributes win *x* amount of points, from color and clarity in the glass to the length of finish (how long the taste lingers) after swallowing.

This scale has been transferred to cigars, but the factors that contribute to a final score are still pretty fuzzy. I've yet to see anyone explain exactly what attributes are considered when a cigar is rated, and how much of the score various attributes comprise. We're going to change that.

When I worked in smoke shops, I saw a lot of people select cigars based entirely on the final point tally. They started with the top-rated cigars and worked their way down. I guess that system worked for them, but with what you now know about cigars, I bet you'll want a rating and review with a little more substance. You may also want to do your own rating and analysis.

When to Forget a Rating

A cigar rating without a meaningful description is about as satisfying as experiencing a basketball game only by reading the final score in the newspaper. Most of the fun is the game: What happened to contribute to that final outcome?

I don't pay much attention to a rating accompanied only by a brief, fuzzy description of a cigar's flavor. I want to know how the wrapper looked, how even the draw was, how evenly the cigar burned, whether it became bitter or harsh tasting toward the end of the smoke—all that good stuff.

I'd also suggest that you forget the ratings of a cigar you really want to try. Just because a cigar received a bad rating from a so-called expert doesn't mean you won't love it, and vice versa. Ratings and descriptions can help you get started and give you something with which to compare your opinion, but the only real measure of whether a cigar is good is whether you enjoy it. It really doesn't matter what anyone else thinks or says.

The role that price should play in rating cigars is another hotly debated issue. Some cigar ratings are weighted for price, and I feel this system is wrong. In some publications, I've seen superior cigars receive lower ratings than lesser smokes because the top smokes were pricey.

I'm the biggest bargain hunter of all, and there's nothing more appealing to me than a great cigar that's also a good value. If I give a great cigar an "85" rating, however, but I don't tell you that I took five points off because of price, you're not getting the whole picture.

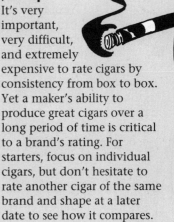

Hot Tip
It's very important, very difficult, and extremely expensive to rate cigars by consistency from box to box. Yet a maker's ability to produce great cigars over a long period of time is critical to a brand's rating. For starters, focus on individual cigars, but don't hesitate to rate another cigar of the same brand and shape at a later date to see how it compares.

As most wine writers do, I prefer to rate the cigar and then examine price, deciding whether or not it's a "best buy." Bottom line: I'd rather have one great $90 cigar than two good cigars, even if the great cigar is pricey. In my descriptive guide to cigars in Appendix A, price plays no role in my overall ratings. But I'm happy to tell you if a cigar is both a great smoke and a good deal!

So forget price-weighted ratings, or ratings that don't give you the inside information. Because I haven't seen any ratings that are this thorough, I'm telling you to do your own scoring and judge for yourself! Let's talk about what goes into describing, and then rating, your stogies.

A Funky, Earthy Taste with a Hint of Berries? NOT!

Many cigar ratings use terms like *coffee, nutmeg, cinnamon, straw,* and *leather* to describe cigars. I think these descriptors may work with wine, but they don't work for cigars. In fact, most cigar makers, and most true aficionados, refuse to apply wine-tasting descriptors to cigars.

In a wine, you can taste tobacco, oak, banana, ripe pears, and a host of other flavors. This is the nature of wine, which is basically a food product. Describing wine in this fashion works.

Tobacco Leaves
"I have never tasted cinnamon in a cigar. Neither have I tasted nutmeg, leather, fruit, or a hint of straw. Cigars taste like cigars, and they should be judged on their body, the quality and age of the tobaccos, and the consistency of construction. These are the things by which you describe a great cigar."

—A cigar company executive

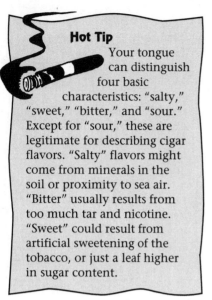

Hot Tip
Your tongue can distinguish four basic characteristics: "salty," "sweet," "bitter," and "sour." Except for "sour," these are legitimate for describing cigar flavors. "Salty" flavors might come from minerals in the soil or proximity to sea air. "Bitter" usually results from too much tar and nicotine. "Sweet" could result from artificial sweetening of the tobacco, or just a leaf higher in sugar content.

I don't find these flavors in cigars, which have such a unique flavor that they defy comparison with any food item. Looking for these tastes in cigars is tomfoolery. If you taste nutmeg or cardamom in your cigar, you have an edge over me and a lot of other cigar experts. Once in a while, you might sense cinnamon, a nuttiness, or spice, but I have failed in years of tasting to associate various herbs, spices, berries, or nuts with cigar leaf.

I'm not saying you won't, at times, taste certain things in a cigar that have a familiar resonance. Some of the fleeting flavors I've identified (some positive, some negative) are cedar, coffee, burned coffee, moist dirt, must or mold, cumin or cinnamon, nuts, and sometimes damp vegetation.

The point is, you don't need to fish around for food adjectives to describe your cigar; plenty of relevant phrases are available. Let's take a look at the truly important flavors and characteristics to concentrate on when tasting and scoring a cigar.

What You DO Taste

You experience a cigar with two basic areas: your tongue and your sinuses. Tongues are amazing instruments, designed to keep primitive humans from eating things that would kill them. Most things that taste bitter are bad for you—maybe even poisonous. Most sweet things are okay to eat. Sour is borderline (some sour things, such as lemons, are good for you), while salty things usually taste good because we need salt to survive.

Using both your tongue and your sinuses, you can detect whether a cigar is peppery or spicy from the "zing" you feel on your tongue and up into your sinus cavities. While your tongue provides very basic readings of taste, your sinuses detect the subtle variations of flavor that are difficult to describe.

How to "Taste" Your Cigar's Aroma

At some point you've probably eaten a meal while suffering from a cold and stuffy nose. Didn't taste like much, did it? Without your sinuses, your tongue can only distinguish salty, bitter, sweet, and sour tastes.

When you smoke a cigar, you detect a lot of subtle flavors as smoke escapes into your sinuses. You can maximize this capability when you taste-test cigars by allowing some of the smoke from your cigar to escape into your sinus passages without inhaling the smoke.

Getting the smoke into your sinus passages takes practice, but you'll know if you have the technique because you'll be able to blow smoke from your nose. I wish I could tell you more about this technique, but it has to be practiced and perfected, not described. When wine tasters are sampling, they draw in air while the wine is in their mouths to more fully distribute the aroma of the wine and draw it into their sinuses. Believe me, the resulting gurgling sound is a lot more unsettling than what you'll do with your cigar!

The best time to taste-test anything—coffee, wine, cigars, you name it—is in the morning. Your taste buds are awake, and you haven't had food or drink that might alter the flavor.

But, hey, this is the real world, and you're probably not going to puff a big, full-bodied Churchill at 8 a.m. So it's perfectly fine to enjoy, and test, your cigar in the appropriate setting—whether that's after dinner with a drink or at a cigar club with friends. To give the cigar every chance to be good, don't smoke it outside or in the car. The wind will affect the burn and may give you an inaccurate reading.

Hot Tip
A "blind" tasting, where you rate and compare several cigars with no bands, only numbers, is the ideal way to rate but is impossible to do alone. If you have a group, one of you might volunteer to buy a few cigars, number and hide the bands, and then reveal the brands after everyone has smoked and scored.

Okay, I've talked enough about how to taste cigars. Let's get started.

How to Describe a Cigar

Take a minute to look at the categories I've included in the blank cigar rating sheet. Feel free to copy this sheet, or the perforated version in the front of this book. (Even the publisher says its okay!)

Rather than spend a lot of time explaining all the categories and what they mean, I'll give you a quick overview of the rating sheet. Then, I'll walk you through how I conducted a cigar taste test. It'll be easier to show you than to tell you.

I've designed my rating form to take you step-by-step through the entire process. I start with where and when you bought the cigar and take you to the finish, or aftertaste, when you set the stub in your ashtray.

You'll notice that the rating sheet contains four main categories, each with a maximum number of points that add up to 100. I use a 100-point scale because it's the most common, and I also provide a letter grade in case you want to see how smart your cigar is!

The four main categories are

➤ Overall Appearance and Presentation of Cigar (20 points maximum).

➤ Lighting and Burning Properties (15 points maximum).

➤ Construction (30 points maximum).

➤ Taste (35 points maximum).

CIGAR RATING SHEET

Cigar Brand_____   Size Name_____

Length/Ring Gauge_____   Purchase Date_____

Box or Individual_____   Smoking Date_____

```
┌─────────────────────────────┐
│ Cigar Band                  │        Packaging_____
│                             │
│                             │        Price (Per Cigar or Box)_____
│                             │
│                             │        Where Purchased _____
│                             │
└─────────────────────────────┘        _____
```

Meal/Beverage _____

Overall Appearance and Presentation of Cigar_____Points (Max. 20)   **Grade**_____

Wrapper Color_____   Consistent Color within Box?_____

Oily/Dry?_____   Veiny/Smooth?_____

Cap Construction _____   Packaging_____

Ease of Cutting _____   Construction (soft, hard?)_____

Lighting and Burning Properties_____Points (Max. 15)   **Grade**_____

Even Initial Light?_____   Even Burn? Initial?_____50%?_____75%?_____

Ash (solid and white/black and crumbly?)_____ Burn rate (fast, perfect, slow?)_____

Resting Smoke (light and even/smouldering?)_____ Require Re-Lighting?_____

Construction_____Points (Max. 30)   **Grade**_____

Initial Draw?_____50%?_____75%?_____ Wrapper Stays Intact?_____

Taste_____Points (Max. 35)   **Grade**_____

Light, Medium, Full-Bodied?_____ Bitter/Harsh/Smooth?_____

Sweet/Salty?_____   Bland/Vegetal/Spicy/Peppery?_____

Describe Any Changes in Body or Flavor_____

_____

Aroma (rich and smooth/strong and acrid?)_____ Finish_____

Comments_____

_____

_____

Total Score/Grade_____

The categories and the importance I give them is my opinion. If you have a different grading scale, feel free to change the points, as long as the maximum score of the categories adds up to 100.

Prime Factors

Some factors are so important to the enjoyment of a cigar that they overwhelm everything else when it comes to rating that cigar. These factors appear in different categories on the rating sheet. And here they are:

➤ A proper *draw*, which ensures you can get proper smoke volume out of the cigar without working too hard.

➤ Properly fermented and aged tobaccos, which means you won't get sick smoking the darned thing.

➤ An even *burn rate*, which means you won't be watching one side of your cigar virtually burning up while the other side lags behind and smolders.

If any of these factors aren't present, the cigar is worthless. Deficiencies in any of these areas should lead to knocking a lot of points off your rating. That's why my cigar rating sheet puts an emphasis on these factors.

Appearance

You know that visual appeal is important, and you know what it can tell you about a cigar. It's your first clue as to what to expect when you smoke the cigar. The various aspects of appearance are worth 20 points maximum. The subcategories I've included are pretty self-explanatory, so let's move on.

Lighting and Burning

A stogie's capability to burn evenly indicates that it's well-constructed. Uneven burning is a nuisance to deal with. A cigar that burns too fast (usually because it's rolled too loosely) means the tobacco will combust at too high a temperature, releasing bitter-tasting chemicals and tar. A cigar that burns too slowly (usually because it's rolled too tightly) will force you to puff harder, overheating the tobacco. A slow-burning cigar is also more likely to go out or smolder. This important category is worth a maximum of 15 points.

Construction

This small and simple category carries a lot of weight, with a maximum 30-point score. Obviously, I put a lot of emphasis on construction. I've attempted to smoke more than my share of great-looking cigars that turned out to be worthless because they were poorly constructed. A cigar that's too loosely filled will burn too hot and, although it's still smokeable, it'll get a low grade from me.

A cigar with little or no draw rates a big, fat zero in this category. Construction and burning are allied, because a badly constructed cigar will probably burn unevenly. However, they can differ; a cigar with a relatively even burn, for example, can be too tightly rolled to draw properly.

Taste

This is by far the most subjective category, but also the most important. Here, you get the chance to decide for yourself whether you think the cigar has a taste that appeals to you. There are some specific things to look for, particularly whether you can smoke the entire cigar without it turning bitter.

As they burn down, a lot of cigars have a tar buildup that makes them turn harsh and bitter. In fact, so many cigars do this that a lot of smokers expect to abandon their cigars anywhere from half to three-quarters through the smoke. Don't accept this from a cigar.

Think of it this way: Would you be just a little bit disappointed if you opened a bottle of wine but could only drink 60 percent of it and had to throw the rest away? Of course you would. I've smoked many cigars to the nub, so I know that a really great stogie will give you a pleasurable smoke until it burns your fingers. If I have to toss a cigar before it's at least 90 percent gone because it gets bitter or harsh tasting, that cigar deserves a major point deduction.

Finally, I don't assign specific numbers to each subcategory, such as the appearance of the ash or the burn rate. You can break down your rating if you like, assigning as many points as you wish to each subcategory as long as they add up to the total for each of the four primary categories.

"Dear Diary..."

Each time you try a new cigar, or revisit a brand, take a few moments to fill out a rating sheet and compile a diary, or log, of your adventures. If you sample enough cigars, you may start to forget what you thought of a particular smoke. This way, you have a permanent record to which you can refer. You can compare your own tastings at a later date, and also compare it to others' opinions.

The best way to learn how to rate smokes is to see how someone else rates them. This section walks you through how I rated a cigar, and how I used my rating sheet to describe the experience.

To make my tasting as close as possible to the experience you might have, I picked a cigar I had never smoked before: the Fuente Fuente OpusX. This cigar is a hard-to-find, relatively new offering from a fine manufacturer.

To let you see more easily how I achieved scores for each category, I've put my individual subcategory scores in brackets. It's your option whether or not you want to use subcategories or just give an overall score.

Here goes.

CIGAR RATING SHEET

Cigar Brand ____Fuente Fuente OpusX____   Size Name _____Robusto_____

Length/Ring Gauge__5 by 50 ring__   Purchase Date __April 22, 1997__

Box or Individual _____Individual_____   Smoking Date __May 4, 1997__

Packaging __Boite Nature/cello wrap__

Price (Per Cigar or Box) US $12.50

Where Purchased CPCC International
____Cigar and Pipe Exposition____

Meal/Beverage **After light meal; smoked with Ferrand XO Cognac**

Overall Appearance and Presentation of Cigar _____20_____ Points (Max. 20)   Grade ____A+____

Wrapper Color **Colorado (4/4)**   Consistent Color within Box? **Yes (2/2)**

Oily/Dry _____**Light Sheen (2/2)**_____   Veiny/Smooth? **Flawless (5/5)**

Cap Construction ___**Excellent (1/1)**   Packaging ____**Very Good (2/2)**

Ease of Cutting **Perfect (2/2)**   Construction (soft, hard?) **Firm -- Slightly hard (2/2)**

Lighting and Burning Properties **15** Points (Max.15)   Grade ___A

Even Initial Light? **Yes (1/1)**   Even Burn? Initial? **Good**   50%? **OK**   75%? **Good (12/12)**

Ash (solid and white/black and crumbly)? **Firm; lt. gray**   Burn rate (fast, perfect, slow)? **Slow but OK (1/1)**

Resting Smoke (Light and even/smoldering)? **Light/even (1/1)**   Require Re-Lighting? **No (1/1)**

Construction ___**26**___ Points (Max. 30)   Grade _____**A-**

Initial Draw? **Good**   50%? **Tight**   75%? **Good (24/27)**

Wrapper Stays Intact? **Split Slightly at end (2/3)**

Taste **35** Points (Max.35)   Grade _____**A+**

Light, Medium, Full-Bodied? **Full-Robust**   Bitter/Harsh/Smooth? _____**Smooth**

Sweet/Salty? **N/A**   Bland/Vegetal/Spicy/Peppery? **Spice/cedar hints**

Describe Any Changes In Body or Flavor
Started medium body and built to more robust at 2 inches

Aroma (rich and smooth/Strong and acrid) **Rich**   Finish **Pleasant**

Comments
Smooth & rich; superior aged leaf throughout; overly firm draw midway diminished smoke volume slightly; large band was tough to remove. Fine smoke. Powerful, complex flavor.

Total Score/Grade   **96/100**   **A**

Appearance and Presentation

First, I jotted down everything related to buying the cigar: size, shape, length, ring gauge, and where and when I bought it. When I purchased the cigar, I compared it to the others in the box and they were identical: all similarly colored and all firmly and evenly constructed. In the cedar box, the large and colorful bands and perfectly matched wrapper leaves made a very nice presentation.

I examined the wrapper: a lovely deep reddish-brown Colorado. Fuente is growing this wrapper leaf in the Dominican Republic, and it's being hailed as one of the most successful efforts so far to grow fine wrappers in that country. In appearance, this is as fine a wrapper as you'll find.

The construction of the cigar seemed flawless, which is typical of Fuente. The cap was seamlessly applied, and the wrapper had a light oily sheen, but was more toward the dry side. I like to see more oil, but it doesn't really matter as long as the wrapper is supple and has some "give" when squeezed.

When I squeezed the cigar, it seemed a bit firmer than I like, but the others in the box were equally firm. There were no spongy spots, but I did have a slight concern about whether the cigar might be too tightly rolled. My judgment call was that it felt fine.

Typical of Fuente, each cigar was encased in a cellophane wrapper. I noted (although I didn't see a need to jot it down), that the cellophane slipped off easily. Had it been too tightly applied to the cigar, as some cello sleeves are (I've never had this problem with a Fuente), I might have had to tug it off and risk tearing the wrapper leaf. Should this have happened, I would have noted it in the comment section.

So, with the exception of the slightly firm construction of the smoke, the appearance and presentation was perfect. Some smokers might take a point off for the cellophane wrappers, because they don't look as stunning in the box as unwrapped cigars. I don't. I gave appearance and presentation 20 out of 20 points, or a solid "A."

Before I began to smoke, I noted when I was smoking it, and what meal came before it. In this case, I had a light stir-fry meal, cleared my palate with some water, and settled down with one of my favorite cognacs. Of course, if you aren't sitting around with pen and rating sheet in hand, you can write notes later from memory. It's best, however, to rate immediately, while the experience is fresh.

Lighting and Burning Properties

Time to fire up! A critical part of enjoying a cigar is how well the cigar burns. As we've discussed, a cigar that doesn't burn evenly is frustrating to smoke. It may also be a sign of poor bunching of the filler tobaccos (remember those bunchers in the factory from Chapter 9?) and uneven aging of the leaf. So in my guide, burning characteristics are worth 15 percent of the total score.

I examine how quickly and evenly the cigar lights when I char the tip, or foot, with my flame. (I'm assuming, of course, that your cigar has been properly humidified before you smoke it. If the stogie's too dry or too moist because you haven't given it the right climate, you can't fault the cigar.) The Fuente Fuente OpusX lit perfectly and evenly.

If you don't have a companion to help you judge aroma, this is the best time to judge for yourself. As the tip begins to give off smoke, use your hand to fan a bit of the smoke to your nose; your ability to really smell a cigar becomes blunted once you start smoking. Why? Beats me, but it's true. You'll be able to smell it, of course, but you want to know how the cigar smells to others around you who aren't smoking. You lose this chance once you start puffing.

The best way to judge aroma is to have someone else smoke the cigar while you smell it. I don't think you want to go to this extreme, do you? But if you're alone and don't have others around you to ask, lightly fanning the smoke toward your nose is the best you can do. If others are with you, you can ask them for opinions on whether the aroma is pleasing.

The rating sheet leaves room for you to grade how even the burn is in the beginning, halfway through, and near the end of your smoking experience. A cigar can start off uneven but settle down into a nice even ring after an inch or so. The cigar can also begin evenly, and then start to degrade.

Ideally, the burn should be perfect at all stages. My Fuente Fuente OpusX started off perfect and even, leaving a firm, light gray ash (also noted). This cigar ash easily reached almost an inch before needing to be gently tapped off the cigar.

Midway through the cigar, the tip began to burn somewhat unevenly, but it wasn't a problem. The cigar then settled back into a perfect and even burn all the way to the end. No points deducted for its burn.

As it rested in the ashtray, the cigar gave off a very light plume of gray smoke. If it had been too loosely rolled, or the filler had been unevenly bunched, it might have smoldered or burned too quickly. The lighting characteristics and burn rate were ideal, so I gave it 15 out of 15 points or an "A" grade.

Construction

This category has few variables, but it carries a lot of weight in my rating. It was here that the Fuente Fuente OpusX showed its only weakness.

The cigar started with a nice draw. The draw became a little too tight halfway through the cigar; perhaps as the tobacco heated up, the filler expanded a bit. This slightly difficult draw, which wasn't enough of a problem to lower my score significantly, was the cigar's only flaw, and I noted it in my comments. The firm draw led me to give the cigar 26 out of a maximum 30 points, or an "A" grade.

Taste

This category has the heaviest weighting, accounting for 35 percent of the total score, but it also contains some of the most complex and difficult-to-describe stogie attributes. This category is also very personal because it deals with your *opinion* of how the cigar tastes. I can smoke a cigar I hate, but I can give it a top rating for construction and appearance if it meets my criteria. I will, however, downgrade such a cigar based on taste.

How do I grade for taste? Generally, I jot down a few notes about taste while I smoke, and add different notes as I taste different things. I like to wait until a cigar is nearly finished before jotting down my final comments about taste, because a cigar's characteristics can change as you smoke. If you like, you might use one rating sheet as a "scratch" copy, and then transpose your final comments to a fresh sheet and to put into your cigar-tasting diary.

As you know, I don't believe in trying to draw parallels between cigars and nuts, fruits, or spices, but you have room in the comments section to note any flavors you detect. I do include some basic descriptions in this section that might help guide you.

The Fuente Fuente OpusX was full bodied, which is no surprise because the Fuentes like to blend heavier-tasting cigars in the Cuban style. Even though the cigar was "heavy," it was very smooth. This taste reflects the thorough fermenting and several-year aging process the tobaccos used in the Fuente Fuente OpusX receive, and I made an appropriate note in the comments section.

Hot Tip

The aftertaste of a *good* cigar will dissipate quickly. The smell won't linger in your curtains or furniture, either. Remember from Chapter 15 how improperly fermented tobacco will still contain traces of ammonia, which cause most of the stench in a bad cigar? If you're testing at home, a good way to test the quality of the cigar is to smoke it in a well-ventilated room and see whether the smell virtually disappears within two hours.

From the first puff to the final stub, the cigar had no trace of harshness or bitterness that would point to insufficient fermentation or aging. Saltiness or sweetness wasn't an issue. Likewise, there was no buildup of dark, bitter tar at the head of the cigar as it neared the finish line—another sign that the tobaccos were perfectly aged.

The cigar was spicy with a bit of pepper, characteristic of the Cuban style. There was no vegetal quality, once again pointing to superior tobaccos that had been sufficiently aged. The cigar did have a hint of cedar, typical of Fuente cigars because they're well-aged in cedar-lined rooms. I noted this flavor in my comments.

I did notice that the cigar started off a bit mild, and then built intensity and increased in body after an inch or so. This characteristic is great in a robusto, which ideally eases you into the smoke and then delivers a lot of flavor in a relatively short time. The change in intensity probably indicates that a slightly lighter filler blend was placed at the foot of the cigar, and heavier tobaccos were used in the remainder of the filler.

As I lay the half-inch stub in the ashtray, my mouth had only the slightest taste of cigar. A bad cigar will leave a sour and bitter aftertaste for up to an hour. The aftertaste of this cigar disappeared quickly. My judgment call was that the taste rated 35 out of a possible 35 points, or yet another "A+."

Comments and Final Scoring

Other than the construction, the Fuente Fuente OpusX was nearly perfect. I loved the luxurious band, but it was glued very firmly and did not readily peel off even as the ash neared the band and warmed the glue. I had to pick off the band carefully, which was a nuisance—but not enough of a nuisance to affect the score. In Chapter 21, I talk more about this little strip of paper, and why it's so important.

A bit of excess glue from the band had oozed onto on the wrapper, creating a very slight tear. Because it had no effect on the smoke, I didn't downgrade for this, but it was a close call. Usually, if I'm having real problems removing a cigar band, I'll leave it on until the very end of the smoke. In this case, the band was so large that I had to remove it to finish the cigar.

The four categories added up to a final score of 96, which is outstanding. I added up the letter grades from each category and gave them a loose weighting, earning the cigar experience an "A."

I never like to rate a brand or line of cigars based on just one cigar, and this Fuente Fuente OpusX provides a perfect example of why. I know the quality and consistency of Fuente cigars is very high, and all cigars are carefully inspected and hand-selected. After this first experience with the Fuente Fuente OpusX, I smoked others of the same line and found the construction to be perfect. You'll notice that in my descriptive guide (in Appendix A), I upgraded my score for the line to a 98.

The same make, type, and year of wine doesn't vary from bottle to bottle because it all comes from the same batch of grapes. The only exception is a very old bottle of wine, which may have improved with age, or turned musty or sour compared with another bottle sampled years earlier.

Each cigar, however, is individual. If you dislike a cigar and try another and it displays the same negative qualities, don't torture yourself by smoking more of them. That brand will probably not measure up, and you should move on. If the cigar you first sample has a few flaws but you like it, keep taste testing.

Blowing Smoke
Even the best makers occasionally turn out a cigar that's not quite perfect—that's the nature of a handmade product. I suggest that you rate several cigars from one line before making your final conclusions about a brand.

The Least You Need to Know

➤ The cigars of most brands taste the same and feature the same construction, regardless of size.

➤ Over time, rate several cigars from the same manufacturer so that you can draw more accurate final conclusions about the quality and consistency of a particular brand.

➤ To build your expertise and knowledge of cigars, keep a diary of the cigars you've smoked and rated.

➤ A "blind tasting" is the most accurate way to rate cigars, but you'll need a least one other person to help you conduct one.

Part 5
Eat, Drink (Smoke), and Be Merry

Many things enhance the pleasure of a cigar and complement your enjoyment. In Part 5, we'll explore some of the activities and issues that swirl around cigars and smoking. We'll take a look at cigar etiquette—everything from when to remove your cigar's band to how to deal with that bar patron who orders you to extinguish your stogie.

Health and smoking is a hot issue, so we'll look at some of the topics related to cigar smoking. We'll talk about how cigars, beverages, and food go together, and which foods and drinks are best with cigars.

To close our cigar adventure, I'll tell you a little about the cigar's first cousin, the pipe. You might enjoy this as a change of pace, and also in seeing the similarities between pipes and cigars. We'll also take a quick tour of what's been said, and who said what, about one of literature's most popular topics: tobacco.

Mind Your Manners

I'll open this chapter by repeating what I said when we first started: Unless you smoke alone, you're asking other people to share and enjoy, or at least accept, your pastime. There's no sense in getting all strung out about cigar etiquette, and I'm sure not going to lecture you about the do's and don'ts of smoking around others.

I would, however, like to share some tricks with you that could make your cigar-smoking experiences more pleasant for you and those around you. Interested? Let's go!

You Can't Tell the Brand Without a Band

I haven't talked much about cigar bands in this book, and for good reason. How much is there to say about a decorative strip of paper wrapped around your cigar? So it has always amazed me that the cigar band gives rise to one of the great debates of cigar etiquette: Do you take it off or leave it on? And if you leave it on, why do you leave it on and when do you take it off?

The most common notion is that a cigar band is placed near the head of a cigar, leaving enough room for you to place the cigar in your mouth without touching the paper. Rumor has it that you should smoke the cigar down to the band, which is a signal that it's time to discard your stogie.

These principles are pretty good, but they don't work. I recently had a Cuban Montecristo No. 2 (a pyramid) where the skinny brown Montecristo band with white lettering was placed too close to the tip for me to smoke without touching. Besides, it slipped right off the pointed cigar head!

I also had a Fuente Fuente OpusX robusto with a luxurious band that was so wide I would have had to discard nearly half the cigar if I had stopped smoking when I reached the top of the band. Bye-bye band; I'm smoking this stogie to the nub!

If I'm smoking a really good cigar, I find I can usually enjoy it far longer than the band would allow me, so I remove band and keep on smoking. A few cigars, such as the Juan Clemente Dominican, place the band at the foot of the cigar. In that case, you have to remove the band to light the cigar. I don't suggest you use the band as a guide to quit puffing!

Some smokers say you're being a show-off if you leave the band on—especially if you're smoking a super-premium stogie that everyone around you covets. If you're concerned with perceived snob factor, take off the band before you start smoking. Frankly, I don't worry about what other people think about what I'm smoking.

Here's how I like to deal with cigar bands. Unless they're too close to the head, I leave them on. I enjoy how an attractive band dresses up a cigar. There's also a practical reason for leaving the band on your cigar until the burning tip draws close: Most cigar bands fit pretty snug around a cigar. Consequently, unless the cigar has dried out and shrunk, you usually can't slip off the band without damaging the wrapper.

Bands are also glued where the two ends meet. Some makers use only a light dab of glue, and in that case you can easily peel off the band. However, many cigar makers use a big dollop of glue, and the only way to remove the band before you light the cigar is to pick at it and tear it off.

If any glue got on the wrapper, you'll risk tearing the wrapper. And as you try to pick off the band, you might rip the wrapper with your fingernail. So why bother? A simpler solution is to smoke the cigar with the band on. As the burning tip gets closer to the band, it usually heats the glue so that you can gently peel off the band. Warm glue is less likely to tear the wrapper.

Besides, with this method, you have a perfectly preserved band you can paste onto your cigar-rating sheet (see Chapter 20) instead of a torn and ratty-looking piece of paper. There, we've just solved the great cigar-band debate. That was easy!

Burning Up

A lot of things can go wrong when you smoke a cigar. Even when you do things right and enjoy a cigar to the very end, your smoldering cigar butt is still a vile-smelling secret weapon. So let's take a minute to look at all the things that happen (or could happen) when you smoke a cigar.

A Study in Shrunken Ashtrays

If you're smoking indoors, make sure you have an ashtray, and make sure that it's big enough to hold the ash from your cigar. Before you light up, size up your ashtray and try to imagine whether your cigar, all chopped up into small pieces, would fit into it. If not, get a bigger ashtray; you don't want ash spilling over the edges.

You also want the ashtray large enough to hold your cigar and still give you enough room to rest the stogie without it touching the ash. If you're stuck with one of those tiny restaurant cigarette ashtrays, you have no choice but to hold the cigar. Try to get a helpful waiter to empty your ashtray part way through your smoke and replace it with a fresh one.

What happens if the ashtray is too small or you don't have one—assuming it's okay to smoke, of course? All I can say is that you gauge your surroundings before you turn that coffee cup, dessert plate, or saucer into an ashtray. The best solution is to ask for one.

The Attack of Old Cigar Butt

I mentioned this briefly in Chapter 1: Cigar butts smell bad. Even the finest cigar, once smoked, should be tossed as soon as possible after the stub has gone out. The chemical elements in a cigar—mostly the nicotine and tar—begin to smell acrid within an hour after being extinguished.

Toss the cold stub and ashes into a covered trash can, flush them, or fling them in the flower bed where they will decompose and feed the roses. If you're in a restaurant and you're going to stay awhile, have the waiter haul away the rubble of your victorious cigar conquest.

Never, ever crush out your cigar stub. Not only does it intensify the acrid scent, it makes the butt smolder and send off an evil-smelling smoke until it mercifully goes out. I'm sure a chemist knows why all this happens, but it's enough to know that you shouldn't do it. Simply let the stub expire in the ashtray, and then dispose of the stub and ashes as soon as possible.

Treatment for the Unfinished Cigar

Once in a while, despite your best plans, you'll have to abandon your cigar before it's finished. Perhaps you're strolling and window shopping and your spouse wants you to go into a store. Maybe that half-time intermission wasn't as long as you expected, or your meal came before you finished your before-dinner smoke.

Whatever the reason, if you're like me, you hate to give up on a perfectly good stogie. Of course, you can toss it. If you'd rather try to save it, however, and you're just popping into a store for a moment, you might be able to find a window ledge on which it can rest momentarily.

Another alternative is a device with the trade name "Cigar Savor." It's a tube that contains a spring-loaded platform. You put your partially finished cigar in the Cigar Savor and close the cap. The metal platform extinguishes your cigar without making it smolder, and you can re-light the smoke a few hours later without the bitter taste usually associated with re-lighting an extinguished cigar. It's a nifty alternative to tossing your smoke.

The Case of the Smoldering Stogie

Sometimes, a poorly rolled cigar will begin to smolder—especially as you near the end of your smoke. Instead of giving off a fine gray plume, it'll start smoking on its own like an autumn bonfire.

The cigar is burning badly, most likely because the filler is too tightly rolled or has become too soggy as the heat from smoking vaporizes the moisture in the leaf. Sadly, you can't salvage this cigar. Place it in your ashtray and hope it dies as quickly as possible before those around start giving you dirty looks.

The Lopsided Patient

One of the most common problems with cigars is an uneven burn. Ideally, your cigar will burn in a perfect, even ring—one sign of a well-constructed cigar. But even among the best brands, you'll occasionally find a cigar that starts to burn more quickly down one side.

This usually happens when there's a spongy spot in your cigar, which signals that the filler wasn't bunched properly. The properly filled side will burn at a leisurely pace, while the looser tobaccos on the spongy spot burn faster because they're getting more oxygen.

See why it's so important to check your cigars for spongy spots before you buy? I'm sure you knew that I had my reasons. I could have explained it to you sooner, but the explanation means a lot more now that you know how a fine cigar is constructed.

If you keep smoking a cigar like this, you'll have a stogie with a black, smoldering scar down one side, while the other side may have a strip of binder and wrapper an inch or more long. Believe me, this burn is messy and even a little dangerous. Sometimes, the hanging end will catch fire, and the piece of wrapper will drop off onto your clothes or favorite chair. In addition, the unevenly burning cigar looks bad and is difficult to smoke.

But wait, there's hope! You may be able to correct this problem and salvage your smoke. As soon as the cigar begins to burn unevenly, set your cigar on the edge of the ashtray and allow it to go out.

When it has stopped smoking, tap off as much ash as possible. Holding the cigar over the ashtray, use your lighter flame to ignite the lopsided, unburned portion. It will probably catch fire, and you should remove the flame immediately because you don't want to roast your cigar. The fire will go out quickly when you remove direct flame from it, and the cigar should burn lightly.

Let this section burn and smoke for a minute; then tap off any ash. You might even hasten the process by gently rubbing the unburned section against the wall of your ashtray. Keep doing this until the tip of the cigar is even. Gently knock off all the ash you can and re-light. The cigar might only have one spongy spot, which you've now by-passed. If so, the rest of the cigar will be okay.

If you buy a brand that keeps burning this way, stop buying it. The maker's rollers obviously don't know how to bunch filler tobaccos properly.

The Split-Wrapper Syndrome

Last but not least, we confront the wounded cigar with a peeling wrapper. Wrappers usually start to peel for two reasons: they were not properly applied at the factory, or the cigar has become dry and the wrapper doesn't have enough elasticity to cling to the binder.

Unraveling wrappers is the most common problem with all cigars. The problem *shouldn't* happen to a premium cigar, but it sometimes does.

If the wrapper starts to peel near the head (usually because you've loosened it when you clipped the head), you may be able to make it behave by discreetly giving it a light moistening with your tongue. There's no need to plunge the cigar into your mouth and soak the whole thing. If the wrapper's salvageable, a couple licks will help hold it in place. You may have to repeat this step a couple of times during your smoke.

If the wrapper starts peeling from the lit end, or continues to unravel despite your moistening, you have two choices: let the cigar go out and toss it, or remove the wrapper. Personally, if it's a tasty cigar, I'll carefully peel off the wrapper, break it into small pieces, and place the pieces in the ashtray.

If you try to smoke a cigar with a peeling wrapper, chances are good that the thin wrapper leaf will catch fire and bits will drop off onto places you don't want burning. A cigar with an exposed binder is not a beautiful thing, but sometimes you gotta do what you gotta do. Remember that the wrapper is mainly a decorative accent, so you'll still enjoy most of your cigar's flavor without it.

"Put Out That Smelly Cigar!"

Bar Patron (disgustedly): "Excuse me, but I find the smell of cigars to be very offensive. I wish you would put it out."

239

Me (smugly): "I'd be happy to, sir, except that you'll notice it isn't lit."

I really had this exchange over my cigar, and countless friends have told me of similar experiences. Some people have a pathological reaction to a cigar, expecting the worst. To be sure, a bad-smelling "el Ropo" filled with ammonia will turn anyone's stomach. Sometimes, that's the only experience with cigars a person has had.

> ### Cigar Esoterica
>
> King James I of England tiraded in 1604: "Is it not both great vanity and uncleanliness, that at the table, men should not be ashamed to sit... making the filthy smoke and stink,...and infect the aire, when very often, men that abhorre it are at their repast?" The next year, he figured he'd make some money for the crown, and levied a big tax on tobacco.

More than a few times, I've asked non-smoking friends to bear with me while I lit up a really good cigar, offering to extinguish it if they found the smell offensive. Generally, their reaction to my cigar has been, "Gee, that doesn't smell bad at all." I keep smoking and take the opportunity to explain why some cigars stink.

Some people, however, find all cigar smoke offensive. Others are legitimately allergic to smoke. Then, of course, there are those who have a somewhat irrational reaction to cigars—like the bar patron who started complaining before I'd even lit up. Some folks have assigned themselves as part of the "smoke police," and just enjoy confronting smokers of all types.

Part of cigar etiquette is being sensitive to those around you as well as to the circumstances. I'm not a combative person, and I won't smoke a cigar in a place where smoking is prohibited—whether or not I agree with that prohibition. Your own judgment is your best guide, but you might find these pointers helpful:

➤ Unless you like a confrontation and are prepared to be kicked out, don't light up a cigar in a restaurant that doesn't allow cigar smoking. To some degree, I can see why restaurants prohibit smoking: The smell of a hearty robusto doesn't sit well if you're eating a raspberry tart. Also, just because you smoke a good cigar doesn't mean the person next to you is smoking a nice-smelling, handmade, premium stogie.

   You'll find that more and more restaurants are cigar-friendly, or at least offer "cigar nights" where smokers can come in and puff away to their hearts' content.

➤ If I'm enjoying a cigar in a place that allows cigar smoking and someone asks me (or orders me) to put out my cigar, I'll quietly and politely note that they are in a smoking section and suggest that they find another seat. I won't put out a cigar if I'm smoking someplace where it's okay.

➤ Some people will tell you to put out your cigar even if you're smoking outside. I tell them it's outdoors, and I have the right to smoke and they have the right to leave. I must say, I don't understand why most open-air sports stadiums will no longer allow you to smoke cigars. Most cigar smokers I know have been careful to adjust their puffing if they see that smoke is wafting directly into the faces of their neighbors.

Still, most parks are now heavily patrolled and you will be asked to put out your cigar or go to the smoking area, which is usually in front of a greasy nacho stand and behind a post. A baseball or football game just isn't the same without a good cigar. I guess that's why I don't go to as many as I used to.

Of course, you always have your "sneaky smoke" cigarillo option in restaurants or bars that allow cigarettes but not full-blown cigars. When and where you smoke cigars, or cigarillos, is a judgment call. A lot depends on your personal taste for propriety versus confrontation!

The main thing to remember is that cigar smoking should be enjoyable for you, and your experience will be much more pleasant if you smoke in a place, and at a time, where you are free to do so without interruption or complaint.

Smoking on the Home Front

Smoking in the house or around loved ones deserves a section of its own. This is a very gray area with no right or wrong answers. If family members don't object to your cigar smoking in the house, you don't have a problem. I suggest sticking to the better-ventilated rooms just to be on the safe side.

To me, there's nothing better than hanging out with the family, sipping a good drink, and smoking my cigar by a roaring fire. Well, maybe smoking on the porch on a Saturday with the morning sun hitting my face. Then again, puffing in my office while I cruise the Internet is pretty cool. Personally, I cherish being able to smoke at home.

Usually, cigar smoking at home involves some negotiation with family members. Maybe it's no cigars before noon or no puffing in the bedroom. In many cases, you can arrange a compromise that works for everyone.

If your smoking bothers family members, either for health reasons such as allergies or asthma, or simply because someone objects to the smell, you have some alternatives.

The Smoking Den

Having a special room reserved for cigar smoking is a classic solution to cigar smoking in the home. Of course, you need enough room at home to set up a special office or den that's all yours.

Some of my friends have set up rooms that are mostly for their personal use, which provides a place where they can smoke cigars. It's a great excuse to establish an office, or just a reading or television room filled with your favorite cigar artifacts.

Banished to the Dungeon

Some cigar smokers must take their smokes to the basement or the garage. If you are in this situation, or are prohibited from smoking anywhere at home, I suppose you just have to make the best of it. Look around for cigar bars, cigar clubs, and cigar-friendly restaurants where you can go alone or with friends.

Many smoke shops have seating areas where you can smoke in comfort, enjoy some good conversation, and pick up a tip or two. Cigars and pipes are important enough to me that I would never give up the option of smoking in my home. But everyone's circumstances are different, which is why no one but you can make these decisions.

When Kids Are Involved

A lot of people choose not to smoke cigars around young children, either for health reasons or because they don't want to do anything that might encourage children to smoke.

You have to handle the etiquette of smoking around kids in the way you think is appropriate. It's worthwhile to make a careful, considered decision.

The Least You Need to Know

➤ It's easiest to remove the cigar band after you've smoked for awhile so that the cigar's heat can soften the glue used to apply the band.

➤ Promptly dispose of cigar stubs and ash.

➤ Sometimes, you can "fix" a badly behaving cigar.

➤ Being considerate of others' concerns about where and when you smoke is a better approach than defiance or confrontation.

Chapter 22

A Votre Sante: To Your Health

In This Chapter

➤ Enjoying cigars in moderation

➤ Facts and fiction about smoking

➤ The lack of scientific information on moderate smoking

Unless you've been residing on another planet, you're aware of the worldwide concern about smoking and health. For most of us, this issue appears to have gained momentum in the early 1980s. In fact, if you study the history of tobacco, you'll discover that smoking and health has been the topic of debate for centuries.

Smoking of any kind is a very personal decision, and there are risks from over-indulgence. I'm not a doctor, nor am I an authority on health. Like many of my friends and cigar-smoking colleagues, I've made a decision to enjoy cigars, despite the fact that it might be healthier not to. It would also probably be safer not to drink, drive a car, or fly in airplanes.

Risk comes with living, and if there's only one point you take away from this chapter, I'd like it to be that you're probably a lot better off if you enjoy cigars moderately—just as you would use caution with alcoholic beverages.

I'm not going to focus on all the studies and test results; you can surf the Internet or visit the library to get details. What I'd like to do is take a look at what's being said about the use of and possible effects of tobacco—specifically cigars.

Enjoy in Moderation

I'm stating the obvious when I say that excessive use of tobacco greatly increases certain health risks. I'd like to offer a concept, however, that often seems to get lost in the great tobacco debate: Excessive use of almost any substance leads to health risks.

Blowing Smoke
Smoking has been given a broad-brush treatment by many health authorities and anti-tobacco advocates. Saying that smoking three or four premium cigars a week is the same as smoking two packs of cigarettes a day is like saying there's no difference between consuming a daily glass of wine and a daily fifth of vodka. There are many ways to use tobacco.

Moderate non-inhaled cigar smoking (and "moderate" is generally considered less than five cigars a week) is probably no more harmful than many of the other everyday risks we take, such as a glass or two of wine with dinner, or eating a rich, heavy meal once in a while, and so on. Many doctors disagree with me, and believe that any and all smoking is dangerous. Other doctors agree with me—I know this because we sit next to each other at cigar dinners!

There are many differing opinions about how much smoke is too much. What I'm saying is that by enjoying tobacco—and many other products, for that matter—in *moderation*, you have a better chance of minimizing any possible health risks.

I've never seen a scientific study that discusses how much nicotine is absorbed through non-inhaled cigar smoking, as opposed to, for example, inhaled cigarette smoking. The few studies done of cigar smokers generally seem to point to moderate cigar smoking as relatively innocuous.

I can't stress this concept of moderate use heavily enough, and the enjoyment of premium cigars really lends itself to moderation for several reasons:

➤ A premium cigar is a special treat to be savored, and anything you constantly consume ceases to be a special treat. I've known a couple of cigar chain-smokers, but they're a rare breed.

➤ The cost of fine cigars makes it relatively prohibitive for all but the very wealthy to consider smoking more than one a day.

➤ Getting the fullest enjoyment from your cigar means not inhaling, which greatly minimizes the amount of smoke, tar, and nicotine that enters your lungs.

➤ Unlike most cigarettes, which have paper and tobacco known to contain a lot of potentially dangerous additives and fillers, premium cigars are an all-natural product. If pesticides are applied at all, they're administered to tobacco crops early in the growing cycle; most pesticides dissipate before the leaves are picked, or they are released during the curing and fermenting processes.

➤ Hedge your bets by being healthy. A number of studies have shown that good diet and exercise is good for everyone, but especially helpful for smokers. They note that it's particularly important to watch your weight, eat veggies and fiber, and take extra vitamin C, which smoking seems to draw out of the system. It's always a good idea to exercise and see a doctor for regular checkups.

Although I can't say I've ever seen these signs in someone who's a moderate cigar smoker, you should certainly get checked out by a doctor (or cut back your smoking) if you:

➤ Have difficulty breathing (you shouldn't have trouble if you're not inhaling) or experiencing shortness of breath

➤ Cough a lot

➤ Feel like you need a nicotine "buzz" from a cigar

➤ Notice any lesions or sore spots in your mouth, which may or may not be related to smoking, but could be irritated by smoke and definitely should be checked out

Your doctor will most likely tell you to stop smoking. That's a very safe thing to say these days. Many doctors will implore you to quit cigarettes, but accept reluctantly the fact that you enjoy an occasional cigar. Of course, you are probably better off if you don't smoke. You have to decide for yourself.

This is a fun book, so if you want, you can skip to the next chapter as long as you remember that *moderation*—and in my book that means a cigar a day or less and no inhaling—is your best bet for the reasonably safe enjoyment of cigars. If you're intrigued by the whole health and smoking issue, however, read on and see if I give you any food for thought.

I won't tell you that smoking tobacco is *good* for you. The fact is, we really don't know how cigars affect our health. Very few scientific studies have looked specifically at the health effects of moderate cigar consumption.

Why Cigarettes and Cigars Are Different

I have many cigarette-smoking friends, and I can see the difference between needing a cigarette and feeling like having a cigar. Nicotine is addictive, and getting it into the bloodstream by inhaling is a potent way to introduce nicotine into the system.

When you smoke a cigar, nicotine does get into the bloodstream through the soft tissues of the mouth and sinus cavities. It's stating the obvious to note that less gets into your system this way, than through the lungs.

So, yes, non-inhaled cigar smoking is a risk. There seems to be general agreement that it's less of a risk than inhaled cigarette smoking of any kind. Your

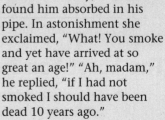

Tobacco Leaves
A lady, one evening, calling on Guizot, a famous French historian of the 18th century, found him absorbed in his pipe. In astonishment she exclaimed, "What! You smoke and yet have arrived at so great an age!" "Ah, madam," he replied, "if I had not smoked I should have been dead 10 years ago."

personal comfort with smoking and health is the key issue. If you feel that you need more information to make an informed decision, then by all means, you should talk with doctors, and read any scientific study you can find, until you reach a comfort level. Only you can make the final decision.

The Answer, Please

There are definitive answers about cigar smoking, but it all depends on who and what you believe. This is still a hotly debated issue, and while the final chapter on heavy, inhaled smoking has probably been written (it's bad for you!), there are still many questions about light to moderate enjoyment of tobacco. What you do is a very personal choice.

> **Blowing Smoke**
> If you know anything about the insurance industry, you know its business is measuring risk and insuring against it. If there's a valid statistic out there, the industry has it. Many, if not most, insurance companies offer pipe and cigar smokers (regardless of how much they smoke) the same health insurance rates as non-smokers, although many charge higher rates for cigarette smokers.

The issue of tobacco and health is clouded, so to speak, by the role that tobacco taxes play in funding government. We cigar smokers pay hefty federal, state, county, and local taxes on our stogies. These taxes help keep politicians' constituents happy, and while many governmental bodies condemn smoking, they readily accept the income it generates.

Of course, Native Americans never taxed tobacco, but ever since Europeans figured out that this simple pleasure could generate revenue, taxes and tobacco have gone hand-in-hand. Although taxes aren't a health issue, they do illustrate the ambivalence governments have historically had about tobacco.

Today, the general government posture is that tobacco is unhealthy. In the past, governments have banned tobacco as evil, vile, and a tool of the devil (maybe because it involved smoke—dangerously close to hellfire and brimstone). Yet the fact that people enjoy smoking and the significant revenue generated by tobacco growing and taxation have caused most governments to take a schizophrenic approach to tobacco. Things aren't much different today!

Cigar-tobacco growing and cigar production doesn't generate much revenue in the United States, but the consumption of cigars does produce a healthy amount of tax revenue. This all makes the issue of cigar smoking and health cloudier than a banquet room at a cigar dinner! I don't expect any answers soon, so I'm going to continue to sit back, relax, and enjoy my cigars in moderation.

The Least You Need to Know

➤ Taking extra vitamin C, eating healthy foods, and exercising are particularly important if you are a cigar smoker.

➤ Enjoy premium cigars in moderation: no more than one cigar per day.

Chapter 23

A Loaf of Bread, a Jug of Wine, and Cigars

In This Chapter

➤ Food and meals that go with cigars

➤ The best time for smoking a cigar

➤ Classic and unusual beverages to drink with cigars

➤ How to plan a "cigar dinner"

My chapter on smoking and health used the French term *a votre sante*, which means "to your health." While it was an appropriate title, this phrase is most commonly used as a toast. So what better way to start off a chapter on different ways for you and your cigar to eat, drink, and be merry?

"Peppered" or "sprinkled" throughout this chapter are four cigar dinner menus I've created that might give you some dinner ideas, along with a brief explanation of the dishes, the cigar selections, and why I've put the two together. If you can't find any of the cigars I've named, use my descriptive guide in Appendix A to find something similar. And if you're intrigued by any of the dishes, you're on your own to find them in a cookbook, or to find a chef to prepare them for you!

After-Meal Smokes

You can smoke a cigar any time of the day. I enjoy a good Saturday-morning smoke as much as a hearty after-dinner cigar. As a rule, smoke lighter cigars earlier in the day and progress to more full-bodied smokes as the day wears on.

Hot Tip
Match the style of your cigar (mild, medium, or full-bodied) to the lightness or heaviness of your meal. In general, that means you'll smoke milder cigars after breakfast, a medium cigar after lunch, and a heavier cigar after dinner. Those are the guidelines, but there are lots of exceptions.

It's quite acceptable to follow a meal—breakfast, lunch, or dinner—with a cigar. A cigar is generally more enjoyable on a full stomach, and having a little food helps ensure that you don't get queasy from your smoke. (Even though you don't inhale cigar smoke, some of the nicotine gets into your bloodstream through your mouth, tongue, and nasal passages.)

I don't get too hung up on what size or style of cigar to smoke after a certain meal. For the most part, it's best to smoke the cigar you feel like smoking! If I eat a heavy dinner and I feel like smoking a mild cigar, that's what I'll smoke. If I eat a light breakfast and feel like a full-bodied double corona (and I have time to enjoy it), I'm going to... Well, you get the idea.

Whatever meal you cap off with a stogie, the key is allowing enough time to savor and complete your cigar. It's tougher to take time to finish a smoke after breakfast or lunch because you're probably going someplace after your meal. If you have a relaxing day planned, with no particular agenda, feel free to enjoy as large a cigar as you like.

The Cigar as a Dinner Companion

Hot Tip
Save larger cigars for after dinner and concentrate on smaller smokes such as the demi-tasse, petit corona, or robusto before your meal. Leave plenty of time to finish your cigar before you sit down to eat. If you have to nibble while you smoke, stick with light, simple foods that don't conflict with your cigar's flavor: smoked almonds, proscuitto (dried ham), or grapes, for example.

I don't know whether you've ever attended, or even heard of, a "cigar dinner," but these are usually events where people eat a good meal and get a bunch of cigars. They can be anywhere from casual to black tie, and they're usually not cheap.

As the final meal of the day, dinner generally gives you the chance to work on a larger cigar such as a double corona or presidente. After dinner is also the most appropriate time to accompany a smoke with a classic drink such as single-malt Scotch or brandy.

I have some definite ideas about what does and doesn't work when matching cigars to dinner meals. As a rule, cigars are best saved for after the meal. If you're feeling excessive, a short before-dinner smoke such as a robusto or even a cigarillo might be a good choice with a drink. I could even stretch to include a mid-meal cigar break, but three cigars is the limit.

Imagine that at a seven-wine-course dinner, you personally had to drink an entire bottle of wine with each course. If you weren't miserable, you'd sure be reeling. That's what having one cigar per course is like. Plus, most handmade smokes take at least a half-hour to finish, and that's a long time to wait between courses.

In addition, your palate quickly experiences sensory overload. You've got food, wine, and a cigar—and then a different-tasting food, wine, and cigar. Your mouth begins to lose any sensitivity to taste.

If you want to smoke a cigar before dinner, or take a cigar break in the middle of your meal, do your best to order something that will clear your palate before you begin smoking. The best choice is a fruit sherbet or sorbet, lightly sweetened or unsweetened. You can also clear your palate with a wine or spirit.

The Classic Meal

My first cigar dinner menu represents the classic rich and heavy meal that is the perfect prelude to a cigar. To turn this menu into a three-cigar dinner, I started with a mixed drink using a heavy, sweet liqueur to lubricate your palate, accompanied by a mild Davidoff 2000 petit corona.

I prefer short smokes before and during dinner, so the after-salad course would include a medium-bodied Fonseca petit corona. After a rich, heavy meal and rich yet delicate soufflé for dessert, the perfect finish is a large, full-bodied cigar such as a PG Belicoso, along with a full-bodied spirit.

CIGAR DINNER MENU 1
RICH AND HEARTY

A SELECTION OF APÉRITIFS, SUCH AS KIR, PERNOD,
OR GREEN CHARTREUSE AND SODA
DAVIDOFF 2000 (petit corona)

SALAD OF ARUGULA AND MIXED CALIFORNIA GREENS, OLIVE OIL, AND
BASLAMIC VINEGAR DRESSING TOPPED WITH A ROUND OF GOAT CHEESE
BREADS
WHITE PINOT GRIGIO OR PINOT GRIS

FONSECA 2-2 (petit corona)
SPARKLING WATER
GRAPEFRUIT OR WHITE WINE SORBET

FILET MIGNON WITH SAUCE BERNAISE
WILD MUSHROOMS WITH FRESH ROSEMARY SPRIGS
STEAMED ASPARAGUS
SYRAH, CABERNET SAUVIGNON OR RED ZINFANDEL

GRAND MARNIER SOUFFLÉ
ESPRESSO

SINGLE MALT SCOTCH OR SINGLE-BATCH BOURBON WHISKEY
PG BELICOSO (torpedo) OR LONSDALE

See? It's possible to make smokes work within the framework of a dinner, as long as you select smaller cigars until your after-dinner smoke.

A Lighter Touch

Although this is a broad generalization, the European and American tradition is to follow a large, rich, heavy meal with a cigar. While after dinner is still the most popular time to enjoy a cigar, many people are eating lighter, healthier meals, so the tradition is changing somewhat.

A full-bodied cigar is still a very appropriate choice after a big dinner, but if you have a light dinner, is it still okay to follow it with a rich, full-bodied cigar? Of course. In the second cigar dinner menu, I show you how.

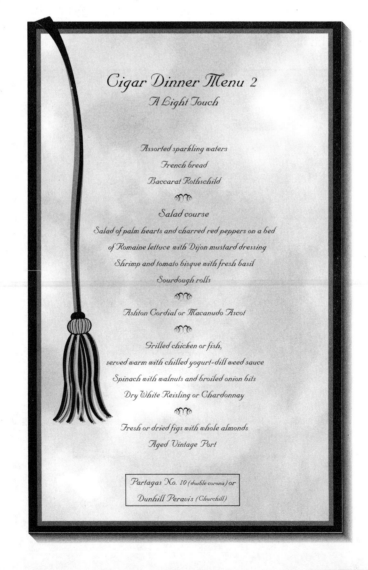

Cigar Dinner Menu 2
A Light Touch

Assorted sparkling waters
French bread
Baccarat Rothschild

Salad course
Salad of palm hearts and charred red peppers on a bed
of Romaine lettuce with Dijon mustard dressing
Shrimp and tomato bisque with fresh basil
Sourdough rolls

Ashton Cordial or Macanudo Ascot

Grilled chicken or fish,
served warm with chilled yogurt-dill weed sauce
Spinach with walnuts and broiled onion bits
Dry White Reisling or Chardonnay

Fresh or dried figs with whole almonds
Aged Vintage Port

Partagas No. 10 (double corona) or
Dunhill Peravis (Churchill)

This dinner shows you can make cigars work even with a light meal. Following a light and sweet cigar such as a Baccarat Rothschild, I'd serve a soup and salad. A medium-bodied smoke like an Ashton Cordial small panatela, or a milder Macanudo Ascot, could stand on its own as a separate course.

A dry white wine would clear your palate and prepare you for something light, such as grilled chicken or fish. For dessert, I'd stay light with fresh figs or fruit, whole roasted nuts, a rich port, and a medium to medium full–bodied smoke such as a Partagas No. 10 (a double corona) or Dunhill Peravis, an elegant Churchill.

A Little Spice

A spicy meal provides an opportunity to use a dessert to give your tingling mouth a rest before lighting up. In the following Mexican-inspired cigar dinner menu, I thought a spicy Te-Amo robusto would match up nicely with a peppery, super-premium tequila made from 100 percent blue agave cactus.

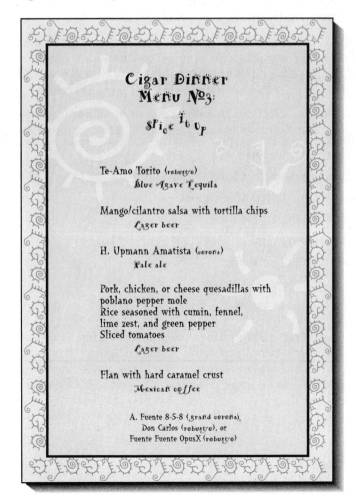

Cigar Dinner
Menu № 3:
Spice It Up

Te-Amo Torito (robusto)
Blue Agave Tequila

Mango/cilantro salsa with tortilla chips
Lager beer

H. Upmann Amatista (corona)
Pale ale

Pork, chicken, or cheese quesadillas with
poblano pepper mole
Rice seasoned with cumin, fennel,
lime zest, and green pepper
Sliced tomatoes
Lager beer

Flan with hard caramel crust
Mexican coffee

A. Fuente 8-5-8 (grand corona),
Don Carlos (robusto), or
Fuente Fuente OpusX (robusto)

A spicy mango/cilantro leaf salsa gets balanced by cooling lager beer, which leads to a medium-bodied yet assertive smoke such as an H. Upmann Amatista, a corona. Smooth pale ale complements the cigar.

After a quesadilla (something resembling a filling sandwiched between tortillas) topped with a medium-spicy pepper sauce and more cold lager beer, an egg-custard flan is smooth and pleasing to the palate. With rich Mexican coffee, an exceptionally robust Cuban-style cigar such as a Fuente would wake up your slightly spice-weary taste buds.

The Cigar as Dessert

Let me briefly mention cigars and sweet desserts. Obviously, a traditional way to finish a meal is with dessert. Sadly, stogies and sweets make a lousy combination.

Let's try a quick visualization exercise. Picture a lit and gently smoking cigar perched next to a piece of strawberry shortcake topped with whipped cream. Do you find that appetizing? If so, you may follow a sweet dessert with a cigar. In general, however, I suggest that if you plan to have an after-dinner cigar, you skip dessert.

If you're planning to have an after-dinner cigar and you still want dessert, avoid any cream-based dish (such as those with whipped cream or ice cream). Cream-based desserts tend to provide a lingering aftertaste that conflicts with the flavors of a cigar. I'd also avoid sugary, syrupy desserts such as tiramisu, fruit pies, and cakes.

If you do want dessert, select one that either has minimal sugar, is egg-based, is nutty, or is slightly bitter. Let me give you some examples of more appropriate cigar desserts:

➤ Grapes, cheeses, and nuts

➤ Plain baked egg custard or Spanish flan

➤ Assorted dark and bittersweet chocolates

➤ Lightly sweetened pumpkin pie

➤ Pecan pie with no topping

➤ Grand Marnier liqueur soufflé

➤ Assorted fruit such as kiwi, grapes, and star fruit

➤ Light fruit sherbet or sorbet

No dessert should be eaten at the same time you're smoking. Finish the dessert, clear your palate with water or an after-dinner drink, and then light up. You want a dessert that's light and quickly cleanses your palate so that you can move on to your cigar without a lingering aftertaste. I enjoy dessert, but if I plan to smoke after dinner, the cigar is usually enough dessert for me.

A Drink with Your Cigar

Throughout this book, I've talked about all the ways that wine and spirits parallel and complement cigars. From growing and processing techniques to finished product, alcoholic beverages seem to go hand-in-hand with cigars.

Before we jump into specifics, I have to tell you that while I might displease some cigar connoisseurs with my rigid feelings about pairing cigars and food, I displease others with my liberal approach to pairing cigars and beverages! For example, a lot of aficionados say that enjoying wine with cigars is a strict no-no. I love wine with cigars, so I'm going to suggest some wines that I believe go wonderfully with a cigar.

And now I'll really make the hard-line traditionalists flip their wigs: I think certain cigars go nicely with beer, coffee, and even soda. Let's take a look at wine and beer first, and then we'll move on to non-alcoholic beverages.

A Jug of Wine

It's fun to try different wines from around the world, testing which flavors stand up to your favorite cigar.

A Bottle of Red

Without question, the best wine with cigars is red wine—the heartier the better. Although red wine hasn't traditionally been paired with stogies, port (an aged red wine fortified with alcohol and sometimes sweetened a bit) is a conventional favorite with cigars.

Some red wines at each end of the strength spectrum aren't as good with cigars. A light red wine such as beaujolais nouveau doesn't mix particularly well with a cigar. "Big" full-bodied red wines (a powerful cabernet sauvignon, for example) tend to numb the taste buds and also overpower the subtle flavors of most cigars. The body has less to do with the grape and more with the particular winemaker's style, so you'll have to experiment or get guidance from a wine merchant on which winemakers favor "big" wines.

Some excellent red wine choices with cigars are red zinfandel wines, Pinot Noir wines, most red table wines from Spain and Italy, red wines using Syrah and Merlot grapes, and California cabernet sauvignon. I'm especially fond of red wines with a slight spicy quality and hints of blackberry. You'll find that character in Syrah grapes (frequently blended with other grapes) and higher quality zinfandel wines.

I like many Spanish red wines because they frequently have a smoky, leathery character that works nicely with cigars. I'm less fond of French red wines with cigars. They tend to be more delicate and subtle, as opposed to the American/California trend toward heartier red wines. The delicate French reds tend to get overpowered by cigars. One exception is the hearty, almost bitter French Côte du Rhone, which easily stands toe-to-toe with any smoke.

On a hot summer day, sangria (a Spanish favorite made with chilled red wine and sliced fruit) is a delicious and refreshing accompaniment to a cigar.

A Bottle of White

Choosing a white wine to accompany your cigar is tougher than choosing a red. Whites are delicate, and they tend to be overpowered by stogies. In my experience, I've found a few types of white wines work well with cigars, although I'm not sure why!

A light, crisp, dry white wine such as the Italian Pinot Grigio complements a cigar because it's so neutral. A rich white French Burgundy has an almost oily, fatty quality that stands up to a cigar. A well-aged, oaky Chardonnay from California or Australia works pretty well with many cigars.

As for sparkling white wines, although I adore them, I don't particularly like them with cigars. I don't know if it's the bubbles, the yeasty quality in sparklers (which creates the bubbles of carbon dioxide), or the acidic taste characteristic of sparkling wines.

When combined with a cigar, sparkling wine or Champagne tends to make my mouth feel unpleasantly dried out. The bubbles numb my palate so that I can't properly enjoy the cigar. Maybe you'll feel differently, and the only way to know is to try.

Sweet white wines such as Semillon or Sauterne aren't bad with very mild cigars. They're too light and delicate to mix well with medium- and full-bodied cigars. Both sweet and dry Riesling white wines are too mild to drink with most cigars, which will overpower their flavor.

A Rustic Meal

You can mix and match red and white wines during a dinner, and your cigar dinner doesn't have to be fancy to be accompanied with wine. Using a countryside theme, I started out cigar dinner menu #4 with a short, medium-bodied La Gloria Cubana cigar with the unofficial drink of Russia: ice-cold vodka, straight up.

The next course features Champagne, which is as tasty with elegant caviar as with country cheeses and pâté. The mid-dinner cigar course needs to be well separated from these strong flavors by a bland consommé or clear broth, and the palate prepared with a red Burgundy or Chianti (Italian red wine). While sipping on this wine, enjoy a medium-mild cigar such as a Cuesta-Rey. Take your time to enjoy a larger cigar such as this Lonsdale.

Feast on a hearty French provincial dish like Cassoulet (a white bean casserole with spices and pork, foul, wild game, or whatever white meats are available) or old-fashioned American chicken and dumplings. Enjoy a very rich white wine like a French white Burgundy.

Warmed by the hearty, simple food, settle back with an after-dinner drink such as Cognac or apple brandy, and light up a full-bodied double corona such as the Punch Gran Cru Diademas.

Cigar Dinner Menu 4
A Countryside Sampler

La Gloria Cubana Minutos
(small panatela)

Iced vodka, straight-up

Toast points and crackers, with
brie cheese, pâte, and caviar
Brut Champagne

Clear consomme
Bread
Red Burgundy or Chianti

Cuesta-Rey No. 1884
(Lonsdale)

Cassoulet of wild game and fowl or
Chicken and dumplings
White Burgundy Wine

Grande Champagne Cognac or Calvados

Punch Gran Cru Diademas
(double corona)

Beer: A Clear Choice

Whenever I've combined beers and cigars I enjoy, the marriage has been very happy.
Some types of beer are better with cigars than others, I think, but I can't say I've ever had
a beer-cigar combination I thought was lousy. The exception might be Weiss beer, which
is very yeasty and has the same acidic tang as sparkling wine.

Although a beer brewer would argue with me, for the purpose of our conversation, let's
say there are three primary categories of beer: *ales, pilsners,* and *lagers.* All are brewed
using very different processes. Pilsners and lagers are bright yellow, light beers. Ales are
generally richer and heavier, ranging from pale yellow to almost black.

With the explosion of micro-breweries, you can choose from thousands of different beers in all these categories. While I can't possibly tell you what beers are good with which cigars, I can give you some general guidelines.

I believe ales go best with cigars, particularly the darker, richer ales like stout, porter, and bitters. Dark lagers also go well with cigars. The flavors of these heavy, rich beers match a cigar. You might even find that at certain points in the flavor spectrum, your cigar and your beer taste very similar.

Drink darker beers and ales when they're cool—never ice cold. These beers have deep, subtle flavors that are lost when they get too cold.

Icy-cold beers tend to deaden your taste buds and your ability to enjoy all the flavors in a cigar. If you consume dark beers at the proper temperature, however, they almost awaken the taste buds.

Light beers such as lagers are good with cigars, but if I want something a little lighter than a dark beer, I prefer a pale ale or red ale. These ales have a slightly higher alcohol content than lagers; usually feature more hops; and have a deeper, richer taste that complements a cigar.

For the same reason I don't like sparkling wine with cigars, I don't like highly yeasty or cloudy beers, such as the German wheat-based Weiss beer. There's something about high yeast content and cigar tobacco that doesn't blend well.

Fortified Wine Has Muscle

Some wine makers just have to make a good thing better, which is how fortified wines began. A fortified wine benefits from the addition of distilled spirits or concentrated, higher-alcohol wine. These wines are aged much longer in wooden casks than regular wine. Fortified wine is available in two varieties, and both are good with cigars.

Very, Very Sherry

This Spanish invention has a nutty flavor, and the production of sherry may have influenced early cigar makers as they developed processes to age and cure cigar leaf tobacco. Like blended cigars, sherry is the product of many different grape crops, combined and aged over several years.

Several types of sherry go well with cigars. I'll give you a brief description of each:

➤ *Manzanilla fina* There's a strong walnut quality to this darker sherry. It's nicely aged and smooth—excellent with almost any cigar.

➤ *Oloroso* and *palo cortado* These sherries are both medium dry, dark, and rich. Either style is superb with cigars.

Any Port in a Storm

Port, another fortified wine, is an ancient and classic type of wine.

Port is available in several types, ranging from the relatively dry *tawny port* to the deep red and sweet *ruby port*. The finest, however, is "vintage" port, which gains richness, color, depth of flavor, and a slight sweetness from years of aging. All types of port taste good with cigars, but a vintage port is best. This fortified wine will age and mature, even in the bottle, for well over 100 years. If you're willing to spend several hundred dollars, you can find such bottles—already aged and ready to enjoy.

If that's a little more cash than you have, look for port labeled "vintage character," which is available at a fraction of the cost of vintage port, but is a high-quality port with enough age to be very mellow. It's a great choice with cigars.

Old port gets its richness and mellowness from aging, while the process is artificially accelerated in younger, cheaper ports by adding more sugar and alcohol to the libation. A cheap port and a fine, aged port hardly taste like the same drink. If you're going to buy a port, be prepared to spend at least $60 for a something well aged from a good manufacturer. Good port is well worth the cost.

High Spirits

Now we've come to the classic accompaniment for cigars: distilled spirits. Your choices in this category are virtually unlimited, so I'm going to concentrate on the spirits that go best with cigars. If I don't mention a favorite drink of yours, go ahead and try a cigar with one!

Before we get started, I'll give you a very general rule of thumb. Drinks that are higher in alcohol or that have more age tend to go better with heavier cigars, while lighter drinks work better with mild smokes. Like everything else we've discussed, feel free to select a cigar and a spirit you like and try them together.

I also suggest that you stick with premium spirits that are in the same "league" as your premium smokes. Usually, inexpensive spirits cost less for the same reason cheap cigars cost less: poorer ingredients, less aging, and more mechanized processing. Inexpensive spirits tend to assault and numb your palate and will almost certainly lessen your enjoyment of a fine cigar.

Brandy and Cognac

Brandies are most commonly distilled from wine, and then aged in wooden casks for several years. Cognac is a type of brandy distilled from grapes grown in the Cognac region of France, and many connoisseurs consider it the finest of all brandies. Brandy is also distilled from other fruits such as pears, cherries, and raspberries. Not surprisingly, they're called fruit brandies. One of the more famous non-grape brandies is Calvados, or applejack, which is distilled from apples.

You can choose from hundreds of brandies and cognacs. These drinks range in age from relatively "young" and fruity V.S. (Very Special) brandy, to more mature V.S.O.P. (Very Special Old Pale), to Napoleon (if it's good enough for the short guy with the emperor complex, it's good enough for me), to the decades-old X.O. (Extra Ordinary) brandy. Other terms are used, but these are the most common.

As you might guess, older, "stronger" brandies match up well with more full-bodied cigars. Younger brandies go especially well with lighter cigars, but let your own taste dictate what you pair together. If you like full-bodied cigars but you don't like X.O. brandy, then by all means seek out a lighter brandy.

When drinking brandy with your cigar, drink it neat (without ice) at room temperature, warmed only by your hand. If you heat it with a flame, which is popular to do, a lot of the subtle flavors and aroma will evaporate. It's best to drink brandy in a glass with a wide body (which lets air reach a large surface area) and a slightly narrow top (to concentrate the aromas).

Scotch Whiskies and Bourbon Whiskies

Whisky is another favorite drink with cigars. Scotch and Canadian whisky is made primarily from barley, and is aged for at least eight years in wooden casks. Bourbon whiskey is made with corn and other cereal grains instead of barley.

Scotch whisky comes in two different forms. *Single-malt* whisky is the product of one particular distillery, and usually has very pronounced characteristics based on the water used for distilling, the type of malt, the environment surrounding the distillery, and the type of wood in which the whisky is aged. Blended scotch whisky is basically a bunch of these single malts mixed together to create an exact taste.

The character of both single-malt and blended whisky is heavily influenced by the length of time the whisky is allowed to age in wooden casks and the type of wood used. Even the youngest whisky you'll find has aged at least eight years in a wooden cask. The oldest you'll find may have aged up to 30 years.

Like brandy, older whisky is usually more mellow, a bit higher in alcohol, and richer and more complex in flavor. The same age rule applies to whiskies as to brandies: older spirits go best with heavier cigars, while younger, lighter spirits go best with lighter cigars.

There's one main difference with whiskies, however, that you need to consider when matching a whisky with cigars. Some whiskies, particularly single malts, have extremely pronounced characteristics such as iodine or smoky peat flavors. These potent flavors can overpower a mild cigar, so you might want to stick with more full-bodied smokes.

Lighter single-malt whiskies go well with any type of cigar, as do most blended scotch and Canadian whiskies, which are usually light and smooth.

You can drink your whisky with ice, but I think a cold drink tends to deaden your palate and lessen your enjoyment of the cigar. I'd suggest you have your whisky "neat," in the same kind of glass you use for brandy.

Most bourbon whiskies are blended, and they can be a very good drink with a cigar if you buy a super-premium bourbon. Cheaper bourbons are harsh; avoid pairing them with a good cigar.

Many whiskies benefit from adding a few drops of water before you drink them. A quarter teaspoon of water can help release additional flavor and aroma. Check it out!

Distilled Spirits, Liquerurs, and Mixed Drinks

I hate to lump a virtual book full of drinks into a few paragraphs, but we have to keep moving. Let me touch on a few drinks I think are tasty with cigars, and I'll leave it up to you to experiment with all the rest.

➤ **Rum**   Although it's thought of primarily as a mixer, a super-premium rum is a superb choice with cigars. Well-aged rum tastes more like fine brandy than the sweet drink you may be used to. You can find a few super-premium brands in larger liquor stores. Be prepared; it will be costly.

➤ **Tequila**   You can enjoy the highest grades of tequila "neat" with cigars. Although top-grade tequila has a very spicy flavor, it doesn't deaden the taste of cigars. In fact, it goes great with spicy cigars, especially Mexican stogies. Stick with top-grade tequila, however, since the lower grades are rough and best left for mixing.

➤ **Grappa**   This Italian spirit is distilled from leftover grape pressings: seeds, stems, and skins. Many grappas are very volatile and "rough." Fine grappas have a floral bouquet and, although they're very firey on the palate, can be excellent on their own and very good with any style of cigar.

➤ **Martinis**   I love both gin and vodka martinis, and I love them with olives or little green tomatoes. However, olives, cocktail onions, and green tomatoes taste awful with a cigar, so stick with a twist of lemon. You might find that a martini made with $2/3$ vodka, $1/3$ melon liqueur, and a splash of vermouth accompanies a cigar nicely.

➤ **Mixed Drinks**   Manhattans, Gin and Tonics, Mint Juleps, Old Fashioneds, and Campari (a bitter aperitif) and soda taste nice with cigars, although they are cold and will deaden your palate a bit. Avoid mixed drinks such as a Tom Collins, which tastes too strongly of lemon. Sweet drinks such as Piña Coladas are too fruity for cigars, but margaritas taste pretty good with stogies.

➤ **Liqueurs and Aperitifs**   Although they're sweet, brandy-based liqueurs such as Grand Marnier and Mandarin Napoleon (both orange-flavored) are delightful with cigars. Drambuie (a whisky-based liqueur) and Benedictine (an herb-flavored drink) taste good with cigars. In general, however, I'd avoid strongly flavored or sweet liqueurs; syrupy, fruit-flavored spirits; or sweet chocolate-flavored spirits. Most of them will either overpower your cigar or not taste good.

The rich, smooth, oily character of most distilled spirits seems to make a good cigar taste even better. And the ritual of sipping at a fine spirit complements the ritual of sipping and savoring a fine cigar. The key is to select spirits you like, cigars you like, and make sure the two complement each other.

Non-Alcoholic Drinks

You don't have to drink alcohol with your cigar. You have several non-alcoholic options, and the most exquisite choice is a rich, full-bodied coffee or espresso. Certain flavors in coffee resonate with and complement cigars.

Although I said I don't like creamy things with cigars, I make an exception with coffee. I like coffee with cream, and even a rich cappuccino (espresso made with steamed milk). As I've said all along, rules are made to be broken! If you like flavored coffee, try it with your favorite stogie and see what you think.

Tea can be good with cigars, particularly a rich, flavorful tea such as China Black. Most herbal teas don't blend well with the flavors of a cigar.

I really can't recommend sparkling beverages with cigars, because the carbonation numbs your tongue and palate. I know that some people drink, and enjoy, club soda, tonic water, or cola with their cigars. It's not for me. If you try a soda with a cigar, I strongly recommend that you avoid drinking fruit-flavored sodas.

Of course, you don't have to drink anything with your cigar! As you smoke, you might just want to occasionally refresh your mouth with some cool, not icy-cold, water.

A Cigar "Party"

Armed with all this information about food and drink, you may want to gather together a few friends and have your own cigar tasting and party. You can do it at home, at a cigar-friendly restaurant, or at a cigar bar or club. You have a lot of options, but to spark some ideas, let me offer a few suggestions.

If you want to have your own tasting at a certain restaurant, and you have enough friends to make a customized evening worthwhile, consider contacting the chef or owner and working out a menu. Most "normal" restaurants wouldn't even consider this idea, but many cigar-friendly establishments will go the "extra mile" to win your business.

I suggest that you have at least six people—a number that makes such an evening worthwhile for a restaurateur to prepare a special meal. The chef may even have fun working with you to create complementary dishes. If the restaurant has a sommelier (wine steward), consider involving him or her in the selection of wines and spirits to accompany your meal and your cigars.

You can host your own cigar dinner and do anything you want for food and drink. You can also conduct a cigar party/tasting with only beverages; this type of party would work well in your home or at a cigar bar. Ideally, everyone will smoke the same cigars and drink the same spirits, which gives you a great opportunity to rate, compare, and discuss your opinions.

Don't try to taste more than three cigars and three spirits during the course of even a long evening: You'll stop being able to taste anything. Even three cigars is pushing the limit a bit, but if you give your tasting 45 minutes to an hour per cigar, you'll probably do fine.

The Least You Need to Know

➤ Cigars are best after a meal.

➤ If you want to have a "cigar dinner," smoke no more than one cigar before, one during, and one after, working from the mildest to the richest.

➤ Richer wines and beers are better with cigars than lighter drinks.

➤ Brandy, port, and whiskey are the classic spirits to accompany cigars.

Put It in Your Pipe and Smoke It

In This Chapter

➤ Pipes: an interesting change of pace

➤ What to look for when buying a pipe

➤ Selecting good-quality pipe tobacco

➤ The equipment you need to get started

Pipes and cigars have coexisted for centuries. Remember the native Arawaks that Christopher Columbus encountered? Some smoked stogies, while others puffed on pipes. Pipes are one of the most ancient ways of smoking tobacco, and they have been made from materials such as stone, clay, reed cane, various woods, calcium carbonate, porcelain, and walrus tusk.

Smoking a pipe with other people traditionally has been an expression of camaraderie, unity, and friendship. Of course you've heard of the *peace pipe*, which was smoked to seal various treaties among Native Americans. Like cigars, pipes are fun when smoked alone, and even more enjoyable when puffed with good friends.

The variety of pipe tobaccos available gives pipe-smoking cigar aficionados, like me, an interesting change of taste (and pace). Pipes can complement your cigar smoking, and can add a whole new dimension to your enjoyment of tobacco. So let's take a quick journey through the world of pipes—a real alternative smoke.

Could Pipes Be Hip?

One of the coolest things I ever saw related to pipes was at a pipe collectors' show. (Yep, a lot of people collect pipes.) I glanced up from my display table to see one of my older collector friends literally nose-to-nose with a young man with a dyed blonde Mohawk haircut and ponytail, a leather biker jacket, and a lot of body piercing. There was at least 50 years difference in age between them.

> **Cigar Speak**
> A **pipe** is a simple device designed to hold your tobacco. The most popular pipe material is **briar**, which is a tough and heat-resistant wood made from the root of a Mediterranean bush.

They were having a very animated discussion, giving the impression that they were arguing about the horrors of body piercing or how the older generation doesn't understand young people. In fact, they were talking about the various smoking properties of pipes and tobaccos, and they couldn't have been happier.

Once in a while, they paused to take a puff on their pipes—the young man's was decorated with feathers and looked like a peace pipe, and the older gentleman smoked a small bent pipe. Those two may have had nothing in common except pipes and tobacco, and they'd probably never run across each other outside of a pipe show. But that day, they made a connection. That's how smoking a pipe can bring people together.

Assorted pipes.

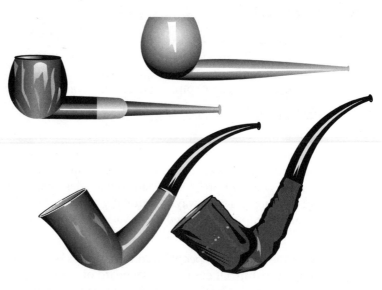

After spending a couple decades with a reputation as "that thing granddad smoked," pipes are making a comeback, and a new generation is discovering their pleasures.

Pipes suffered right alongside premium cigars, which declined in sales until the mid-1980s.

Many people think of pipes as something for old people in the same way that they view cigars as raunchy-smelling things being chewed by a bunch of old guys in a poker game. The enjoyment of pipes and cigars seems to have skipped an entire generation.

Carved meer-schaum pipes—one new (right) and one darkened after years of puffing.

A pipe lets you enjoy premium tobacco in moderation. In this regard, it's on par with enjoying a handmade cigar. I could write another *Complete Idiot's Guide* about pipes. With only one chapter, however, I'll instead touch on a few of the most basic points about pipes and pipe smoking.

Pick a Pipe, but Not Any Pipe

Of course, if you're going to smoke a pipe, the first thing you'll need is a pipe. Unlike cigars, which are gone once you smoke them, a good pipe is something you can keep forever. One reason pipes are becoming popular is that for the price of a box of premium cigars, you can buy a very nice pipe that you can smoke over and over.

Find a good-quality pipe. Just as you'd take a pass on inexpensive machine-made cigars, take a pass on pipes you find in drug stores or on "bargain bin" pipes at a smoke shop. The odds are that if you find a pipe for less than $40, it's not going to give you the best experience possible.

Cigar Speak
Every pipe has a **bowl** for holding the burning tobacco, a **shank** that keeps the bowl away from your mouth and allows the smoke to air cool, and a **stem** that you put in your mouth for puffing. The most popular pipe material is **briar**.

Let's talk a little about what makes a good-smoking pipe. Every pipe has a *bowl* for holding the burning tobacco, a *shank* that keeps the bowl away from your mouth and allows the smoke to air cool, and a *stem* that you put in your mouth for puffing. The most popular pipe material is *briar*, which is a tough and heat-resistant wood made from the root of a Mediterranean bush.

The parts of a pipe.
Courtesy J.T.& D.
Cooke pipes.

PARTS OF A PIPE

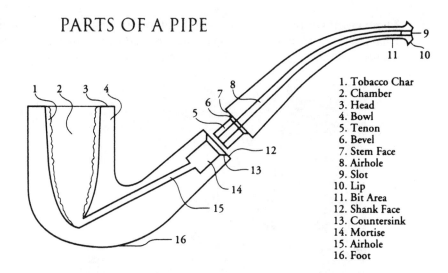

1. Tobacco Char
2. Chamber
3. Head
4. Bowl
5. Tenon
6. Bevel
7. Stem Face
8. Airhole
9. Slot
10. Lip
11. Bit Area
12. Shank Face
13. Countersink
14. Mortise
15. Airhole
16. Foot

Pipes come in many different shapes and sizes, but most have either a bent shank or a straight shank. The shape doesn't make a significant difference in how the pipe smokes. Just pick a shape you like, one that feels good when you hold it.

Straight shank pipe.

Bent shank pipe.

Focus your search on a *briar* pipe with a stem made of Lucite (a plastic) or *vulcanite*, which is hard rubber. (Briar, a heat-resistant wood, is by far the most commonly found pipe material.) Look for a pipe with "grain" all the way around the bowl. Grain makes the pipe look like a finely figured piece of furniture. If a pipe is "bald," or has large spots with no grain, don't buy it.

Even though a briar pipe looks like a solid piece of wood, it's really filled with microscopic holes that allow moisture to escape and air to get in. These holes help keep the tobacco in the bowl from getting soggy, because moisture is released as pipe tobacco burns just as it's released when you smoke a cigar. A slight porosity in the wooden bowl helps keep your tobacco cool, and cool smoke is just as important in a pipe as it is in a cigar. A piece of wood without grain probably won't breathe as well as one with grain, and your pipe won't smoke as cool.

The "Look" of a Pipe

Pipes can be given three basic treatments. The first is called *smooth*, in which you can see the grain of the wood. This kind of pipe looks like the top of a wooden dresser or dining room table. The straighter the grain of a smooth pipe, the more you can expect to pay because straight grain is extremely rare in chunks of briar root. Some straight-grain pipes look like somebody drew pencil lines up and down the bowl, but this effect is just for looks and has no effect on how well the pipe smokes.

The second possible treatment for pipes is called *sandblast*, in which the bowl of the pipe gets a high-pressure blasting with sand to create a pitted, rough surface. The craggy appearance is really appealing. These sandblasted pipes are often stained with a darker color, but sometimes they're left almost a natural, blonde wood color.

Many pipe smokers think that sandblasted pipes smoke even cooler than smooth pipes because the bumps and crevices create a greater surface area for the air to reach. In my experience, sandblast pipes do tend to smoke a little cooler.

Sandblasted and smooth pipes come from the same wood, but a maker usually charges less for a sandblasted pipe because these pipes can cover up flaws in the wood. Small "pits" or holes are common in briar, but they mar the appearance of a smooth pipe. Manufacturers can, however, salvage a marred bowl by sandblasting it and making it rough and bumpy.

Cigar Speak
The exterior of pipes comes in three basic finishes. **Smooth** pipes are like polished furniture. **Sandblasted** pipes have been sprayed with sand at high pressure to make them rough and pitted on the outside. The surfaces of **carved** pipes are designed to resemble sandblasted pipes.

A third treatment involves carving the entire bowl with a sharp tool in a way that mimics the sandblast appearance—without subjecting the pipe to sand. Many Italian-made briar pipes are finished this way, and they can be beautiful and smoke very cool, just like a sandblast. It takes some handiwork and time, but carved pipes are still generally less expensive than smooth pipes because carving is another way to salvage a flawed piece of briar.

Look around a smoke shop; you'll see pipes in all different colors; from red and golden yellow to very deep brown. The color you pick is purely aesthetic; color is not indicative of the smoking quality of the pipe.

Finding a Good Pipe

Many fine pipes are being made today, and many manufacturers offer a number of different quality grades and prices based on the appearance of their wood. You can spend hundreds of dollars on just one briar pipe, but you don't have to! Some of today's cigar makers, such as Savinelli, Ashton, Butera, Stokkebye, and Dunhill, also make fine pipes.

> **Blowing Smoke**
> Avoid buying a pipe that is part smooth and part carved; the maker was probably trying to cover up a flaw by carving a decorative design. As a general rule, high-quality pipe makers don't use this technique; their pipes are either entirely smooth, sandblasted, or carved.

Some brands that have high-quality briar pipes for $100 or less include Ferndown, Savinelli, Don Carlos, Sasieni, Comoy, and Nording. There are many other fine brands, but most of their products run more than $100. You can purchase any of them with confidence, but if you want to start your pipe experience without spending a lot of money, you can find good briar for less.

My best advice to you is to talk with someone at your smoke shop who knows pipes, and most smoke shops have at least one person—often the owner—who's particularly knowledgeable about pipes. Many smoke shops carry special brands that use good briar and represent a very good value—perfect for the beginning pipe smoker. Look to the retailer for guidance in selecting your pipe and tobaccos, and also in how to pack tobacco in a pipe, light it, and keep it burning.

Tobacco: Go for the Best

The tobacco you smoke is the most important aspect of pipe smoking. With cigars, tobacco is everything; with pipe smoking, you've first gotta have a pipe to hold the tobacco. But if you smoke crummy pipe tobacco, you'll probably be very disappointed, especially if you're getting used to smoking cigars made from the finest tobacco in the world.

Let me take a moment to relate my first experience with pipes, which illustrates my point. I started off on Cuban stogies, then lost my way temporarily by smoking cheap cigars. I finally found a few good smoke shops and got back on track with premium cigars. I got interested in pipes mostly because my then–father-in-law constantly puffed on a pipe, and he always seemed pretty relaxed and contented. I was really getting into cigars, and the idea of a pipe also intrigued me.

I bought a relatively inexpensive pipe at the smoke shop where I bought my cigars. Although I know now that the pipe wasn't the best quality, it would have been fine if the shop owner had given me the same advice I'm going to give you.

I bought what's called *aromatic tobacco*, which is usually sprayed with a glycerin-based flavoring agent that may smell of anything from chocolate or cherries to mint and mango. I say "smell" rather than taste because although those around you smell the flavoring agent, you taste very little of it. Smoking cherry-flavored tobacco is not like smoking a bowl of cherries.

I didn't have much trouble lighting and smoking the pipe (which is a problem for a lot of first-time pipe smokers), but the taste of that tobacco sure was a turnoff. The tobacco bit my tongue, the flavoring agents tasted bitter, and the very moist tobacco in my bowl left a gurgling residue that I occasionally drew up through my pipe into my mouth.

To this day, I find that glycerin-based flavoring agents have a harsh and bitter chemical taste; flavoring agents are usually used to cover up the taste of inexpensive tobaccos. If you've gotten used to premium cigars, I think you'll be very disappointed if you try smoking aromatic tobacco.

> **Cigar Speak**
> Pipe tobacco is usually shredded and cut to pack into the bowl of a pipe. Thousands of different varieties of pipe tobacco leaf are available, and blended together to create thousands more combinations. There are two basic styles of pipe tobacco. **English style** means only the natural, unflavored tobaccos are used. Pipe tobacco may also be enhanced with flavors: fruit, nuts, vanilla, chocolate, mint, and so on. These are called **aromatic pipe tobacco**.

I struggled through a few ounces of that aromatic pipe tobacco and was ready to give up the pipe and just stay with cigars. I did eventually discover *English style* (natural, unflavored) pipe tobacco, however, which delivered the same kind of flavor I loved in premium, handmade cigars.

Pipe Tobacco Styles and Brands

Aromatic is by far the most commonly available form of pipe tobacco, but it's worth the trouble to go to a local smoke shop and look for tins of English style tobacco. Many retailers also carry their own English style blends in jars.

Although you'll need to ask your retailer for assistance finding an available tobacco that suits your taste, I can recommend a few commonly available brands that, for the most part, make only natural, unflavored tobacco:

➤ Balkan Sobranie

➤ Butera

➤ Dunhill

➤ Lane Limited

➤ McClelland's

➤ Peterson

➤ Rattray's

➤ Three Nuns

Pipe tobacco has different "strengths," just like cigars. There are rich and full-bodied blends, usually made with tobaccos grown in Asia and the Middle East, and lighter, milder blends, made with tobaccos grown predominantly in Virginia. The best thing for you to do is try some different blends. Many larger smoke shops actually offer free samples of their own pipe tobacco blends, so all you need is a pipe to be able to sample to your heart's content.

Don't expect pipe tobaccos to taste anything like cigars.

What would it be like if you crumbled up your cigar and smoked it in a pipe? Not real good, I'm afraid, because pipe tobacco has to be cut up properly in order to burn evenly. Also, for some reason, a good cigar just tastes better as a cigar. I've tried cutting up cigars into my pipe bowl, but the results weren't very tasty.

You can, however, find a few pipe tobaccos that incorporate cigar leaf with other tobaccos to give some of that unique "cigar" taste. I do like cigar-leaf tobacco in my pipe.

Finally, the finest pipe tobacco is relatively inexpensive compared to premium cigars. Good pipe tobacco costs about $25 per pound, but that's a lot of tobacco! Generally, you'll buy pipe tobacco in vacuum-sealed four-ounce or eight-ounce tins, which last a moderate pipe smoker (someone who smokes about a bowl or two a day) a week or two. Smoke shops with jars of loose tobacco blends will let you buy and bag as little as an ounce at a time.

I suggest that you start by purchasing only small amounts of pipe tobacco. You'll then have a better chance to sample different tobaccos and see what you like. Also, pipe tobaccos dry out just as cigars do, so you don't want to buy too much until you have a pipe tobacco humidor.

Because pipe humidors are simple jars, they generally cost a lot less than cigar humidors. You want to find one with a tight seal to keep in the moisture, but pipe tobacco isn't nearly so delicate as are cigars. And you can also use zip-seal plastic bags, which will keep a few ounces of tobacco moist for several weeks—long enough to finish the tobacco.

Firing Up Your Pipe

Many people get discouraged when they first smoke a pipe because they can't keep the tobacco burning. There is a little technique to lighting a pipe and keeping it burning, but it isn't rocket science. Lighting a pipe does take a little more practice than lighting a cigar, but you'll get the hang of it.

When you fill a pipe with tobacco, you're performing much the same task as the cigar bunchers and rollers who create your cigars. Remember that when a cigar is rolled too tightly, you can't draw enough air through it, and when it's rolled too loosely, it burns hot and fast. The same principle is true for filling a pipe. Your job is to fill the pipe with the right amount of tobacco, and pack it down just right, so that it burns perfectly and evenly.

Filling Your Pipe

This section is a quick lesson in filling a pipe. In addition to your lighter, pipe, and tobacco, you'll want to have two very simple and inexpensive tools:

➤ **A pipe tamper, or pipe tool**   This tool has a flat end, called a *tamper,* that is used to press your tobacco into the bowl when you light up and as you smoke. (When pipe tobacco heats up, it wants to spring up and out of the bowl, so you need to keep it in line by packing it down periodically.) The other end is called the *pick,* and you use it when you're finished smoking to clean out all the bits of tobacco from your bowl. You can buy very fancy and expensive pipe tools, but you can also find ones for 50 cents that work just fine.

➤ **Pipe cleaners**   You can use these inexpensive gadgets to make really cool animals and stick figures, but they got their name because they're used to clean pipes. After you're finished smoking, you run one of these cleaners through the air hole of your pipe, which swabs out moisture and help keeps the pipe from clogging and getting smelly. Pipe cleaners are also useful while you smoke; they keep moisture out of the pipe's air hole. Pipe cleaners are cheap, so buy a pack of 50 and use them liberally.

Pipe tools.

Cigar Speak
Pipe accessories consist of a **pipe tamper**, or **pipe tool**, which has a flat end, called a **tamper**. You use the tamper to press your tobacco into the bowl when you light up and as you smoke. **Pipe cleaners** are used to swab out your pipe to avoid moisture build-up in the air hole.

To fill a pipe, simply hold it over your can or bag filled with tobacco. You trickle tobacco into the bowl until it's full, and then you use your thumb to press the tobacco until it's packed firmly but still springs back. This technique leaves space for sprinkling in a little more tobacco until the pipe is full. Finally, you press down lightly until the tobacco is about a quarter-inch from the top of the bowl. You're ready to smoke. Most beginning smokers make the mistake of pressing down too firmly on the tobacco, which means you won't be able to draw in enough air to keep the tobacco lit. The problem is the same as with a tightly rolled cigar: no draw.

To test how good a job you've done, try to draw air through the pipe before you light it. If you feel that same nice, firm flow of air (a little resistance, but not much) that you've experienced with a perfectly rolled cigar, you've probably packed your bowl just right.

If drawing air through the pipe seems too easy, add just a little more tobacco and press everything down a little bit more firmly. If you can't pull any air through the pipe, simply use the other end of your pipe tamper to pick out the tobacco, return it to the tin or bag, and try again. The tobacco should come to within a quarter inch of the top, but not all the way. You'll see why when you light the pipe.

Lighting Your Pipe

Just as you start your cigar off by making sure the entire tip is evenly lit, you want to do the same with a pipe. When you think you have the tobacco packed just right, use your lighter or a wooden match to light the top layer of tobacco in your pipe bowl. You want to avoid paper matches for the same reason you avoid them for lighting a cigar (refer back to Chapter 3).

Tobacco Leaves
Thy brown and polished bowl I'll fill with care,
And then, with lips pressed close unto thine own—
No lover drinks a sweeter draught, I sear
I'm happier than a king upon his throne!
—from *To My Pipe* by Edwin Carlisle Litsey

Steadying the pipe with one hand and holding it in your mouth, draw in puffs of air slowly and evenly. The technique is much the same as the one you use to light a cigar.

Don't puff furiously; just draw in gently and pull the flame down to the tobacco. Move the flame around to light all the tobacco. The tobacco in the bowl will start to spring up as it heats, which is why you want to leave enough room at the top: so that the tobacco doesn't spill over the bowl.

Stop lighting for a moment, and use your tamper to push the springy, glowing tobacco back in place. There should be a fine, even gray coating of charred tobacco on the top of the bowl. Not surprisingly, this coating is called the *charring light*.

Unlike a cigar, you'll need to re-light your pipe tobacco at this point because the tamping has probably made the tobacco go out. Hold your lighter about a half-inch from the tobacco and use the same gentle puffing process to re-light it. When the entire surface tobacco starts to flame up, it's sufficiently lit. It's now time to start puffing and enjoying.

Settling In for a Good Smoke

Like cigars, pipes will go out if you don't puff on them. Also like cigars, you should let a pipe "rest" between puffs so that the tobacco doesn't heat up and burn your tongue. It's better to have to re-light your pipe several times and ensure you're smoking "cool" than to puff too much and burn your mouth with hot smoke.

As you smoke, lightly tamp your tobacco down to keep too much air from getting in. You may want to tip your pipe over an ashtray to let any loose ash fall out of the pipe bowl. The advantage of smoking English-style tobaccos over the aromatic types is that they release less moisture, and you won't have to tamp your pipe as often. English-style tobaccos burn more evenly than aromatic, so you won't end up with a soggy mass of tobacco at the bottom of the bowl; this gunk is called *dottle*.

Just puff merrily away, and visually check your bowl occasionally to see how far down the tobacco has burned. You want to smoke your tobacco as close to the bottom of the bowl as possible, but you have to puff a little more slowly toward the end. If at any time your bowl gets so hot that it's uncomfortable to hold in your hand, set your pipe down and let it cool off for several minutes.

Although briar wood is very durable and heat resistant, it will burn if it gets too hot. A pipe with a flaw, or one that has been puffed too vigorously, may develop a black spot on the outside of the bowl. This sign indicates that the wood has been charred. The heat will eventually eat through the wall of your pipe's bowl and reach the outside, destroying your pipe. A carefully smoked pipe, however, should last for decades.

Tobacco Leaves

Tobacco smoke, like silken web,

Suspended in the restful airs,

To me and mine, in soothing rhymes

A dainty, artless burden bears;

Let cares rage on—let hopes renew—

The yesterday, tomorrow be—

But we are wise, the smoke and I;

We cease regrets and troubles flee.

—from A.B. Tucker's *Smoke Dreams*

Tobacco Leaves

"Honest men, with pipes or cigars in their mouths, have great physical advantages in conversation. You may stop talking if you like, but the breaks of silence never seem disagreeable, being filled up by the puffing of the smoke..."

—from *The Social Pipe* by William Makepeace Thackeray

273

Giving Your Pipe a Rest

When you think you've smoked the tobacco about as far as you can, you can either immediately pick out the ash and the few remaining bits of tobacco, depositing them in an ashtray, or allow your pipe to cool off before cleaning it. Don't leave residue in your pipe for more than a few hours. Run a pipe cleaner through the air hole, making sure it gets all the way into the bowl. (You can see the tip of the pipe cleaner inside the bowl.)

Let your pipe dry out by resting it with the bowl up. It's best to let the pipe dry with the stem slightly higher than the bottom of the bowl. Give a pipe at least a day to dry out, or those little microscopic pores can get clogged, which will make your smoke hotter and bitter tasting.

If you start to enjoy regular pipe smoking, you'll probably want to buy at least one other pipe so that you can "rotate" your pipes. You might even want to find a pipe rack or "nest" in which to rest the pipe. You can find pipe racks and pipe nests in most smoke shops that carry pipes.

As you smoke your pipe, you'll notice that the inside of the bowl will start to develop a hard black crust called the *char*. The char is good because it helps absorb moisture and further cools your smoke. It's made of the charcoal and various residual materials from your burning tobacco.

Of course, too much of a good thing can be bad. In time, you'll have to trim down the char or it'll completely fill up the inside of your bowl and you won't have any room left for tobacco. Your best bet is to ask your tobacconist for some help in how to keep the char in check. Until you start to build up this protective coating (about four to six bowl-fuls), you'll want to smoke extra slowly and carefully to avoid burning the exposed wood inside the bowl.

What's It Like to Smoke a Pipe?

Smoking a pipe is a different experience from smoking cigars, although the two have many similarities. Just as you shouldn't inhale a cigar, you should sip at a pipe without inhaling the smoke. You want to savor the fine tobaccos and enjoy them in moderation—as you would a fine cigar.

If you plan to leave home with your pipe, you'll have to bring the pipe, a tamper and lighter, some pipe cleaners, and a small bag for your tobacco.

You can have a "quick smoke" more easily with a pipe than a cigar. If you're running errands, it's easy to give your pipe a minute to go out, and then slip it in your pocket when you enter a store. Try that with a stogie! When you get back outside, just re-light the pipe and go on your way. As with a cigar, you don't want to let your pipe go unlit for more than a half hour or the tobacco will start to get bitter tasting.

Smoking a pipe is also a different experience from smoking a cigar, and although it's very difficult to explain, at times my mood calls for a contemplative pipe instead of a cigar. Because cigars and pipes render different experiences, I enjoy having the option.

I've also found that fewer people object to the smell of pipe smoke than cigar smoke. If you find a relatively mild-smelling pipe tobacco, you might have more luck enjoying your pipe in places that would object to the invasive smell of a cigar.

Pipes can offer an interesting alternative to cigars, and if you find yourself eyeing the pipe section of your local smoke shop, don't be afraid to ask questions. You'll find that shop attendants and even other pipe smokers will usually be pleased to give you pointers. Since the first humans put tobacco in ceremonial pipes thousands of years ago, a fellowship and bonding related to pipes began that continues to this day.

> **Tobacco Leaves**
> Break the red stone from this quarry, Mould and make it into peace pipes, Take the reeds that grow beside you, Deck them with your brightest feathers, Smoke the calumet together And as brothers live hence forward!
>
> —from *The Calumet* (the peace pipe) by Henry Wadsworth Longfellow

The Least You Need to Know

➤ To match the experience of smoking a premium cigar, buy a high-quality pipe and pipe tobacco.

➤ Look for a pipe made of briar, with "grain" all the way around the bowl. If a pipe is "bald," or has large spots where there is no grain, don't buy it.

➤ Get help and guidance from your local cigar and pipe retailer on how to properly fill and light a pipe.

➤ Smoke a pipe slowly and easily, just as you'd smoke a fine cigar.

Blowing Literary Smoke

In This Chapter

➤ Finding and enjoying cigar-related literature

➤ Famous cigar smokers, fictional and real

➤ Keeping the cigar flame burning

I'd like to leave you with one final way to enhance your cigar-smoking experience, and that's with the rich variety of literature written about cigars and tobacco. It's nice to know that thousands of writers and celebrities have shared your passion for cigars and left behind their opinions and wisdom for you to enjoy.

Thousands of books have been written about tobacco, cigars, and pipes—everything from poetry to scientific papers. Movies such as *Havana* and *Smoke* provide a visual portrayal of the world according to cigars. Great writers, from Mark Twain, an avid stogie-puffer, to J.M. Barrie, author of *Peter Pan*, have extolled the cigar and Lady Tabacum.

The Scent of a Good Cigar

One of the finest pieces ever written about cigars describes the pleasure of smelling, not smoking, a good cigar. I'd like to share this whole poem with you because it's one of the classics.

The Scent of a Good Cigar

What is it comes through the deepening dusk,—
    Something sweeter than jasmine scent,
    Sweeter than rose and violet blent,
More potent in power than orange or musk?
    The scent of a good cigar.
I am all alone in my quiet room,
    And all the windows are open wide and free
    To let in the south wind's kiss for me,
While I rock in the softly gathering gloom,
    And that subtle fragrance steals.
Just as a loving, tender hand
    Will sometimes steal in yours,
    It softly comes through the open doors,
And memory wakes at its command,—
    The scent of that good cigar.
And what does it say? Ah, that's for me
    And my heart alone to know;
    But that heart thrills with a sudden glow,
Tears fill my eyes till I cannot see,—
    From the scent of that good cigar.

—Kate A. Carrington

Penned many decades ago, this poem tells about the fond memories and gut-level emotions a cigar can evoke. Finding treasures like this is one of the delights of discovering tobacco-related literature. It's another way of "connecting" with past and present generations that have experienced the pleasure and passion of fine tobacco.

The World's Most Popular Topic?

Literature on cigars, pipes, and tobacco ranges from the famous *Counterblaste to Tobacco* (written by England's King James I) to ambivalent acceptance by J.M. Barrie in *My Lady Nicotine* to glowing praise from Rudyard Kipling and Mark Twain. In between these classics are research papers, down-home narratives, catalogues, and histories.

A Counterblaste to Tobacco, penned by King James I in 1604, is an ornery and arrogant missive against tobacco. Although King James is best known for sponsoring the King James Version of the Bible, he wasn't a very enlightened man when the subject turned to cigars. I'd like to share a couple of his comments with you.

Cigar Esoterica

Sir Walter Raleigh was one of tobacco's earliest supporters. The first time his servant saw him smoking his pipe, the servant thought he was on fire and tried to put him out by dousing him with water. King James I more effectively doused Sir Walter's flame by accusing him falsely of treason and having him hanged. Raleigh mounted the steps of the scaffold calmly smoking his pipe.

"For tobacco being a common herb, was first found out by some of the barbarous Indians to be a preventative against the pox, whereunto these barbarous people are very much subject, what through the uncleanly...constitution of their bodies...," wrote the king, not realizing that it was the Europeans who carried these diseases and gave them to native peoples, who had no immunity.

James continued: "...shall we, I say without blushing, abase ourselves so far as to imitate these beastly Indians, slaves to the Spaniards, refuse to the world, and as yet aliens from the holy Covenant of God?"

The old boy argued that hot tobacco robbed the "cool and humide" brain of its vital fluids, making men stupid and barbaric. Even though he was the king, most English men and women ignored him and the use of tobacco continued to grow.

Other writers over the centuries have delved into the production and pleasures of cigars and tobacco. Through literature you can follow the history of tobacco, or tobacco trade. You can have a lot of fun settling down with an old (or new) book, a nice glass of your favorite "whatever," and a premium, hand-made smoke.

One of my favorite works in my very modest collection is a hardcover book, named *Obsequio de la Fabrica de Cigarillos—Á Sus Favorecedores* (Our Favorites) that I acquired at a pipe and cigar show. Published in the late 1800s by Por Larrañaga, it was presented to the best customers of Havana cigar retailers and features females in various states of dress and undress. It's simply a book of naughty photos—no text. It's a period piece, and is precious because it captures the highly secret sensualism of an era that was, on the surface, so straight-laced.

Tobacco Leaves

Sublime tobacco!

Divine in hookas, glorious in a pipe,

When tipp'd with amber, mellow, rich, and ripe;

Like other charmers, wooing the caress

More dazzlingly when daring in full dress.

Yet thy true lovers more admire, by far,

Thy naked beauties—give me a cigar!

—from *The Island*, Canto II, by Lord Byron

You can find some tobacco-related literature at almost any library, but I'm afraid most of it will be books written about why people should not smoke cigarettes. You may also find books about cigars and tobacco at used or collectible bookstores; they are sometimes under literature or poetry, sometimes in the medical section, and other times just scattered around the store. Smoke shops carry books, and smoke-shop owners may be able to give you the names of collectors who amass cigar and tobacco literature.

The Cigar as a Clue

One of the most enduring and endearing images of the cigar smoker in literature is Sherlock Holmes, the famous sleuth created by Sir Arthur Conan Doyle.

Holmes smoked everything: pipes, cigars, and cigarettes. He smoked cigars often enough to warrant carrying a cigar case, and offered them to his colleague Dr. John Watson on occasions such as their train ride to Exeter in "The Adventure of Silver Blaze." He smoked cigars at his famous home, located at 221B Baker Street.

Doyle never tells us whether Holmes preferred fine Havanas or the strong Indian stogies frequently smoked by the people Holmes encounters in his adventures. Holmes did, however, prefer to store his smokes in a coal scuttle. Watson usually kept a supply of fine Havanas for himself and visitors (but he didn't keep his supply in the coal scuttle).

The Trichinopoly cigar, mentioned by Holmes in "The Sign of Four," was rolled in Holland using very strong and harsh Indian tobaccos, while "birds eye" was a type of pipe tobacco. What's amazing is how accurately Sir Arthur really researched his tobaccos and built his knowledge into the Holmes stories.

> **Tobacco Leaves**
>
> "I enumerate a hundred and forty forms of cigar, cigarette, and pipe tobacco, with coloured plates illustrating the difference in ash. It is a point which is continually turning up in criminal trials, and which is sometimes of extreme importance as a clue. To the trained eye there is as much difference between the black ash of a Trichinopoly and the white fluff of bird's eye as there is between a cabbage and a potato."
>
> —Sherlock Holmes, discussing his monograph on tobacco ash, from "The Sign of Four"

Some Famous (Real) Cigar Smokers

Although Sherlock Holmes may be one of the most famous and interesting cigar smokers in literature, plenty of real celebrities have and do enjoy a good cigar. Actors, politicians, and famous business people have publicly demonstrated their fondness for a good stogie.

Cigars are all the rage with celebrities these days. Some, like Arnold Schwarzenegger, have been enjoying stogies for years. I owned and published a pipe and cigar magazine, *The Compleat Smoker*, in the early 1990s—when cigar smoking wasn't very popular. I recall that when doing my magazine and planning to run celebrity shots, I received a desperate plea from Arnold's agent that I not run a photo of him smoking a cigar because they were trying to downplay his love of a good cigar. Times have changed, and Arnold isn't hiding his love of cigars any longer!

Many sports celebrities enjoy cigars, from Michael Jordan and Scottie Pippin (celebrating an NBA championship), to hockey player Wayne Gretzky, who seems to enjoy the finer things in life. It takes a little courage for a sports celebrity to enjoy a stogie in public because someone inevitably criticizes them for being a bad role model. I think they're good role models because they're showing how to enjoy tobacco in a responsible and moderate way.

I have to chuckle at how many celebrities claim to smoke Havanas almost exclusively. I'm sure they can both obtain and afford them, but I'm still trying to figure out where they manage to find all these marvelous Cuban smokes. My cigar connoisseur friends, many of whom travel abroad more often than I, agree with me that it's hard to find a good Cuban smoke. It's a mystery to me.

One of the most beloved cigar-smoking celebrities was George Burns, who passed up Havana smokes in favor of machine-made El Producto cigars. He said the looser-rolled cigars stayed lit during his stage act, while the long-filler Havanas went out between puffs. Burns lived to be 100 and smoked at least 10 cigars a day for more than 70 years. He outlived most of his contemporary celebrities and, as he liked to joke, the doctors who told him to give up his beloved martinis and cigars.

Many great authors, politicians, and historical figures have also enjoyed cigars. Cigars were a staple of U.S. presidents Ulysses S. Grant and John F. Kennedy, gangster Al Capone, New York City Mayor Fiorello LaGuardia, poet Lord Byron, and World War I–era German Chancellor Otto von Bismarck.

Sir Winston Churchill was seldom without a cigar. During a German air raid on London, the manager of the Dunhill shop where Churchill kept his stash telephoned him at 2 a.m. to assure Churchill that his stogies were safe.

Sir Winston, a thrifty man, smoked many different brands because he received so many complementary cigars from manufacturers who wanted to claim that Churchill smoked their cigars! The large 8-inch, 50-ring cigar came to be called a "Churchill" shape in his honor.

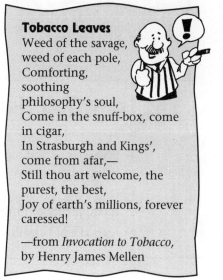

Tobacco Leaves
Weed of the savage, weed of each pole,
Comforting, soothing philosophy's soul,
Come in the snuff-box, come in cigar,
In Strasburgh and Kings', come from afar,—
Still thou art welcome, the purest, the best,
Joy of earth's millions, forever caressed!

—from *Invocation to Tobacco,* by Henry James Mellen

> **Tobacco Leaves**
> Edward VII, Prince of England, loved cigars, but even a prince can't always have his way. His mother, Queen Victoria, banned smoking cigars in court. On the day he assumed the throne and became king, Edward announced to those with him: "Gentlemen, you may smoke."

> **Tobacco Leaves**
> "I vow and believe that the cigar has been one of the greatest creature-comforts of my life—a kind companion, a gentle stimulant, an amiable anodyne, a cementer of friendship."
> —from *The Social Pipe,* by William Makepeace Thackeray

Your Place in History

As we near the end of our adventure through the world of cigars, it's interesting to think about how much in common we have with the celebrities, historical figures, and "commoners" who have enjoyed a good cigar. An ancient Mayan or Arawak puffed smokes for basically the same reasons we do: Cigars satisfy some basic need for good taste, relaxation, and camaraderie.

Smoking is an ancient and simple pleasure, and cigars are tobacco in its simplest and most basic form. Millions have puffed and savored cigars without knowing how tobacco is grown or cured; how cigars are made; or any of the other tidbits you've learned while reading this book.

You don't need to know any of this to enjoy a cigar, but I hope all the things we've talked about will significantly enhance your knowledge and enjoyment of cigars. I know a little about a lot of things, but I've had the exciting opportunity to become an expert in tobacco. From literature and lore to sampling and scoring, it's one of my passions.

Thanks for the opportunity to share my passion with you. I hope you've caught a little of my "cigar fever," and that this book helps fire up a long and happy quest for that perfect smoke.

The Least You Need to Know

➤ Thousands of books have been written on tobacciana.

➤ It's easier to find tobacco-related literature from specialists and at used book stores than at the library.

➤ Don't worry if celebrities talk about the Cuban cigars they smoke and you can't get them; plenty of fine stogies are out there.

➤ A good smoke with a good book or magazine is a great way to relax.

The Descriptive Guide to Cigars

Here, you'll find brief descriptions of the strength and attributes of nearly 100 non-Cuban brand cigars. New brands are being added every month, but I've done my best to cover all the established brands, and the newcomers I think stand a chance of hanging around for awhile. I rate entire lines of cigars, not just single cigars or one size. I haven't scored or described a line unless I've had the chance to sample several sizes in order to check for brand consistency.

> **Country of origin** follows each brand name. I include no Cuban brands because it's impossible to rate lines that are as inconsistent as the Havanas have become. Because most manufacturers outside Cuba use blends of tobacco from many countries, I don't put as much weight on the country of origin as in the overall strength rating. Countries are abbreviated as follows:

COS—Costa Rica
DOM—Dominican Republic
HON—Honduras
JAM—Jamaica
MEX—Mexico
NIC—Nicaragua
PAN—Panama
USA—United States

> **Strength** rating helps you identify the relative strength of the brand.

> **Scores and grades** give you two different ways to see how I judged a brand of cigars, and I use the same categories as my rating guide in Chapter 20. I'm not afraid to use

the full spectrum of scoring, so a superb line of cigars can earn a near-perfect 98 or "A+," while other lines may get a "D" or 70. You'll find that my good ratings, particularly in the 90s, are higher than you'll see in some other publications, but I think a great brand deserves a near-perfect score.

➤ **Descriptions** include a discussion of notable positives and negatives, as well as basic categories (**Appearance, Lighting & Burning, Construction, Taste**). I've based my ratings and grades on the same rating sheet you'll find in Chapter 20, but for the sake of space, I've provided only a brief summary of each cigar brand's flaws and strengths. "Taste" is more heavily weighted in my grading, so a low mark for taste will pull down the overall grade considerably.

I don't break out individual sizes within a brand, unless I know a particular size incorporates a different blend. Different-sized cigars within the same line usually feature the same blend of filler tobaccos and the same overall characteristics of quality and construction. If a maker has two or more distinctive lines, such as Macanudo and Macanudo Vintage, I differentiate them for you.

Overall, my comments focus on the flaws more than the excellences for the simple reason that I assume a premium, handmade smoke is excellent in all areas unless it proves otherwise!

➤ I've included a very general **price code** at the end of each description. My ratings are not influenced by price, but I'll let you know if I think a line is overpriced or a good deal. While specific prices are not listed, a quickie per-brand rating is included as follows:

$= Modestly priced line ($3–$6/cigar)

$$= Medium priced line ($5–$8/cigar)

$$$= Pricey ($6.50–$12/cigar)

$$$$ = Très Pricey ($8–$25/cigar)

Price within a particular line of cigars is influenced by size: In general, cigars will be consistently priced from the largest to the smallest. As a general rule of thumb, there is no such thing as a particular size that represents a particular value. I like to imagine, cheapskate that I am, that I get the most "smoke time" for my money with double coronas and Churchills, but I have no real evidence to back up that conclusion!

➤ *Best Buy* means that the cigar combines quality, taste, consistency, and price.

➤ *Great Smoke* means that the cigar is one of my personal selections for a top cigar, regardless of price.

The Descriptive Guide to Cigars

Ashton (DOM)

Strength: Medium
Lighting & Burning: 13/15 (A-)
Taste: 33/35 (A-)

Appearance: 18/20 (A-)
Construction: 26/30 (B)
Final Grade: 90/100 (A)

The regular line of Ashtons is well constructed (by Fuente) and features silky Connecticut shade-grown wrappers. Occasionally these wrappers are so delicate that they crack when smoked. Ashtons also feature an excellent, sweet maduro wrapper on several sizes. The wrapper makes a considerable difference in flavor, but Ashton maduros are in very short supply. The line features a wide variety of sizes and usually burns well. The Cordial is one of the best small cigars around. *Great Smoke* **$$**

Ashton Cabinet Selection (DOM)

Strength: Medium
Lighting & Burning: 13/15 (A-)
Taste: 32/35 (B+)

Appearance: 19/20 (A)
Construction: 26/30 (B)
Final Grade: 90/100 (A)

The Cabinet Selection line is good, using more aged tobaccos than the regular Ashton line, which lends a smoother character. They sometimes display uneven burning characteristics. They are perhaps not worth the difference in price. *Great Smoke* **$$$**

Avo Uvezian Regular and XO Series (DOM)

Strength: Robust
Lighting & Burning: 15/15 (A+)
Taste: 34/35 (A)

Appearance: 20/20 (A+)
Construction: 29/30 (A)
Final Grade: 98/100 (A+)

This is a beautifully constructed cigar. The natural wrappers are usually luscious and oily. The line offers the unusual belicoso, petit belicoso, and pyramid shapes. The XO is purported to use more aged tobaccos, but I don't notice much difference in flavor between the two lines. Then again, I don't know how you can improve much on the regular Avo line. The cigar is manufactured by Hendrik Kelner, one of the world's finest cigar makers. The cigars are subjected to many quality control checks, and I've never seen a bad one. Being a full bodied cigar, it isn't for the faint of heart, but it's always smooth, made with vintage tobaccos. *Great Smoke* **$$$$**

La Aurora (DOM)

Strength: Mild
Lighting & Burning: 10/15 (B)
Taste: 22/35 (D)

Appearance: 15/20 (B-)
Construction: 22/30 (C-)
Final Grade: 69/100 (C-)

This Cameroon-wrapped cigar once had a great reputation, but today the consistency is so highly variable that it cannot be listed among the contenders. The tobaccos consistently show signs of being too young. A positive sign is that family member Guillermo León has made a major commitment to returning the La Aurora and Leon Jiminez brands to their former glory, and it will be very exciting if he succeeds. **$$**

Baccarrat (DOM)

Strength: Very mild
Lighting & Burning: 13/15 (A-)
Taste: 32/35 (B+)

Appearance: 17/20 (B+)
Construction: 25/30 (B-)
Final Grade: 86/100 (B+)

This cigar is very interesting with a very sweet taste that I'm sure is from naturally sweet cigar leaf rather than an artificial means. It's consistently well made, although it burns a little hot because the tobacco is a bit too loosely rolled. The wrappers are a little dry, but it's a very pleasant and interesting smoke. *Best Buy* **$$**

Bances (HON/USA)

Strength: Mild
Lighting & Burning: 13/15 (A-)
Taste: 26/35 (C-)

Appearance: 14/20 (C+)
Construction: 26/30 (B)
Final Grade: 79/100 (B)

Bances tends to lack any complexity in flavor, but it's a relatively well-constructed brand with good consistency. The tobacco usually shows moderate lack of aging. It's inexpensive for a handmade stogie, but bland. **$**

Bauza (DOM)

Strength: Medium
Lighting & Burning: 13/15 (A-)
Taste: 28/35 (D)

Appearance: 14/20 (C+)
Construction: 26/30 (C+)
Final Grade: 79/100 (B-)

Although made by Fuente, this is a half-step above a bundled cigar and not much attention seems to be lavished on it. Construction is spotty and the cigars sometimes burn unevenly. It lacks any distinguishing flavor. Wrappers are dull and papery. **$**

Belinda (HON)

Strength: Mild
Lighting & Burning: 13/15 (A-)
Taste: 22/35 (D)

Appearance: 15/20 (B-)
Construction: 20/30 (D)
Final Grade: 70/100 (C-)

A lot of smokers disagree with me on this cigar. I have not had much success finding consistently constructed, smooth-smoking Belinda cigars, but perhaps I'm looking in the wrong places. Belindas are deficient in quality, often showing spongy construction and rough wrappers. They tend to burn unevenly. The tobacco is green, albeit smokable. **$$**

Jose Benito (DOM)

Strength: Mild
Lighting & Burning: 13/15 (A-)
Taste: 25/35 (D)

Appearance: 15/20 (B-)
Construction: 23/30 (C-)
Final Grade: 76/100 (C+)

Pleasant and undistinguished, with inconsistent and dry wrappers, the tobacco shows signs of insufficient quality and aging. **$**

Bering (HON)

Strength: Mild
Lighting & Burning: 14/15 (A)
Taste: 26/35 (C-)

Appearance: 15/20 (B-)
Construction: 25/30 (B-)
Final Grade: 80/100 (B-)

A few years ago, the maker introduced a handmade version of this formerly all machine-made line. It's a nice, mild smoke, but the flavor lacks much complexity. The wrappers are attractive but dry, the filler tobacco is nice and generally well-aged, and construction is consistently good. **$**

Borhani (COS)

Strength: Medium to medium-full
Lighting & Burning: 7/15 (C-)
Taste: 22/35 (D)

Appearance: 20/20 (A+)
Construction: 20/30 (D)
Final Grade: 69/100 (C-)

Assembled in Costa Rica, the Borhani incorporates tobaccos from several countries. It's a great-looking cigar with a simple but eye-catching yellow band. The cigar tends to burn unevenly, however, which is a great disappointment because the wrappers are gorgeous, dark, and oily. The tobaccos inside are young, and become sharp and bitter during smoking. It apparently lacks the aged leaf necessary to be a great smoke. It could improve and mellow with a couple of years in your humidor, but aging won't help the construction. **$$$**

Butera (HON)

Strength: Full-bodied
Lighting & Burning: 14/15 (A)
Taste: 32/35 (B+)

Appearance: 20/20 (A+)
Construction: 27/30 (B+)
Final Grade: 93/100 (A)

This robust cigar is consistently well made using attractive, smooth colorado claro wrappers. Some smokers say they detect bitterness, but I never have, and I've smoked many Buteras. I do notice a faint, almost seaweed resonance, which is not at all unpleasant. Mike Butera is a world-class U.S. pipe maker, and his cigars reflect a commitment to quality. Made in limited quantities, they're tough to find, but worth the hunt. *Great Smoke* $$$$

Caballeros (DOM)

Strength: Medium-mild
Lighting & Burning: 12/15 (B+)
Taste: 28/35 (C)

Appearance: 17/20 (B+)
Construction: 22/30 (C-)
Final Grade: 79/100 (B-)

Caballeros are generally well made with shade-grown wrappers, but they lack complexity in flavor and tend toward an overly tight draw. The aging of the filler tobaccos is somewhat inconsistent, but good enough to have attracted a loyal following. *Best Buy* $$

Las Cabrillas (HON)

Strength: Medium
Lighting & Burning: 12/15 (B+)
Taste: 20/35 (D)

Appearance: 16/20 (B)
Construction: 20/30 (D)
Final Grade: 68/100 (C-)

This cigar suffers from inconsistent construction and shows consistently underage tobacco that gives it a vegetal and sometimes bitter character. $

Calixto Lopez (Philippines)

Strength: Medium-mild
Lighting & Burning: 13/15 (A-)
Taste: 20/35 (D)

Appearance: 14/20 (C+)
Construction: 17/30 (D)
Final Grade: 64/100 (D)

This is an inexpensive cigar, with a taste to match. The wrappers are dry and papery, and the tobaccos are harsh. $

Canaria D'Oro (DOM)

Strength: Mild
Lighting & Burning: 14/15 (A)
Taste: 31/35 (B)

Appearance: 16/20 (B)
Construction: 25/30 (B-)
Final Grade: 86/100 (B+)

Among mild cigars, this is one of the nicer selections. It also benefits from aging at least six months, and will develop additional flavor in your humidor. I have some that are three or four years old, and I'd swear they're better for the aging. Crammed into boxes, the cigars show a lot of box pressure (square instead of round), which is a flaw. Many smokers say the cigar is bland. However, it is an older, established brand and has proven itself over the years with consistent flavor and quality. It combines good taste with a low price. *Great Smoke & Best Buy* $

Casa Blanca (DOM)

Strength: Mild
Lighting & Burning: 14/15 (A)
Taste: 31/35 (B)

Appearance: 18/20 (A-)
Construction: 26/30 (B)
Final Grade: 89/100 (B+)

This is a nice-looking cigar that comes with both a very dark maduro and an attractive natural shade-grown wrapper. It's well-constructed and smooth-burning. If you're into really thick cigars, the line features the Jeroboam, an outrageous 10 inches with a 66 ring gauge (a 50 ring is the outer limits for most cigars) and a half Jeroboam at 5 inches by 66 ring that looks somewhat obscene. Mild and usually well-aged cigars, they have a somewhat bland flavor, but are still great, mild smokes. *Best Buy* **$$**

Juan Clemente (DOM)

Strength: Medium-full
Lighting & Burning: 14/15 (A)
Taste: 23/35 (D)

Appearance: 19/20 (A)
Construction: 23/30 (C-)
Final Grade: 79/100 (B-)

This cigar features a band applied to the foot of the cigar instead of the usual placement near the head. It's beautiful looking, but I find that these cigars become very tarry and bitter halfway through the smoke, which is inexcusable for a premium cigar. **$$$$**

Credo (DOM)

Strength: Medium
Lighting & Burning: 14/15 (A)
Taste: 31/35 (B)

Appearance: 18/20 (A-)
Construction: 27/30 (B+)
Final Grade: 90/100 (A)

Since being introduced a few years ago, this cigar seems to have maintained a high level of quality and consistency. It has a complex and interesting flavor, excellent construction, and pleasant greenish-brown Connecticut shade-grown wrappers. The cigars feature offbeat names like Arcane and Pythagoras. *Great Smoke* **$$$**

Cruz Real (MEX)

Strength: Medium to medium-full
Lighting & Burning: 13/15 (A-)
Taste: 28/35 (C)

Appearance: 14/20 (C+)
Construction: 23/30 (C)
Final Grade: 78/100 (B)

Typical of Mexican-made smokes, the Cruz Real line has somewhat dry wrappers and tastes like the tobaccos were not aged sufficiently. Among Mexican-made cigars, this relative newcomer seems like one of the best. I haven't smoked enough of them to judge long-term consistency. **$$**

Cuba Aliados (HON)

Strength: Full-bodied
Lighting & Burning: 14/15 (A)
Taste: 32/35 (B+)

Appearance: 19/20 (A)
Construction: 24/30 (C+)
Final Grade: 89/100 (A-)

The chocolate-brown EMS wrappers on these cigars are shiny, and the hard-to-find natural wrapper is nice, too. The supply of these smokes is spotty—and recent cigars I've seen have spotty wrappers, as well. The overall quality is good, but it may be degrading because of a shortage of leaf. The line features lots of sizes, including an excellent Churchill and hard-to-roll pyramid shape. Even burning and very smooth for a robust cigar, with no bitterness. The tobacco seems consistently well fermented and aged, and the price is very reasonable. If Cuba Aliados has a flaw, it's that too many cigars are too tightly rolled. *Best Buy & Great Smoke* **$$**

Cubita (DOM)

Strength: Mild
Lighting & Burning: 13/15 (A-)
Taste: 27/35 (C)

Appearance: 16/20 (B)
Construction: 23/30 (C)
Final Grade: 79/100 (B-)

This line offers a relatively mild but interesting smoke, slow and even burning until the final inch or two. If you toss the cigar with a couple of inches left, it would get a higher rating. However, I detected increasing harshness on some samples as the cigars burned past halfway, and a tendency to burn unevenly with a couple inches left. **$$**

Cuesta Rey (DOM)

Strength: Mild
Lighting & Burning: 13/15 (A-)
Taste: 31/35 (B)

Appearance: 18/20 (A-)
Construction: 27/30 (B+)
Final Grade: 89/100 (A-)

This is a very pleasant line made for M&N Cigar by A. Fuente y Cia. It's well made, extremely consistent, and available with natural or maduro wrappers that are generally a bit on the dry side. It is a good, but not a great or complex smoke. For the money, however, it's an excellent value. *Best Buy* **$**

Davidoff Nos. 1–3, Aniversario 1 and 2, Ambassadrice (DOM)

Strength: Medium-mild
Lighting & Burning: 15/15 (A+)
Taste: 33/35 (A)

Appearance: 20/20 (A+)
Construction: 30/30 (A+)
Final Grade: 98/100 (A+)

Davidoff produces several lines of cigars featuring different blends. These cigars are the mildest of the Davidoff series, but still have a lot of body and flavor. In price-weighted ratings, Davidoff cigars get downgraded because of their extremely high price—they are one of the most expensive smokes available. Price aside, every aspect of every Davidoff is nearly perfect because of high-quality tobacco, good construction, and meticulous quality control. The natural, Connecticut shade-grown wrappers are excellent and consistent in color and quality within each box, but will vary considerably from box to box—from olive green to a rich colorado rosa. Most wrappers are oily and silky. *Great Smoke* **$$$$**

Davidoff 1000 Series (DOM)

Strength: Medium
Lighting & Burning: 15/15 (A+)
Taste: 33/35 (A)
Appearance: 20/20 (A+)
Construction: 30/30 (A+)
Final Grade: 98/100 (A+)

The entire Davidoff line is made by Hendrik Kelner, who also manufactures two of the world's other great smokes, Avo Uvezian's Avo and Paul Garmirian's PG. This Davidoff series offers a little spice and a medium body you expect to find only in more robust cigars. Filler tobaccos are well aged and mature. To my mind, the major flaw (other than price) in this series is that most ring gauges in the Davidoff line are thinner than I like (30 to 42) to get sufficient smoke volume. Only the #5000, at $5^{1}/_{2}$ inches by 46 ring, has a satisfactory circumference. *Great Smoke* **$$$$**

Davidoff Gran Cru Series (DOM)

Strength: Medium-full
Lighting & Burning: 15/15 (A+)
Taste: 34/35 (A)
Appearance: 20/20 (A+)
Construction: 30/30 (A+)
Final Grade: 99/100 (A+)

As far as the rating goes, second verse same as the first! Although fuller than other Davidoffs, the smokes in this series are not what you'd call robust, but they do have body and very pleasant spice. This series was developed as the Dominican alternative to Davidoff's discontinued Cuban line, and it upholds the tradition. The quality is impeccable but, once again, I find the ring gauges of the five sizes (40 to 42) too thin. The cigars' length-to-width balance is close to perfect. *Great Smoke* **$$$$**

Davidoff Special and Double "R", Special "T", and Tubo (DOM)

Strength: Robust
Lighting & Burning: 15/15 (A+)
Taste: 34/35 (A)
Appearance: 20/20 (A+)
Construction: 30/30 (A+)
Final Grade: 99/100 (A+)

These are the fullest-bodied cigars offered by Davidoff—and my favorites. The ring gauges of these three are wider, allowing more smoke volume. The Special R ($5^{1}/_{2}$ inches by 50 ring) is a superb robusto, the Double R (7 inches by 52 ring) is excellent, and the Special T is one of the best pyramid shapes you'll find. The Tubo is a bit thin at 6 inches by 38 ring, but each comes in a white tube and is wrapped in cedar and makes a nice gift. *Great Smoke* **$$$$**

Diana Silvius (DOM)

Strength: Medium
Lighting & Burning: 14/15 (A)
Taste: 33/35 (A-)

Appearance: 19/20 (A)
Construction: 28/30 (A-)
Final Grade: 94/100 (A)

This cigar is well made, with good body and relatively complex taste. It has a cedar resonance from marrying time in cedar aging rooms. *Great Smoke* **$$$**

Don Diego (DOM)

Strength: Mild
Lighting & Burning: 15/15 (A+)
Taste: 32/35 (B+)

Appearance: 17/20 (A-)
Construction: 30/30 (A+)
Final Grade: 94/100 (A)

This is an old-line brand and, amazingly to me, overlooked by many cigar smokers because it isn't new and sexy. I'll take established and consistent any day! Made by Consolidated Cigar Co. and overseen by the quality-conscious Richard DiMeola, it's a bastion of consistency. If there's a drawback, it's that the flavor is very mild and not particularly complex, but not every cigar has to knock your ears off. As a mild smoke, its Macanudo is equal at a much lower price. The line offers lots of shapes and sizes. The coffee-and-cream colored, natural shade-grown wrappers are a bit on the dry side, but are very consistent in color and quality. Only a couple of shapes come in maduro. *Best Buy & Great Smoke* **$$**

Don Juan (DOM)

Strength: Mild
Lighting & Burning: 13/15 (A-)
Taste: 20/35 (D)

Appearance: 17/20 (B+)
Construction: 23/30 (C)
Final Grade: 73/100 (C)

A lot of smokers like this cigar, but others complain it is both bland and bitter. It doesn't have a complex or interesting flavor, but the line does carry a reasonable price tag. The aging of the tobacco seems somewhat inconsistent. Don Diego, Baccarat, Macanudo, and Cuesta Rey are all better mild cigars. **$$**

Don Lino, Don Lino Habano Series, Don Lino Colorado Series (HON)

Strength: Medium-mild
Lighting & Burning: 11/15 (B)
Taste: 25/35 (C-)

Appearance: 19/20 (A)
Construction: 24/30 (C+)
Final Grade: 79/100 (B-)

This line has rapidly grown in popularity since its introduction a few years ago, but I find all of the Don Lino cigars to smoke somewhat harsh, hot, and bitter. Even the Colorado and Habano Reserve lines, which feature different blends and use more vintage tobacco, are somewhat harsh. Because so many people like them, I strongly suggest you try them for yourself. **$$$**

Don Tomas (HON)

Strength: Very full-bodied
Lighting & Burning: 14/15 (A)
Taste: 18/35 (D)

Appearance: 19/20 (A)
Construction: 28/30 (A-)
Final Grade: 79/100 (B-)

This is a heavy, old-style Honduran line of cigars. Many smokers, including me, would call it harsh and strong, which it has always been. It's consistently well made with attractive dark wrappers, but the taste of the tobaccos shows signs of brief aging and is almost unpleasantly peppery. It's a favorite of some, but it isn't what I'd call a "polished" cigar. If you like a "rough and ready" stogie, you might like the Don Tomas line. **$$**

Don Tomas Special Edition (HON)

Strength: Medium
Lighting & Burning: 14/15 (A-)
Taste: 30/35 (B)

Appearance: 13/20 (C)
Construction: 28/30 (A-)
Final Grade: 85/100 (B+)

The five sizes in the special edition line are very different in flavor and strength from the regular Don Tomas. The special edition line is relatively mild and well-constructed. It's a bit harsh, but it's still an interesting cigar because it combines a mild smoke with that dryish, peppery, Honduran cigar-making style. The natural wrappers can be incredibly blotchy and unattractive, but some are smooth and creamy. Inconsistency earns a slap on the knuckles with teacher's ruler, and the score and grade gets lowered. **$$$**

Dunhill (DOM)

Strength: Medium
Lighting & Burning: 13/15 (A-)
Taste: 32/35 (B+)

Appearance: 19/20 (A)
Construction: 29/30 (A)
Final Grade: 93/100 (A)

This is a flavorful, medium-bodied line using well-aged tobaccos and featuring only natural wrappers. The line includes Dunhill Dominicans as well as Dunhill Canary Island cigars, which are assembled in the Canary Islands. The Canary Island smokes are supposedly milder, in the Canary Island tradition, but I can't tell a difference. The Dunhill line offers several tubed selections, good for gifts and traveling. Dunhills strike a nice balance between lengths and ring gauges, creating very attractive cigars with a preponderance of larger ring gauges (48 to 50). Although they are very well made and even-burning, some smokers find they lack a degree of character and complexity. They used to be pricey, but everyone else has caught up to them and Dunhill now represents a decent value. *Great Smoke & Best Buy* **$$$**

Dunhill Montecruz Sun Grown (DOM)

Strength: Medium
Lighting & Burning: 14/15 (A)
Taste: 31/35 (B)

Appearance: 16/20 (B)
Construction: 26/30 (B)
Final Grade: 87/100 (A-)

This cigar offers dark, sun-grown, natural wrappers, which have a slightly stronger and more vegetal, asparagus flavor than shade-grown wrappers. (This flavor isn't bad, but it is unique.) The Montecruz line occasionally can be a little harsh and the wrappers are inconsistent, ranging from oily to dry. It does have a unique flavor, however, and thus represents a true change of pace in your cigar-smoking repertoire. *Best Buy* **$$**

8-9-8 Collection (DOM)

Strength: Medium
Lighting & Burning: 11/15 (B)
Taste: 26/35 (C-)

Appearance: 18/20 (A-)
Construction: 23/30 (C)
Final Grade: 78/100 (B-)

I've notice an unpleasant, slightly metallic taste throughout the smoke. The construction of the cigars tends toward spongy, but the overall draw is good and the burn rate is reasonably even. I've noted signs of lack of aging in the filler tobaccos. **$$$**

El Rey del Mundo (HON)

Strength: Medium to heavy
Lighting & Burning: 13/15 (A-)
Taste: 22/35 (D)

Appearance: 18/20 (A-)
Construction: 24/30 (C+)
Final Grade: 77/100 (C+)

To my taste buds, the El Rey is a harsh and heavy cigar. Because I've seen it described as everything from mild to heavy, somebody has to be wrong. You'd better try it for yourself. The El Rey has a peppery, biting taste that some smokers crave. Construction and quality is inconsistent. If you smoke enough of them, you'll find that some are good, but many are not. It's a classic old-style Honduran cigar with harsh tobacco—which I don't like. **$**

El Sublimado (DOM)

Strength: Mild
Lighting & Burning: 14/15 (A)
Taste: 33/35 (A-)

Appearance: 19/20 (A)
Construction: 28/30 (A-)
Final Grade: 94/100 (A)

Made for Hardy Cognac in the Dominican Republic, this is an interesting cigar because the leaf is cured in rooms with Hardy Cognac. (The cognac is not applied directly to the leaf.) This is the only premium cigar cured with fine spirits, but there's barely a hint of the brandy. There's also a single-malt whiskey-cured El Sublimado, the flavor of which is very faint. The spirit's smell on the unsmoked wrappers is more pronounced than in the actual smoking. The construction is excellent, and most of the natural wrappers are rich and oily, but some are papery. The El Sublimado line offers several sizes. It's an extremely expensive smoke, and if you can't taste much Cognac flavor, it's a lot to pay for a mild cigar. *Great Smoke* **$$$$**

La Finca (NIC)

Strength: Medium
Lighting & Burning: 12/15 (B+)
Taste: 20/35 (D-)

Appearance: 14/20 (C+)
Construction: 23/30 (C)
Final Grade: 69/100 (C-)

Like many Nicaraguan cigars that use a considerable amount of Nicaraguan tobacco, occasional cigars in this line can be good, but the quality from cigar to cigar is highly inconsistent. Nicaraguan tobacco crops haven't recovered from that country's civil war, and even when good leaf is produced, it's often skimmed off by top makers in Honduras and the Dominican Republic. **$**

Flor de Florez (DOM)

Strength: Medium
Lighting & Burning: 13/15 (A-)
Taste: 24/35 (C-)

Appearance: 17/20 (B+)
Construction: 24/30 (C+)
Final Grade: 78/100 (B-)

This is an attractively wrapped line of cigars with a middle-of-the-road flavor and decent construction. It's pleasant, not too expensive, and a nice, average cigar. **$**

Flor de Florez Cabinet Selection (DOM)

Strength: Medium to medium-full
Lighting & Burning: 13/15 (A-)
Taste: 32/35 (B+)

Appearance: 18/20 (A-)
Construction: 26/30 (B)
Final Grade: 89/100 (A-)

This line is a step up from the regular Flor de Florez, and uses some very nice, aged tobaccos. Because it's a relative newcomer, I wonder whether it can maintain the quality it now shows. I hope so, because the wrappers are attractive and relatively oily, and the cigar is well constructed with a smooth, even draw. *Great Smoke* **$$$**

Fonseca (DOM)

Strength: Medium
Lighting & Burning: 14/15 (A)
Taste: 33/35 (A-)

Appearance: 19/20 (A)
Construction: 28/30 (A-)
Final Grade: 94/100 (A)

This brand, which has a marketing tie-in with Fonseca port, took off like a rocket in the early 1990s and never looked back. There's a Cuban Fonseca, so don't get the two confused. Interestingly, people seem to either love it or hate it, and some smokers find it harsh, but I haven't noticed this trait. I would say the line shows body and some spice. To smokers of mild cigars, the Fonseca is too heavy. For those who like full-bodied cigars, this is a milder alternative that still shows character. The triangular is one of the most reasonably priced pyramids available, and it's very well made. Recently, I've had a few Fonsecas that show signs of green tobacco and tend toward some bitterness, but I'm hoping that with a top-notch maker like Manuel Queseda at the helm, this cigar will remain great. *Great Smoke & Best Buy* **$$**

La Fontana (HON)

Strength: Medium-full
Lighting & Burning: 12/15 (B+)
Taste: 27/35 (B)

Appearance: 15/20 (B-)
Construction: 25/30 (B-)
Final Grade: 81/100 (B-)

There's nothing distinguishing about this brand, except for the sizes named after great Italian artists, musicians, and scientists. **$$**

Arturo Fuente Regular Line (DOM)

Strength: Medium
Lighting & Burning: 12/15 (B+)
Taste: 31/35 (B)

Appearance: 18/20 (A-)
Construction: 27/30 (B+)
Final Grade: 88/100 (A-)

This is a solid brand with lots of sizes and shapes, excellent construction, and good value. In its price range, this is one of the most reliable, consistent cigars you'll find. The cigars are blended to have some spice, and some smokers find them a bit harsh. Box to box, however, you'll get the same consistent taste over and over because Fuente controls much of its tobacco crop, and then blends in leaf from other nations. The company also properly ages its tobaccos. *Best Buy* **$**

Arturo Fuente Chateau and Double Chateau (DOM)

Strength: Medium-full
Lighting & Burning: 13/15 (A-)
Taste: 34/35 (A)

Appearance: 19/20 (A)
Construction: 28/30 (A-)
Final Grade: 94/100 (A)

Most smokers don't know this, but these two cigars, one a Rothschild and the other a double Rothschild, have a different, spicier blend than the regular Fuente line. The Rothschild, or robusto, is one of the best on the market, packing a lot of punch in a short smoke. Rothschilds are individually wrapped in cedar, which accentuates the cedar flavor they get from spending time in Fuentes' cedar-lined aging room. They come in a natural Connecticut shade-grown wrapper and a hard-to-find maduro wrapper. *Great Smoke & Best Buy* **$$**

Arturo Fuente Hemingway Series (DOM)

Strength: Medium-mild
Lighting & Burning: 15/15 (A+)
Taste: 34/35 (A)

Appearance: 20/20 (A+)
Construction: 28/30 (A-)
Final Grade: 97/100 (A+)

With an impeccable Cameroon wrapper, the cigars in this series exhibit the height of the cigar-roller's art with a tapered foot and head: the classic and seldom-found "perfecto" shape. If anything, the cigars are occasionally rolled too lovingly and tightly, so the draw can be a little firm. The lush "Masterpiece" (9 inches by 52 ring) is a celebratory cigar at a very reasonable price. *Great Smoke & Best Buy* **$$$**

Arturo Fuente Don Carlos Reserve Series (DOM)

Strength: Full-bodied
Lighting & Burning: 15/15 (A+)
Taste: 34/35 (A)

Appearance: 19/20 (A)
Construction: 28/30 (A-)
Final Grade: 96/100 (A+)

Although the selection of sizes in this line is extremely limited, as is supply, the cigars show the usual excellent Fuente construction. The robusto is excellent. *Great Smoke* **$$$**

Fuente Fuente OpusX (DOM)

Strength: Robust and full-bodied
Lighting & Burning: 15/15 (A+)
Taste: 35/35 (A+)

Appearance: 20/20 (A+)
Construction: 26/30 (B)
Final Grade: 96/100 (A+)

If you like a very spicy, powerful, Cuban-style cigar, the Fuente Fuente OpusX fits the description. It's well made, using very aged tobacco with noticeable hints of cedar aging. The construction can occasionally be overly firm, but the cigar is made with high levels of consistency and care. The cigar has a large band that must be removed to finish the cigar, so be careful not to tear the dark, oily, Dominican-grown EMS wrapper. It's a hard-to-find and expensive smoke, but is one of the heartiest Cuban-style cigars you'll encounter. *Great Smoke* **$$$$**

Gispert (DOM)

Strength: Medium
Lighting & Burning: 13/15 (A-)
Taste: 31/35 (B)

Appearance: 18/20 (A-)
Construction: 25/30 (B-)
Final Grade: 87/100 (A-)

This cigar is only available to smoke shops that are members of a special tobacconists association. If you patronize a shop that carries it, you'll find a very nice, smooth line of cigars that uses well-aged tobaccos and is well constructed. It's a good smoke at a reasonable price. *Best Buy* **$$$**

La Gloria Cubana (US)

Strength: Medium to full
Lighting & Burning: 11/15 (B)
Taste: 27/35 (C)

Appearance: 15/20 (B-)
Construction: 24/30 (C+)
Final Grade: 77/100 (C+)

This line isn't one of my highest-ranking brands for one reason: The caliber of the tobaccos is hopelessly inconsistent. If he gets good leaf, manufacturer Ernesto Carillo can make one of the best cigars around. I've had La Glorias that were like a dream and others that were a nightmare of green tobaccos. That's why the taste rating for the brand is so low. It used to be an inexpensive smoke and worth the risk of an occasional bad stogie, but it has become both expensive and hard to find, taking away any advantage it once enjoyed. **$$$$**

The Griffin's (DOM)

Strength: Mild
Lighting & Burning: 12/15 (B+)
Taste: 30/35 (B-)

Appearance: 16/20 (B)
Construction: 25/30 (B-)
Final Grade: 83/100 (B)

The lack of large ring sizes in this brand is frustrating if you like the smoking characteristics of a thicker cigar. Most Griffin's run 38 to 44 ring gauge. Some smokers find the cigar bland, but as a mild cigar, I think it's complex and interesting. My favorite is the Prestige. At 8 inches by 48 ring, it's a good value. Construction of the line is good, but the natural shade-grown wrappers are inconsistent and sometimes papery. I've even come across the rare, reddish tan, and oily colorado rosa wrappers on this brand. $$$

Henry Clay (DOM)

Strength: Medium
Lighting & Burning: 13/15 (A-)
Taste: 22/35 (D)

Appearance: 13/20 (C)
Construction: 23/30 (C)
Final Grade: 71/100 (C)

Some folks really like this cigar, and it's easy to find. It has a gnarled, dark wrapper and I find it gets bitter. It's inexpensive, but in this league, I much prefer the Munniemaker machine-made tubed cigar, which uses all Connecticut tobacco and is just as dark and ugly as the Henry Clay, but smoother. Box pressure makes the cigars square. $

Thomas Hinds (HON)

Strength: Medium-full
Lighting & Burning: 12/15 (B+)
Taste: 30/35 (B)

Appearance: 18/20 (A-)
Construction: 25/30 (B-)
Final Grade: 86/100 (B+)

When this cigar first came out, it was one of the least expensive premium smokes around, and it was delicious. I bought boxloads, which I'm still enjoying. (See why it pays to have a humidor?) The introductory price was raised, and the quality and consistency of the filler tobaccos seem to have diminished slightly in the past couple years. Still, the Hinds features a good range of standard sizes and nice, thick ring gauges on all sizes. The line has a smooth natural Ecuadorian wrapper, double binder, and primarily Honduran filler. The cigars burn evenly, and although they are Honduran, they aren't strong or peppery. The line is worth your while to try to find it. $$$

Thomas Hinds Nicaraguan Selection (NIC)

Strength: Medium
Lighting & Burning: 13/15 (A-)
Taste: 26/35 (C-)

Appearance: 17/20 (B+)
Construction: 27/30 (B+)
Final Grade: 83/100 (B-)

Among the blended cigars being made with primarily Nicaraguan tobaccos, this line is consistently well made and has nice, subtle flavors. It tastes a little rough and dry, however. It might improve with aging; the tobaccos seem a little short on finished aging but generally seem well-fermented. **$$$**

Hoyo de Monterrey (HON)

Strength: Full
Lighting & Burning: 14/15 (A)
Taste: 27/35 (C+)

Appearance: 16/20 (B)
Construction: 26/30 (B)
Final Grade: 83/100 (B)

This regular Hoyo line is somewhat harsh and overly peppery, consistent with-old style Hondurans. If you like strong Honduran smokes *a la* Don Tomas and Punch, the Hoyo is the best of that bunch. **$**

Hoyo de Monterrey Excalibur (HON)

Strength: Full
Lighting & Burning: 14/15 (A)
Taste: 33/35 (A-)

Appearance: 18/20 (A-)
Construction: 28/30 (A-)
Final Grade: 93/100 (A)

The Hoyo Excalibur line is easy to distinguish from regular Hoyos by the label, which says "Excalibur" and Roman numeral sizes I through VII. This cigar is full-bodied, but the tobacco is well fermented and aged and very smooth. Both the English claro and maduro wrappers are attractive. Even the smaller Excaliburs are tasty and smooth. More expensive than the regular Hoyo line, the Excalibur is still an excellent value. *Great Smoke & Best Buy* **$$**

Joya de Nicaragua (NIC)

Strength: Medium
Lighting & Burning: 12/15 (B+)
Taste: 22/35 (D)

Appearance: 15/20 (B-)
Construction: 27/30 (B+)
Final Grade: 76/100 (C+)

This was once a fine line, but the civil war of the 1970s and 1980s virtually destroyed the tobacco fields. Joya has always relied heavily on Nicaraguan tobacco, and while the fields are beginning to recover, there isn't enough supply of aged leaf to fill these cigars. They're generally harsh cigars, without much complexity. **$$**

Leon Jiminez (DOM)

Strength: Full
Lighting & Burning: 11/15 (B)
Taste: 20/35 (D)

Appearance: 14/20 (C+)
Construction: 23/30 (C)
Final Grade: 68/100 (C-)

Made by La Aurora, this brand exhibits the same inconsistency of tobacco you'll find in La Aurora. This is a very heavy cigar, but also bitter, with lots of tar. Here's hoping Guillermo Léon can return the line to former glory. **$$**

JR Ultimate (HON)

Strength: Full-bodied and robust
Lighting & Burning: 14/15 (A)
Taste: 31/35 (B)

Appearance: 19/20 (A)
Construction: 25/30 (B-)
Final Grade: 89/100 (A-)

This cigar is heavy but smooth. It had some quality-control problems for a couple years, particularly related to the loss of Honduran leaf to blue mold, but returned to its former quality and consistency a few years ago. Now, it seems as if the exclusive retailer, Lew Rothman of JR Cigars, cannot get enough leaf to even begin to keep up with demand for the Ultimate. The line offers a multitude of sizes and wrappers, including jade. *Best Buy* **$$**

Jose Llopis (PAN)

Strength: Medium-full
Lighting & Burning: 13/15 (A-)
Taste: 28/35 (C)

Appearance: 18/20 (A-)
Construction: 23/30 (C)
Final Grade: 82/100 (B)

It's hard to find this line, which features good cigars at reasonable prices. Well constructed, with a tendency to be too firm, the line features somewhat dry wrappers and an even draw. **$$**

Licenciados (DOM)

Strength: Medium-mild
Lighting & Burning: 12/15 (B+)
Taste: 26/35 (C)

Appearance: 18/20 (A-)
Construction: 25/30 (B-)
Final Grade: 81/100 (B)

Individual cigars in this line have received some high ratings in cigar publications, which I don't agree with. While it's a tasty, reasonably priced line, it can't compete with the top brands. It tends to be harsh due to underage tobaccos. It can be very good, and has developed a devoted following, but if it were more consistent, it would be a much better cigar. It features a Dominican filler, Honduran binder, and consistently average to dry Connecticut shade-grown wrapper. It lacks complexity, but is a good value, burns evenly, and is reliable and pleasant as an "everyday" smoke. *Best Buy* **$$**

Macanudo (JAM/DOM)

Strength: Mild
Lighting & Burning: 14/15 (A)
Taste: 33/35 (A)

Appearance: 19/20 (A)
Construction: 28/30 (A-)
Final Grade: 94/100 (A)

The country of assembly is listed as Jamaica, famed for mild stogies, but much of the tobacco is Dominican. The Macanudo line is one of the most consistent, well-constructed brands you'll find. Many veteran smokers think they're far too bland, but if you enjoy mild cigars, or occasionally feel like a break from heavier cigars, this is a great smoke from

General Cigar Co. Macanudos come in a huge variety of shapes, a few with a maduro wrapper option, but most with Connecticut shade-grown wrappers. The small Ascots (4$^1/_8$ inches by 32 ring) are great small smokes, while large sizes such as the Prince Philip (7$^1/_2$ inches by 49 ring) are good values. Value in the rest of the line depends on the particular shape. *Great Smoke & Best Buy* **$$$**

Macanudo Vintage Collection (JAM/DOM)

Strength: Mild to medium
Lighting & Burning: 14/15 (A-)
Taste: 31/35 (B)

Appearance: 19/20 (A)
Construction: 28/30 (A-)
Final Grade: 92/100 (A-)

This line offers a distinctly heartier flavor than the regular Macanudo line. It comes with a super-premium price, and it isn't on a par with some of the other smokes in its price league. While its tobaccos are well-aged, the blend isn't very interesting or complex. **$$$$**

Montecristo (DOM)

Strength: Medium
Lighting & Burning: 13/15 (A-)
Taste: 31/35 (B)

Appearance: 18/20 (A-)
Construction: 24/30 (C+)
Final Grade: 86/100 (B+)

This new introduction is yet another effort to borrow classic Havana names and use them in non-Havana cigars. It's a good-looking line, with a bit of spice. The samples I've tried burned somewhat unevenly. Time will tell whether this brand can maintain consistency. **$$$**

Montecruz (See Dunhill Montecruz)

Montesino (DOM)

Strength: Mild
Lighting & Burning: 12/15 (B+)
Taste: 31/35 (B)

Appearance: 17/20 (B+)
Construction: 26/30 (B)
Final Grade: 87/100 (B)

For an inexpensive, handmade, boxed cigar line just one step away from a no-name bundled smoke, this is a great cigar. It's not a big-time smoke, but it's a very pleasant "golf smoke" or low-cost supplement to bridge the gap between more expensive stogies. *Best Buy* **$**

Nat Sherman (DOM/HON)

Strength: Mild to robust
Lighting & Burning: 14/15 (A)
Taste: 33/35 (B+)

Appearance: 18/20 (A-)
Construction: 28/30 (A-)
Final Grade: 93/100 (A)

This brand, sold primarily through the Nat Sherman store in Manhattan, is tough to rate because the line contains cigars with different tastes and strengths. I've smoked many different Shermans, and they're consistently well made and delicious, from mild to the most robust. Like everything in New York, the cigars are expensive. **$$$**

New York (MEX)

Strength: Medium
Lighting & Burning: 12/15 (B+)
Taste: 24/35 (D)

Appearance: 17/20 (B+)
Construction: 23/30 (C)
Final Grade: 76/100 (C+)

This is a sub-brand of the Te Amo line, and the cigars are pleasant, average Mexican smokes. I feel like my bias against Mexican cigars is showing, but I find the taste somewhat harsh. **$$**

Dominican Olor (DOM)

Strength: Medium-mild
Lighting & Burning: 13/15 (A-)
Taste: 30/35 (B-)

Appearance: 17/20 (B+)
Construction: 26/30 (B)
Final Grade: 86/100 (B)

This well made cigar features good, smooth tobaccos. There isn't a lot of age behind Olor, but there isn't meant to be, nor is it priced as a great smoke. It's an excellent choice for an "everyday" cigar, or for something mild and pleasant on a weekend morning. *Best Buy* **$**

Onyx (DOM)

Strength: Medium
Lighting & Burning: 12/15 (B+)
Taste: 25/35 (C-)

Appearance: 15/20 (B-)
Construction: 25/30 (B-)
Final Grade: 77/100 (C+)

With its black oscuro wrapper, this cigar has created quite a sensation among maduro lovers and has developed a regular following. Today's shortage of maduro leaf makes it harder than ever to have a brand that features only maduro wrappers. The wrappers are relatively dry, especially for maduro, and not as naturally sweet as the best maduro leaves. The cigar frequently burns unevenly, but the flavor is very consistent from beginning to end, and there's no tar buildup. It tends to taste stale, and the aroma to those around you is also pungent and slightly stale. Still, smokers whose taste I respect enjoy the Onyx, so you may just have to try this cigar and decide for yourself. **$$**

Oscar (DOM)

Strength: Medium full
Lighting & Burning: 12/15 (B+)
Taste: 30/35 (B)

Appearance: 19/20 (A)
Construction: 27/30 (B+)
Final Grade: 88/100 (A-)

This cigar straddles the border between smooth sophistication and a peppery Cuban-style pizzazz. The flavor is nicely balanced and the tobaccos are consistent. Its aroma is pungent, so smoke these only with cigar-loving friends. It's an attractive brand with a Connecticut shade-grown wrapper. **$$$**

PG/Paul Garmirian (DOM)

Strength: Robust
Lighting & Burning: 15/15 (A+)
Taste: 35/35 (A+)

Appearance: 19/20 (A)
Construction: 30/30 (A+)
Final Grade: 99/100 (A+)

Another product of Hendrik Kelner's Dominican factory (like Davidoffs and Avos), every PG exhibits the relentless quality control of Kelner and its creator, Paul Garmirian. It's a robust, spicy, Havana-style brand and is extremely consistent and beautifully constructed. Production is very limited, and the brand isn't widely distributed. It was the first line to offer the tapered-tip Belicoso, a shape that's now all the rage among smokers. The PG "Bom-Bones" (3½ by 43) has won acclaim as one of the best small cigars made. The ring gauges are thick to maximize smoke volume. Despite being robust, the cigar smokes smooth. The shade-grown wrappers are excellent. This is one of the finest brands available. Although it's expensive, the price is reasonable compared with other super-premium smokes, given the quality and consistency. *Great Smoke* **$$$$**

Padron 1964 Anniversary Series (NIC)

Strength: Medium
Lighting & Burning: 13/15 (A-)
Taste: 20/35 (D)

Appearance: 17/20 (B+)
Construction: 26/30 (B)
Final Grade: 76/100 (C+)

This line, featuring all Nicaraguan tobacco, has received a lot of acclaim since its recent introduction. I think it shows signs of green tobacco and harshness, and there's a distinct damp-wood flavor I didn't like. This is a good example of a cigar I'd like to try several times in the future to make a better assessment. **$$$$**

Partagas (DOM)

Strength: Medium
Lighting & Burning: 14/15 (A)
Taste: 33/35 (A-)

Appearance: 18/20 (A-)
Construction: 27/30 (B+)
Final Grade: 92/100 (A)

This brand from General Cigar (which also makes Macanudo) has been, like Macanudo, a time-tested standard of quality and consistency. It's a nice choice because it has character and complexity, and it's one of the few lines still using the Cameroon wrapper, which has been hard to get in recent years. Because of this supply problem, some Partagas wrappers have looked a bit "shaggy" in the past, but wrapper quality seems to be improving. The cigar has a rich taste, yet isn't robust, which gives those who don't enjoy a "heavy" cigar the chance to enjoy the sensation of a full-bodied smoke. Some of the cigars exhibit squaring due to box pressure. *Great Smoke & Best Buy* **$$**

Petrus (HON)

Strength: Medium-full
Lighting & Burning: 13/15 (A-)
Taste: 28/35 (C)

Appearance: 18/20 (A-)
Construction: 25/30 (B-)
Final Grade: 84/100 (B+)

I haven't sampled and observed as many of these as I would like in order to judge the entire line. The ones I have smoked are moderately complex and a bit vegetal, but the tobacco seems well aged. I have heard complaints about spongy construction, and burning is a little uneven but acceptable. **$$**

Pleiades (DOM)

Strength: Mild
Lighting & Burning: 12/15 (B+)
Taste: 31/35 (B)

Appearance: 18/20 (A-)
Construction: 23/30 (C)
Final Grade: 84/100 (B+)

This is a pleasant, mild cigar with some complexity. The binder and filler exhibit fine and consistent construction, but the thin shade-grown wrappers tend to crack and unravel. **$$$$**

Por Larranaga (DOM)

Strength: Medium-mild
Lighting & Burning: 14/15 (A)
Taste: 28/35 (C)

Appearance: 18/20 (A-)
Construction: 26/30 (B)
Final Grade: 86/100 (B+)

This is a re-creation of the classic Cuban extolled by Rudyard Kipling in a famous poem. Wrapped individually in cedar with a gold band and pretty shade-grown wrapper, it makes a beautiful impression. However, I have found the brand shows some harshness and signs of insufficient aging. **$$$**

Primo del Rey (DOM)

Strength: Mild
Lighting & Burning: 10/15 (B-)
Taste: 24/35 (D)

Appearance: 11/20 (D)
Construction: 22/30 (D)
Final Grade: 67/100 (D+)

Mottled wrappers and spongy construction get the cigar off on the wrong foot. The cigars have a somewhat strong and acrid quality, with a distinctive hay-like barnyard character. The flavor tends to improve toward the end, but they burn unevenly getting there. **$**

Primo del Rey Club Selection (DOM)

Strength: Mild
Lighting & Burning: 12/15 (B+)
Taste: 28/35 (C)

Appearance: 16/20 (B)
Construction: 23/30 (C)
Final Grade: 78/100 (B-)

This series, with a white, red, and gold band, is distinctly better than the regular Primo brand. There is still a bit of the barnyard about the Club Selection, and it still burns somewhat unevenly due to spongy construction. **$$**

Punch (HON)

Strength: Strong
Lighting & Burning: 14/15 (A)
Taste: 20/35 (D)

Appearance: 19/20 (A)
Construction: 28/30 (A-)
Final Grade: 82/100 (B+)

Punch gets you right at the base of your throat. This is a harsh, rough, strong cigar that will tickle burned-out taste buds and overwhelm normal palates. It is, however, incredibly well-made and consistent. It's loved by many and hated by many. It is not a subtle cigar. Obviously, my low score for taste reflects my own very negative opinion. Try one for the experience and form your own opinion. **$**

Punch Gran Cru (HON)

Strength: Full-bodied
Lighting & Burning: 14/15 (A)
Taste: 33/35 (A-)

Appearance: 19/20 (A)
Construction: 28/30 (A-)
Final Grade: 94/100 (A)

The Gran Cru series is an entirely different creature from the regular Punch line. You have to be careful when you buy to look for the special bands—either a Punch band combined with a miniature Honduran cigar tax seal, or a red-and-gold Punch label with a black stripe at the bottom. The blend of high-quality Honduran, Dominican, and Mexican tobaccos is subtle and reflects thorough fermenting and aging. It's a beautifully constructed cigar and is consistent box after box. The Gran Cru is also an excellent value. *Great Smoke & Best Buy* **$$$**

Ramon Allones (DOM)

Strength: Medium
Lighting & Burning: 13/15 (A-)
Taste: 25/35 (D)

Appearance: 12/20 (C-)
Construction: 27/30 (B+)
Final Grade: 77/100 (C+)

This brand has been around for a while, but I sense underage tobacco and some consistent harshness. The wrappers are relatively dry and unattractive. There's nothing particularly striking, good or bad, about this brand. **$$**

Romeo y Julieta Vintage (DOM)

Strength: Mild to medium
Lighting & Burning: 14/15 (A)
Taste: 31/35 (B)

Appearance: 20/20 (A+)
Construction: 29/30 (A)
Final Grade: 94/100 (A)

From the initial appearance of the silky, shade-grown Connecticut wrappers to the final draw on a small stub, this cigar bespeaks quality. It is always in short supply, for good reason. It has been the immediate favorite of many smokers since its introduction a few years ago. There is subtle spice, yet the cigar is still mild. *Great Smoke* $$$$

Royal Jamaica (DOM)

Strength: Mild
Lighting & Burning: 13/15 (A-)
Taste: 31/35 (B)
Appearance: 17/20 (B+)
Construction: 27/30 (B+)
Final Grade: 88/100 (A-)

When this brand was produced by the Gore family in Jamaica, it was one of my favorites. It featured a secret flavoring process that gave Royal Jamaicas a unique taste. When the Gore's factory was completely destroyed by Hurricane Hugo, the brand was sold to General Cigar Company, and production shifted to the D.R. The cigars just don't taste the same. They're still pleasant and mild, however, and an enjoyable smoke. They offer a maduro wrapper, but all Royal Jamaica look a bit rough and dry. *Best Buy* $$

Santa Clara (MEX)

Strength: Mild
Lighting & Burning: 14/15 (A)
Taste: 29/35 (C+)
Appearance: 18/20 (A-)
Construction: 27/30 (B+)
Final Grade: 88/100 (A-)

This is a relatively smooth-smoking and attractive cigar, considering it's all Mexican tobacco. There is a bit too much bitterness and tar toward the end, but it's one of the best Mexican-made smokes available. *Best Buy* $

Saint Luis Rey (HON)

Strength: Medium
Lighting & Burning: 13/15 (A-)
Taste: 30/35 (B-)
Appearance: 20/20 (A+)
Construction: 27/30 (B+)
Final Grade: 90/100 (A)

This relatively new entry is yet another brand using the name of a classic Havana cigar. It's a tasty smoke, and the line so far seems very consistent. If this continues, it could be a long-term winner. *Great Smoke & Best Buy* $$

Santa Damiana (DOM)

Strength: Medium-mild
Lighting & Burning: 13/15 (A-)
Taste: 27/35 (C-)
Appearance: 18/20 (A+)
Construction: 28/30 (A-)
Final Grade: 86/100 (B+)

This brand has generated a lot of excitement since its introduction a few years ago. It's beautifully made with smooth Connecticut shade-grown wrappers. I find it's a little bitter and harsh, especially toward the end. It could be slightly underage tobacco, but it's still a good smoke. $$$

Sosa (DOM)

Strength: Medium   **Appearance:** 14/20 (C+)
Lighting & Burning: 12/15 (B+)   **Construction:** 22/30 (C-)
Taste: 25/35 (C-)   **Final Grade:** 73/100 (C)

Spongy construction is the biggest downfall of this brand. Veiny, poorly constructed wrappers detract from the appearance. This brand seems to exhibit inconsistent fermentation and aging of tobaccos. **$$**

Savinelli Extra Limited Reserve (DOM)

Strength: Medium to full   **Appearance:** 20/20 (A+)
Lighting & Burning: 15/15 (A+)   **Construction:** 29/30 (A)
Taste: 33/35 (A-)   **Final Grade:** 97/100 (A+)

This cigar is superior in every way. The line features hearty tobaccos with a bit of spice and very consistent appearance and flavor. If you enjoy this cigar, whose namesake is a top-line Italian pipe maker, you will enjoy it time and again because the line maintains the highest quality control. *Great Smoke* **$$$$**

Signet (DOM)

Strength: Mild   **Appearance:** 18/20 (B+)
Lighting & Burning: 12/15 (B+)   **Construction:** 28/30 (A-)
Taste: 31/35 (B)   **Final Grade:** 89/100 (A-)

This new entry from Lane Limited, which has a solid reputation for consistency, is very tasty, with interesting spice for an essentially mild cigar. Given the manufacturer's decades-long commitment to quality, this could be a winner. *Best Buy* **$$**

Te Amo (MEX)

Strength: Medium   **Appearance:** 17/20 (B+)
Lighting & Burning: 12/15 (A-)   **Construction:** 27/30 (B+)
Taste: 26/35 (C-)   **Final Grade:** 83/100 (B-)

This cigar is very consistently made at a reasonable price, but the Mexican tobacco is harsh. It's widely available with several wrapper styles. The maduro-wrapped cigar tastes a little sweeter than the natural wrapper. *Best Buy* **$**

Temple Hall (DOM/JAM)

Strength: Mild   **Appearance:** 20/20 (A+)
Lighting & Burning: 14/15 (A)   **Construction:** 29/30 (A)
Taste: 31/35 (B)   **Final Grade:** 94/100 (A)

This is the café latte of cigars: smooth, rich, and creamy. It's one of the best mild cigars available, yet exhibits a level of complexity that's unusual for a mild cigar. The construction is consistent and excellent and the wrappers are attractive silky shade-grown Connecticut leaf. Some Temple Hall sizes are also available with an attractive sweet maduro wrapper. This cigar ages well and improves in richness and complexity after a year or two in the right conditions. The belicoso shape is expensive but offers incredible oily, silky wrappers. Temple Hall has been an East Coast favorite for years, and is being discovered (slowly) by the rest of the country. If you can find it, Temple Hall is probably one of the finest mild cigars you're likely to find. *Great Smoke* **$$$**

Tressado (DOM)

Strength: Mild
Lighting & Burning: 13/15 (A-)
Taste: 29/35 (C+)

Appearance: 17/20 (B+)
Construction: 27/30 (B+)
Final Grade: 86/100 (B+)

With a pretty Indonesian wrapper and mild but interesting filler tobaccos, Tressado is a very affordable everyday smoke. Its mild but engaging flavor is great if you're just starting out with cigars. *Best Buy* **$$**

Troya (DOM)

Strength: Mild to medium
Lighting & Burning: 14/15 (A)
Taste: 28/35 (C)

Appearance: 18/20 (A-)
Construction: 28/30 (A-)
Final Grade: 88/100 (A-)

Introduced as a premium boxed cigar at a bundle cigar price, Troya has succeeded in that it's a fine and pleasant smoke. The blend and construction is very consistent. The tobaccos are nicely fermented, but the cigar seems a little short in the final aging and marrying. *Best Buy* **$$**

La Unica (DOM)

Strength: Mild
Lighting & Burning: 13/15 (A-)
Taste: 29/35 (C+)

Appearance: 17/20 (B+)
Construction: 26/30 (B)
Final Grade: 86/100 (B+)

Basically, this bundled cigar has been treated as a boxed cigar. It's a very nice cigar and certainly a good value. There's a tendency toward slightly spongy construction. It features an attractive Connecticut shade-grown wrapper and most sizes are available in maduro. A very good value. *Best Buy* **$**

H. Upmann (DOM)

Strength: Medium
Lighting & Burning: 14/15 (A)
Taste: 32/35 (B+)

Appearance: 20/20 (A+)
Construction: 28/30 (A-)
Final Grade: 94/100 (A)

The Upmann used to feature a great Cameroon wrapper, but the shortage and inconsistent quality of Cameroon prompted the maker, Consolidated Cigar Company, to switch to an attractive Indonesian wrapper. The taste isn't quite the same, but H. Upmann remains a standard of consistency and reliability. It never turns tarry or bitter, and is widely available at an exceptionally reasonable price. *Great Smoke & Best Buy* **$$**

V Centennial (HON)

Strength: Medium-full
Lighting & Burning: 14/15 (A)
Taste: 28/35 (C)

Appearance: 19/20 (A)
Construction: 28/30 (A-)
Final Grade: 89/100 (A-)

Although made in Honduras, the V Centennial is less robust than many Hondurans due to blended tobaccos from the Dominican Republic. It features smooth Connecticut shade wrappers. It lacks some complexity, but it's a pleasant smoke and offers a pretty torpedo shape. *Great Smoke & Best Buy* **$$$**

Vueltabajo (DOM)

Strength: Mild to medium
Lighting & Burning: 12/15 (B+)
Taste: 25/35 (C)

Appearance: 17/20 (B)
Construction: 26/30 (B)
Final Grade: 80/100 (B-)

This is a highfalutin' name for a cigar that has nothing to do with Cuba's Vuelta Abajo other than the Cuban seed tobacco it features, like most other non-Havana cigars. There's some harshness present. **$**

Zino (HON)

Strength: Medium to full-bodied
Lighting & Burning: 12/15 (B+)
Taste: 31/35 (B)

Appearance: 18/20 (A-)
Construction: 28/30 (A-)
Final Grade: 88/100 (A-)

This is a spicy, Honduran-style cigar that isn't overpowering, yet is relatively robust. The wrappers are a little dry and the average ring sizes are relatively thin (34 to 44). The line offers a nice panatela, if you like thinner cigars. The tobacco is well aged and the cigars never turn harsh or bitter. The foil-wrapped Classic Brazil and Classic Sumatra offer different tobacco tastes, if you enjoy Brazilian and Sumatran tobaccos. **$$$**

Best Buys

Baccarrat
Caballeros
Canaria D'Oro
Casa Blanca
Cuba Aliados
Cuesta Rey
Don Diego
Dunhill
Dunhill Montecruz Sun Grown
Fonseca
Arturo Fuente Regular Line
Arturo Fuente Chateau and Double Chateau
Arturo Fuente Hemingway Series
Gispert
Hoyo de Monterrey Excalibur
JR Ultimate

Licenciados
Macanudo
Montesino
Dominican Olor
Partagas
Punch Gran Cru
Royal Jamaica
Santa Clara
Saint Luis Rey
Signet
Te Amo
Tressado
Troya
La Unica
H. Upmann
V Centennial

Great Smokes

Ashton
Ashton Cabinet Selection
Avo Uvezian Regular and XO Series
Butera
Canaria D'Oro
Credo
Cuba Aliados
Davidoff Nos. 1–3, Aniversario 1 and 2,
    Ambassadrice
Davidoff 1000 Series
Davidoff Gran Cru Series
Davidoff Special and Double "R,"
    Special "T" and Tubo
Diana Silvius
Don Diego
Dunhill
El Sublimado

Flor de Florez Cabinet Selection
Fonseca
Arturo Fuente Chateau and Double Chateau
Arturo Fuente Hemingway Series
Arturo Fuente Don Carlos Reserve Series
Fuente Fuente OpusX
Hoyo de Monterrey Excalibur
Macanudo
PG/Paul Garmirian
Partagas
Punch Gran Cru
Romeo y Julieta Vintage
Saint Luis Rey
Savinelli Extra Limited Reserve
Temple Hall
H. Upmann
V Centennial

Best Buys/Great Smokes

Canaria D'Oro
Cuba Aliados
Don Diego
Dunhill
Fonseca
Arturo Fuente Chateau and Double Chateau
Arturo Fuente Hemingway Series

Hoyo de Monterrey Excalibur
Macanudo
Partagas
Punch Gran Cru
Saint Luis Rey
H. Upmann
V Centennial

Cigar Speak Glossary

8-9-8 packaging   This refers to cigars that are packed in a box three layers deep, with nine cigars in the middle and eight on the top and bottom rows.

aging   Storing stogies under humidified conditions for extended periods of time. Many cigar makers combine cigars for several months before shipping to allow the tobacco to "rest" and the flavors to blend. Individuals can also age cigars in humidors. Subtle mellowing can develop with aging.

air curing   The process of hanging freshly picked tobacco leaves in open-air, covered barns to dry in the breeze. This allows the flavors of the tobacco to concentrate, and the unwanted chemicals to dissipate. (See also *heat curing*.)

bales   After tobacco leaves have finished fermenting, they are packed up in a bale made from the tough sheath of the palm tree and encased in burlap, which provides a home for the leaves while they age, and also serves to transport them safely.

band   A colorful strip of paper applied around the cigar, usually near the head, that identifies the maker.

binder   A leaf of tough, coarse tobacco that holds the filler tobacco in place, which is then covered by a leaf of wrapper tobacco.

blending   Most cigars are blended, which means manufacturers use tobaccos from all over the world to achieve the desired balance of flavor and strength.

body   See *strength*.

box pressure   Certain cigars are pressed so tightly into a box that they assume a slightly square shape. Most premium cigars are carefully packed into boxes to retain their original round shape.

boxes   Cedar cigar boxes are generally called boite nature, which is French for "natural box." There are also a variety of paper-covered cardboard and basswood boxes.

bunchers   Some cigar factories use employees who specialize in assembling the "guts" of premium cigars and wrapping them in a binder. Bunchers are often apprentice rollers, or less skilled than full-fledged rollers.

bundled cigars   Sometimes cigars are sold in bundles of 10 or 25, rather than in a box. Bundling and wrapping in plastic saves money, so less expensive smokes, or "seconds," are bundled. Bundled cigars can be a good deal.

cap   See *flag*.

cedar   Cedar can impart a delicate and pleasing woody flavor to tobacco. Cedar is used to make cigar boxes, and to line the walls of humidors and cigar aging rooms.

chavetta (or **tuck**)   A specialized crescent-shaped knife that is one of the cigar-roller's only tools. It's used to cut the leaf, pack the filler into the cigar, and shape the stogie.

cheroot   A small cigar. A century ago, cheroots were often smoked using a decorative holder.

cigar bar   A place with comfortable seating and/or tables where you can buy individual cigars and accompany them with drinks.

cigar drill   A type of cutter. See also *pinhole cutter*.

cigarillo   A "small cigar," generally not much bigger than a cigarette. It's made from cigar-leaf tobacco, but due to its small size, it generally contains short filler to promote proper, even burning.

climate   A critical part of growing good cigar leaf. Even slight differences in temperature and rainfall will make the same type of tobacco plant have a different flavor.

cohiba   A variation of the term for tobacco used by natives of the Caribbean hundreds of years ago. The word *cohiba* was used to name Cuba's best and most famous brand of cigar—which was created for Fidel Castro.

color   Refers to the shade of the leaf used to wrap your cigar, which can range from light green to almost jet black. All shades have specialized names, such as natural, Colorado, or Maduro.

consistency   The hallmark of a premium cigar brand, meaning that almost every cigar you buy over the weeks, months, and years will be well constructed, use properly aged tobaccos, and feature almost identical wrapper colors within a box (for visual appeal).

curing   See *air curing*.

cutter   A device used to remove or puncture the cap of tobacco used to seal the tip of a cigar. There are numerous types of cutters, and several styles of cuts.

debudding   The process of nipping off the flower buds that sprout from the top of a tobacco plant, forcing the plant to expend all its energy to grow bigger, better leaves.

fermentation   When air-cured tobacco leaves are placed in large piles and allowed to heat up, the process is called fermenting, bulking, or sweating the tobacco. Tobacco fermentation is basically highly controlled composting, and releases many chemicals and impurities that would otherwise ruin the tobacco's flavor.

fillers   See *long filler* and *short filler*.

flag or **cap**   The head of a premium cigar is covered by a "flag" of tobacco, which is carefully applied at the end of the cigar-rolling process. If applied properly, the flag is smooth, feels good in your mouth, and helps prevent the wrapper from unraveling.

foot   The business end of the cigar—the end that you light.

free zone   An area of a country specifically set aside to receive shipments of foreign products—the only place where free movement of non-domestic materials is allowed. Because of free zones, Caribbean-based cigar makers can legally import tobaccos and other materials for use in creating their smokes.

handmade cigar   A cigar created primarily by individuals, not machines.

head   This is the end you smoke. It's covered by a piece of tobacco, called a "flag," or "cap."

heat curing   Accelerating the natural drying process of tobacco using heat. Without sufficient time for flavors to concentrate, this process results in a leaf with less flavor and richness than air-cured leaves.

homogenized tobacco product   Pulverized and reconstituted tobacco blended with natural binders. It's used as the wrapper for a number of cigarillos.

humidor   An enclosed device that keeps cigars in a tropical climate. A humidor can be a huge walk-in room, a box made of wood or Plexiglas, or something as simple as a sealed plastic bag—anything that maintains the relatively high level of airborne moisture, or humidity, cigars require to keep from drying out.

hygrometer   A device used to read and measure humidity levels.

length   The length of your cigar is measured in inches or millimeters.

long filler   Long-filler cigars are filled with long leaves of tobacco.

machine-made cigar   A cigar made primarily by a machine. The filler in most machine-made cigars is short filler, or tobacco scraps.

nicotine   This chemical, in its pure state, is colorless and highly poisonous. It also has the characteristic smell of tobacco. Tobacco contains a very small percentage of nicotine, and cigar leaf contains among the smallest amount of nicotine of all tobacco. Only about 2 percent of the leaf's content is nicotine.

packing   Premium cigars come packed in two ways—square pack and round pack. All handmade cigars are round when they're made, and a round pack preserves this shape. Some cigars are pressed into a box so tightly that they take on a square shape.

pinch test   An easy way to check the construction of your cigar is to lightly "pinch" the cigar between your thumb and index finger. It should feel firm, but not hard. If it feels like a piece of wood, or if you feel a soft, spongy spot, choose a different cigar.

pinhole cutter (or **cigar drill**)   A cutter that creates a small air hole in the head of the cigar through which you draw smoke.

pipe   A simple device designed to hold your tobacco. The most popular pipe material is briar, which is a tough and heat-resistant wood. Another popular pipe material is meerschaum, a white calcium-based mineral.

pipe cleaners   These are used to swab out your pipe to avoid moisture buildup in the air hole.

pipe finishes   The exterior of pipes come in three basic finishes. Smooth pipes are like polished furniture. Sandblasted pipes are rough and pitted on the outside. The surface of carved pipes are designed to resemble sandblasted pipes.

pipe tobacco   Usually shredded and cut to pack into the bowl of a pipe. There are two basic styles of pipe tobacco; English style means only the natural, unflavored tobaccos are used. Pipe tobacco may also be enhanced with a variety of flavors: fruit, nuts, vanilla, chocolate, mint, and so on. These flavored tobaccos are called aromatic pipe tobacco.

premium or **super-premium cigar**   This is a cigar made by hand and worthy of praise because it's a brand that's consistently excellent from one cigar to the next and from box to box.

puncture cutter   This type of cutter, when inserted into the head of a cigar, removes a plug approximately $1/4$ inch across, creating a large air hole while still preserving the smooth, rounded head of the cigar.

ring gauge   Measures the thickness of a cigar in $1/64$-inch increments. A 32-ring cigar would be a half-inch in diameter.

rollers   Experienced rollers apply the cigar wrappers. In some tobacco factories, a few master rollers apply wrappers only. In other factories, rollers are responsible for making entire cigars.

scissors cutter   This cutter looks like a pair of scissors, but with special blades for cutting a cigar. It delivers a straight cut.

seconds   Cigars that are rejected by manufacturers for a variety of reasons are frequently sold as "seconds." They are often packaged economically, and sold at a significant discount to the company's firsts. The flaws, however, may be so insignificant that the seconds represent an excellent value.

shape   The shape of a cigar is the length balanced with a particular ring gauge. Some standard combinations of length and ring gauge exist—such as corona or robusto.

short filler   The middle of a short-filler cigar is filled with scraps of tobacco, rather than long leaves. Virtually all short-filler cigars are made by machines.

sizes Cigars are classified by their length and girth, or ring size. There are certain combinations of length and girth that are standard, and many of these have special names. Three examples are the robusto (short and thick); the mid-sized corona (moderately slim and in the middle of the cigar length spectrum); and the double corona, sometimes called a Churchill, which is long and relatively thick.

straight or **guillotine cut** This most common of all cuts lops off the head of a cigar in a straight, clean line, allowing air to be drawn through the cigar. A straight cut can be made using a cutter with one blade, or two blades.

strength or **body** The relative strength or body of your cigar means whether it's mild, medium, or full-bodied.

stripping Stripping tobacco means removing the thick stem that attaches the tobacco leaf to the stalk. After the stem is stripped, the tobacco leaf dies, and its growth process essentially stops.

tamper A pipe tool, which is used to press your tobacco into the bowl when you light up and as you smoke.

tercio A burlap-wrapped bale (about the size of a hay bale) containing aged individual tobacco leaves. The tercio is used to protect and transport the tobacco, and also to store the tobacco during the aging process.

tobacciana A general term that refers to smoking-related collectibles and memorabilia. From advertisements to books to six-foot cigar-store Indians, tobacciana includes an almost unlimited variety of items.

tobacco plant The tobacco plant is divided into three basic sections. The top leaves, which comprise the corona, are small and somewhat harsher because of their exposure to the sun. The lower leaves are called volado, and they burn well and have higher nicotine content. The prized middle leaves are the largest, and are called seco.

tobacconist A tobacconist is distinguished from a mere cigar retailer by several things: a wide selection of brands and sizes; proper humidification for the stock; a strong working knowledge of cigars, tobacco, and brands; and a selection of smoking-related accessories such as cutters, lighters, and humidors.

v-cut A top-to-bottom slice that creates a v-shaped wedge through the head of the cigar.

Vuelta Abajo Roughly pronounced *voo-el-tah ah-bah-o*, this region of Cuba is the world's most famous cigar leaf-growing real estate.

wrapper A silky leaf of tobacco that makes your cigar look and feel attractive.

young or **green tobacco** Tobacco that has been insufficiently cured, fermented, and aged. Proper processing removes many chemical compounds that make tobacco harsh and strong. Smoking even the best tobaccos, without proper maturation and mellowing, will make you sick.

Index

C

321

D

When You're Smart Enough to Know That You Don't Know It All

For all the ups and downs you're sure to encounter in life, The Complete Idiot's Guides give you down-to-earth answers and practical solutions.

The Complete Idiot's Guide to Buying Insurance and Annuities
ISBN: 0-02-861113-6 ▪ $16.95

The Complete Idiot's Guide to Managing Your Money
ISBN: 1-56761-530-9 ▪ $16.95

Complete Idiot's Guide to Buying and Selling a Home, 2E
ISBN: 0-02-861959-5 ▪ $17.95
Available November 1997!

The Complete Idiot's Guide to Doing Your Income Taxes 1997
ISBN: 0-02-861958-7 ▪ $16.95
Available January 1998!

The Complete Idiot's Guide to Making Money with Mutual Funds
ISBN: 1-56761-637-2 ▪ $16.95

The Complete Idiot's Guide to Getting Rich
ISBN: 1-56761-509-0 ▪ $16.95

You can handle it!

Look for The Complete Idiot's Guides at your favorite bookstore, or call 1-800-428-5331 for more information.

The Complete Idiot's Guide to Learning French on Your Own
ISBN: 0-02-861043-1 ▪ $16.95

The Complete Idiot's Guide to Dating
ISBN: 0-02-861052-0 ▪ $14.95

The Complete Idiot's Guide to Cooking Basics, 2E
ISBN: 0-02-861974-9 ▪ $16.95
Available November 1997!

The Complete Idiot's Guide to Hiking and Camping
ISBN: 0-02-861100-4 ▪ $16.95

The Complete Idiot's Guide to Learning Spanish on Your Own
ISBN: 0-02-861040-7 ▪ $16.95

The Complete Idiot's Guide to Gambling Like a Pro
ISBN: 0-02-861102-0 ▪ $16.95

The Complete Idiot's Guide to Choosing, Training, and Raising a Dog
ISBN: 0-02-861098-9 ▪ $16.95

The Complete Idiot's Guide to Trouble-Free Car Care
ISBN: 0-02-861041-5 ▪ $16.95

The Complete Idiot's Guide to the Perfect Wedding, 2E
ISBN: 0-02-861963-3 ▪ $17.99

The Complete Idiot's Guide to Trouble-Free Home Repair
ISBN: 0-02-861042-3 ▪ $16.95

The Complete Idiot's Guide to Getting into College
ISBN: 1-56761-508-2 ▪ $14.95

The Complete Idiot's Guide to the Perfect Vacation
ISBN: 1-56761-531-7 ▪ $14.99

The Complete Idiot's Guide to First Aid Basics
ISBN: 0-02-861099-7 ▪ $16.95

You can handle it!